Edubooks by Kathy S. Thompson

A Journey through the Triangle of Canada, Britain,
and America
Afterlife Envision
Brown Flowers in Gloucester (Drama)
Counseling Helps (27 Helps)
Creeping Greed
Crimes, and Rehabilitation (and The Gap Theory)
Crime, Crime Awareness, and Crime Prevention, including the Mafia
Diary of a Drug Addict
8 Drama Stories: Twists and Turns
Funeral Planning, Memorial Services, and
Coping with Grief
Global Warming Causes, Solutions, and Theories
I Care For My Cats (and Other Animals)
Landscaping a Small Lot
Letters to England
Living and Travelling in the South-West
Political Write-ups
Racial Equality
13 Science Fiction Stories: Separate Worlds
Sex Trends in Society
Shingles are Awful
Stair-Temple Sites/Chilean Easter Island
Stonehenge and Other Stone-Placement Sites
Taking a Shower—Shower Savvy
The Case Study—Case by Case
The Equal Personage Concept of Children and Youth (EPCCY)
The Gap Theory for Mental Assessment and Treatment
The Outdoor Perils of Cats
The Surgery Experience
Three Careers and a Driven Life: The Life of My Father
Travellers (Sci Fi)
Writers and Writing

Poems and Short Works Books (57 in each)

Going through Life Poems and Short Works
Getting through Life Poems and Short Works
Next Poems and Short Works
Straggler Poems and Short Works
Isolates Poems and Short Works
Extra Poems and Short Works
Final Poems and Short Works
Spare Poems and Short Works

Young Readers Books

Charlie and Mom Cat (early readers)
The Cygnet (young readers, and all ages)
Madame Spider (tweens, teens, and all ages)
Philpot and the Forest Animals (young readers, and all ages)

LANDSCAPING a Small Lot

KATHY S. THOMPSON, M.A.

authorHOUSE

AuthorHouse™
1663 Liberty Drive
Bloomington, IN 47403
www.authorhouse.com
Phone: 833-262-8899

Published by AuthorHouse 12/23/2021

ISBN: 978-1-7283-5875-8 (sc)
ISBN: 978-1-7283-5874-1 (e)

Library of Congress Control Number: 2020906519

Print information available on the last page.

Any people depicted in stock imagery provided by Getty Images are models, and such images are being used for illustrative purposes only.
Certain stock imagery © Getty Images.

This book is printed on acid-free paper.

Disclaimer

The author makes no claim to the accuracy of details in this book. The author has attempted to remove any noted errors and has checked out what could be checked out as well as possible. Efforts towards accuracy have been made but the author makes no claim to there being full and complete accuracy of the book's contents. Any errors brought to the attention of the author will be corrected in the future.

CONTENTS

Apology.. ix

Writer's Note... xi

Tools and supplies you will need for gardening and
landscaping a small lot or any lot (some will be optional)— xiii

1. Introduction: foundation—the home/the lot 1

2. Planting and transplanting 50

3. Remove the unwanted, start selecting, and get started............. 79

4. Plan for variety, with plantings and rocks 115

5. Lot chores and projects 171

6. Choices, choices, and more choices 196

7. Maintain your investment 237

Index.. 265

APOLOGY

I know this book is not perfectly written. Though I majored in English as an undergraduate, I've forgotten some grammar, plus some grammar and even spelling rules have changed over the years and I have not kept up with those new ways, although, many of them are optional. Still, grammar can get to be a little muddled in the mind. So, apologies for any and all imperfections. Just getting the book out was the priority. Therefore, you may find some irregularity, in that the book was not professionally edited. I hope there's no typing errors (but my eyes are not so good). So, apologies go out for any and all oversights or undersights. There may be some repetition, too. Some is purposely there, to drive in a point. Some is accidentally there but is put in a different context. Because I was working on more than one book at a time, I would sometimes forget what I had already written so I occasionally put the same information in twice—almost always in a different context. Also, this book was a bit of a rush job. Because the book was somewhat rushed, all sentence construction may not be immaculate but most of the content generally makes sense in so far as I know.

Furthermore, you may think some text information does not directly relate to the included covered subjects. There is, perhaps, some borderline material in there. With what may seem extraneous, if you give it more thought, you would likely make the connection that the material does relate to the overall subject and certainly to what is generally being covered in the text. There are one or two covered areas that may be more remotely related to the principal subject but

I wanted to add in those subjects and felt that they were connected. All points made tie in with the overall subject, and they generally or specifically relate. Some points that were made do, more than others. I tried to be thorough; I am a detail-oriented writer. Putting so many details in so the book would be more comprehensive was not always so easy to do and so the organization of the book is not quite all that I would have wanted it to be, but I'm not unhappy with it. Mainly, I got everything in that I wanted in and that was my priority. Again, this book was a little rushed.

WRITER'S NOTE

There are only seven sections because the book is intended to be a quick read. It is somewhat of a reference book, though, because much is packed into it and it covers a great deal. The book is concise, but generally thorough in relaying some essentials for gardening and for planning out and establishing a landscape. Points are made that relate to these tasks. The warmer and hotter areas in the southern American states (and in Hawaii) are the more at-issue locations that are noted in the book, but the main points can be applied to any lot, anywhere in the world and regardless of year-round temperatures. Points made relate to all areas in the United States and all countries but some coverage relates to South and South-West USA vegetation.

When planning a landscaping, there doesn't have to be any general sequential pattern to the planning. There can be, but there doesn't have to be. Also, some people will plan out the sequencing very carefully while others will randomly go about doing the projects. One course of action that is taken is to plan out where the trees, rock-enclosed areas, shrubs, and larger plantings will go, and once that has been concluded, then other areas around the lot that are still open can be planned out, using other rock-enclosed areas, more plantings, some pots and yard ornaments, and whatever else is desired and chosen.

Landscaping any lot, especially a blank one, is a process. It evolves, and even if there has been careful planning, there can still be improvisation along the way. Those doing the gardening and the landscaping should allow themselves some latitude and be open to altering and changing when it appears to be best to do so. With gardening and landscaping, it is look, see, assess, decide, do, and inspect. Then it will be leave alone, alter, or change, as time goes by.

TOOLS AND SUPPLIES YOU WILL NEED FOR GARDENING AND LANDSCAPING A SMALL LOT OR ANY LOT (SOME WILL BE OPTIONAL)—

long-handled pruner
long-handled clipper
shovel
tight-toothed rake (for leaves)
open-toothed heavy-duty rake (for small rocks and dirt)
pitchfork (to loosen dirt)
saw—large
saw—small

3-prong garden fork or digger
cutters or old pair of scissors
hand clippers or grass edger
spade
table knife (old one) (to cut weeds down at roots)
one-piece tongs (to pick up thorny cactus pieces)
toothbrush (to remove dirt from cactus)
nut pick (to get to debris between cactus quills)
barbecue skewer (to reach into plant areas to loosen or remove leaves, etc.)

oscillator (a hose-attachment type)

hose (one or two)

wheelbarrow

ladder—two types (A-shaped, and straight and tall)

old rubberized garbage can lid—one or more (for temporarily shoveling dirt or putting

cactus on)

several pots and planters

potting soil, mulch, compost

plastic bags/sacks and unwanted cardboard boxes (for placing debris)

old potholders (for handling cactus)

flat throw pillow (old one) (to protect knees)

plant covers (for frost)

cap or hat (to protect from wind and sun)

welder's gloves (for handling cactus—or, use tools to each side.)

gloves—cloth and/or rubber

It is better if you can keep all these items in one area so they can be found and retrieved fairly quickly. There may be other useful items, not listed, but many of those just-noted items are gardening staples—for the most part and they are recommended. You can buy some of them as you go along but some of them you will need from day one. Electric or power tools are optional.

Some people carry a gardening bag around with them while they are working in the yard. These bags have compartments to the sides and you put gardening hand tools in them. Usually, gardening bags are lined with plastic so if the tools are a little dirty, it is not a problem. There's a large inside area of the bag, too, and all kinds of items can be put in this main, central area. If you look at the page that lists tools and items needed for landscaping and gardening, you can determine for yourself what items can be put in a gardening bag. All gardening bags have handles, and are washable. I received mine as a gift and it was a pleasant surprise. A gardening bag can make gardening a little easier. You keep it in your shed, or in your home if you have no shed.

Sometimes you don't have all your yard and landscape materials out when you start to work in the yard. You might think you do, but you may end out taking on additional tasks or projects you hadn't planned on taking on, that particular day. So often, one thing will lead to another. This has happened to me many times. I ended out making more trips to the shed or to another area to get what I needed. Anyone who does landscaping and yard work should have a shed where they can keep all needed supplies. In this day and age, you'll need a good lock on the shed door—perhaps even two locks, especially if you have power tools inside. Some people even have a greenhouse, where they can keep yard tools and supplies in with their potted plants. (Insects aren't quite as prevalent in a greenhouse and this is one of the benefits of having a greenhouse, when you work with pots and plants.)

If you have a small lot, you can still install a greenhouse and/or a shed. Both come in, or can be made in different sizes and shapes. I had a concrete floor put under my shed and it fits my shed's dimensions. I have metal tie-downs that go over my shed. They are secured by long metal bars that are hammered into the ground. The metal stakes are to the sides, hammered in at an angle, and metal cables are attached to the tie-downs and they go over the top of the shed. You can use two or three sets of these tie-downs and two or three cables. The stakes were hammered in to some depth. The stakes have loops at the end that the cables can go through. At the connection area, special attachments and bolts are used on the cable to make it tight so it will all stay together. The cable has to be vinyl-coated.

My shed is metal, which I prefer to the new materials they're using to make sheds, but to each his or her own. All my gardening items are kept to the front of the shed, along the shed walls, to the right and the left. Some are on shelves. The tall, thin gardening tools are on the floor, and are upright. The door to the shed is large and has two panels that slide open. I usually only open the one side, or the other. I keep all my empty plastic pots on the deck, usually, but tools should not be on the deck or patio or out in the open. Some of them can be quite valuable, and, they all add up. A shed or greenhouse, with a good lock (or locks) is the best way to go. Some people keep some of their tools in their homes.

INTRODUCTION: FOUNDATION— THE HOME/THE LOT

This book applies to landscaping any lot or land area, including a mobile home lot. Landscaping a mobile home lot is how I learned what I learned and why I am able to bring forward what I've learned. If you have another kind of lot to landscape, other than a mobile home lot, feel free to jump on board because the book content will be applicable to any sized lot, really. The material covered can be for house lots, too, and for business-property lots. In fact, much of what is in the book could easily apply to business property lots, since business property lots are generally on the smaller side. Usually, it's the building that takes up a lot of the space. The information covered in the book can be useful in a number of settings, in whole or in part. Plus, you never know if and when you might buy a mobile home, which is what quite a few people end out doing. You never know if or when a friend or relative will, either, and they might enjoy the book and benefit from reading it. Apartment dwellers never know when they might move to a home of any type, which has a lot.

For mobile home lots, once the mobile home is put on a lot, and skirting, awnings, and a deck or patio is added, the yard will, nonetheless, look barren and blank. If a mobile home owner suspects they'll be there for a while, they may as well get started right away and plan out their lot. Whether the lot any home is on is owned or not, most people want to have an attractive-looking lot or yard. They want an area that can be enjoyed. Obviously, if you don't own the lot, you may need to first get permission to do certain things to the lot, from the owner. (You may want to get it in writing.) The owner might help you with some or even all of the costs, too, but, if it is not your lot, you should not be putting too much of your own money into it, since you'll eventually be moving. Driving in and out of the lot or yard, and walking around outside, causes most people to realize that their land area should look nice. It's not about keeping up with the Joneses, either. It's about making an area nice for yourself and your loved ones so the area can be enjoyed. Enjoyment of life is what it's all about. Some people will even hire a Landscape Architect to help them with designing a landscape, because they very much plan to be outside a good deal of the time. There are also other professionals that can be hired. Some of them have college degrees, while others don't.

Landscaping refers to creating a yard or outdoor area that ends out having ample and selected plantings. Landscaping includes highlighting the yard or outdoor areas with rocks, bricks, pavers, concrete blocks, yard decorations, potted plants, lights, and miscellaneous other. Landscaping can include planning and preparing a pool area, a children's play area, a patio area, a shed, and some garden areas. Landscaping essentially includes gardening but gardening doesn't always include for landscaping. Garden areas can include plants, flowers, vegetables, and even fruit. This book does not cover vegetable and fruit gardens, per se, but regardless, vegetables and fruit can be a part of any landscaping.

With mobile homes, any or all of the noted features can be a part of the landscaping, but landscape features are generally planned and completed on a somewhat smaller scale, if a lot is a small size.

Many houses are on small lots to begin with so the amount of leftover lot amount for landscaping can be quite small but they aren't usually quite as small as mobile home lots are. A singlewide mobile home tends to have more extra lot space (for landscaping and gardening) than a doublewide has, and a triplewide mobile home tends to have less lot space (for landscaping and gardening) than both doublewide and singlewide mobile homes have. Mobile homes in mobile home parks rarely have more lot area or land than mobile homes on land owned by the owner or owners have. Landscaping can be done on any sized lot, and all landscaping will have to be maintained and will sometimes need some repairing or restoring.

Gardens are fun to plan out and work on, but they can be utilitarian when you are able to produce edible food. In certain areas in England, people, especially immigrants, are granted an allotted plot of land in an area with other plots for other people. These allotments are farmed so that the families of the gardeners will have more food to eat. The plots are fenced in, and are usually side by side. This is not communal gardening, because each plot and garden belongs to separate individuals. There is a waiting list for these plots of land. Also, they aren't all that big. But, they can yield good food. The gardeners often compare notes so if they create a garden, and any of their friends or relatives do, as well, they will be able to regularly compare notes with one another in hopes that they can all make their overall production even better. Comparing gardening notes with anyone, at any time, is always a good idea. It can never hurt. Watching gardening shows on television can also be helpful. You want to pick up as many tips as you possibly can.

When deciding on what to plant, realize that some plantings you can buy locally or order from the Internet can be invasive species. Invasive species are plants (and also animals) that originate in one area of the world but are brought in to another, further-away area that has a different eco-system, and the translocating interrupts that second eco-system in diverse ways, and often, in negative ways. Such plantings would include groundcover, shrubs, mushrooms/toadstools, flowers/wildflowers, plants, bushes, and trees. Certain foreign plantings are all-right to plant, in some areas, but you have to be in the know about which ones are all-right and which ones aren't. The fewer invasive species plantings there are in a country, the better. They can cause problems, of some type or another. They may not be as safe as generic plantings would be.

People like to plant fruit and vegetables in a garden or around their lot. They will establish a plot—square or rectangular—and plant rows (usually) of whatever they are able to grow or want to grow. Planted trees can yield certain kinds of fruit (and nuts), but trees take a while before they yield any fruit (or nuts). Growing fruit or nut trees can be a specialty and there are lots of tricks to it. It has to be done correctly from day one. Obviously, there are many commercial fruit and nut tree growers, and they tend to do everything right or they couldn't sell the products. Some commercial growers have gone organic or started off being organic growers. On a small residence lot, usually only one or two nut trees are grown and they are usually put in special places.

When a garden is being planned, there is more than one way to do the watering. It can always be done by hand, each and every time. It can be done by leaving the hose in different spots from time to time and using a slow-drip method. It can be done by way of using an irrigation plan—generally with indented rows. A drip system can be installed, or even a spray system. The spray system can be on the ground, or it can even be an overhead one. An overhead system is used in some areas for agricultural watering. An overhead system of spraying is not commonly used for private gardens, but it could be and some of these can be computerized. In this day and age, timers are used with watering systems.

Organic gardening is popular these days. With organic growing, there are no synthetic pesticides or fertilizers. With non-organic gardening, even when fruit or vegetables grown in a garden or coming off of a tree are washed, there is still a measurable pesticide load (though it is greatly reduced from washing). Therefore, people like to grow organic food, and they will take time out to establish such a garden on their lot. Since especially around 2000, this has been on the increase. Common organically-grown fruits are peaches, apples, cherries, strawberries, pears, and grapes. Common organically-grown vegetables are spinach, lettuce, potatoes, celery, carrots, peppers, and peas. I'm sure I've missed some, but those are some of the usual ones.

Allotment gardening goes on in other European countries besides England. (It should be going on in the USA more than it is.) Sometimes a family will rent the land for generations, even. A plot can be extremely large. Some plots are large enough to be communally shared, and some of them are communally shared. Some families are allowed to, and are able to sell their fruit and vegetables; some of them aren't, though. Some who aren't do anyway. There can be vandalism at these places, and crime. Gardens get raided. There is some communal or community gardening in America, but you don't hear about it much. Factors relative to working and running these communal areas can vary. If allotments or community or communal gardening is available in any area near you, if you are interested, check it all out. All such lots need pre-work before anything is even planted, though, and all gardens need regular maintenance. Depending on weather and seasons, there will be a time for soil preparation, cultivating, planting, maintaining, and harvesting. In other words, there will be a growing season.

Often, with allotment gardening, vegetables are grown. Vegetable gardening is a large subject; only a little about it is presented in this book. In the main, ground preparation is important. Compost will be needed—some kind of mulch—and periodic manuring would be helpful. You do not want vitamin deficiency and one of those deficiencies is calcium. Relative to any lot, you have to monitor and inspect lawn and garden areas often—for vitamin deficiency, worms, crawler insects, and flyer insects. There can be other kinds of insects, too, like, the hoppers. On-time watering is quite important. Some allotment growers are going to the organic and will, absolutely, use no commercial pesticides. They might concoct a natural pesticide that may not end out poisoning all insects.

Pesticides have come under considerable scrutiny. Europe has been quicker to get rid of certain ones than the United States has. Some think the EPA is in the hands of certain big companies that make these pesticides. Pesticides get into the food itself, and, they get into the ground so new food growths get them into their system. The United Kingdom has banned certain pesticides from being sold, and they've also established co-operation amongst plant sellers to not sell plants that have been pre-sprayed by certain pesticides. Neonics, a class of pesticides, is a particular problem to plants, our food, and to insects.

20' x 20' (6m x 6m), 10' x 15' (3m x 4.5m), and 10' x 10' (3m x 3m) are typical sizes of gardens on smaller lots, wherever they are found. Garden plots can be square or rectangular but dimensions and shape can vary. With a mobile home lot, if a doublewide is on the lot, there will be little room for a garden (compared with if a singlewide is on the lot). There can still be some room, though. Decide if sun amount will be best on the one side or the other, of the house or the mobile home layout. Check the soil on both sides because soil composition can vary around any lot. Check the shading relative to time of day, but keep in mind that you can add and install shading by planting trees or building wood or canvas canopies.

It is not so hard to put a vegetable garden in, on a lot. If you are a novice, you should probably start with a 4' x 4' or 5' x 5' plot. To keep animals away from digging in it, or from eating the leaves or veggies, it should be fenced in, somehow. You can fence out further away from the actual garden. Portable fencing, if you think you want to enlarge the plot, would be best. You can cover over the fencing at times, if it becomes necessary (for shading purposes).

Some vegetables start better by using small plants. With others, seeds are fine to use. The soil has to have good drainage and the soil composition or mix should be of good quality. The vegetable plants will need from five to ten hours of sunlight a day, depending on the temperature. Some vegetable plants can thrive in containers if there is adequate area for root growth and the draining works well. Certain container plantings will need to have a pole or trellis installed so the plant can climb up as it grows. You'll want to put up poles or trellises on any ground plot, too, if they are needed. Trellises help to provide some shade, as well.

Some fruit can be grown on the smaller lots, along with some vegetables. Common non-organic vegetables grown in gardens are potatoes, squash, cucumbers, tomatoes, turnips, carrots, peas, and lettuce. There are plenty of others, too, whether they're common or uncommon. Tomatoes are popularly grown. They have lycopene in them. Lycopene is a biochemical that makes tomatoes red. It, supposedly, helps to prevent cancer, reduce depression, and it helps the skin. It can lower cholesterol and prevent brain cells from slow damage—so, does it help prevent Alzheimer's? Some say, yes. I suppose something that is an antioxidant is also a biochemical. In any event, tomatoes are one of those wonder foods...kind of like broccoli. It is an antioxidant that can be of help to skin that gets expose to the sun. It's always good to try a variety of vegetables.

Keep in mind, too, that anything red, yellow, or orange may have carotenoids, which are vital for good health like green vegetables are (spinach, broccoli, kale, et al.). Sweet potatoes have the beta-carotene in them. Both sweet potatoes and yams do. Beta-Carotene can destroy free radicals that could damage skin cells. Carotene converts to Vitamin A, and it is the Vitamin A that can help slow down aging signs. Broccoli can slow down aging signs, too, particularly regarding the skin. It is because of the Vitamin C found in broccoli that collagen production is increased. Bell peppers are good for that, too, but broccoli is grown more often in private gardens than bell peppers are. So often, fruit comes from trees, but some fruit is grown via the ground—watermelon, for example. Most berries tend to come from large plants or bushes. Both blackberries and raspberries have ellagic acid in them that can give some UV protection to people so their skin wrinkles less. Conceivably, berries can be considered a vine fruit, but only certain kinds of berries are. Not many berries actually come from trees. Growing both fruit and vegetables in a garden, and eating them, garden fresh, is advantageous, relative to health.

If you are planning to establish a food-producing garden, because of Global Warming slowly coming in, you might want to think about regularly growing whatever is more drought resistant, especially if you live in the Sun Belt areas that do not tend to get humid—the non-coastal areas, mainly. You will not have to use up so much water on them, when you grow these crops. They tend to require watering less frequently, too. Drought-resistant crops are noted on the Internet. They really do not include most vegetables and fruit that we are used to eating. The seeds for these plantings can be hard to get ahold of, in some cases. They can come from other countries.

Though many of the drought-resistant crops grow in other countries, you can get at least some seeds and plantings for them in the United States. There are many Internet nurseries. Many of the drought-resistant crops are ones that have to be grown on very large land areas and not in smaller gardens but some can be grown inside of garden plots. You just have to go through, make some selections and order what you want to <u>try</u> to grow in your garden. As per usual, it may or may not be successful. With certain seeds and plantings, you know they will succeed in your soil and your area, but you also know that certain other ones will be iffy and hit and miss. Some of the drought-resistant crops are barley, black-eyed peas, cassava, chia, chickpeas, cowpea, flax, green gram, groundnut, millet, pigeon pea, seed bank, sorghum, soybeans, sweet potato, tarwi pea plant, and Tepari bean.

Dry-type gardening is referred to as xeriscaping. Water is conserved because of the drought-tolerant plants. Water use is assessed state by state. Some people use more water on their gardens than other states do, on average. The different states are able to figure out the average amount of water use per gallon per person per day but the specific amount that each person uses cannot be determined. Still, some gardens will require more gallons of water per day and whereas one garden might require fifteen gallons per square foot, another one might only require three gallons per square foot, during the same amount of time. Parts of California, Arizona, Utah, Nevada, and Texas are very dry and so the people there may want to consider growing drought-resistant garden vegetation or crops.

Some people will grow different vegetables and fruits in together so that taller plants will help to shade the shorter plants. The taller plants should be more drought-resistant than the shorter plants. This is a strategy, for better garden success. The strategy is known as intercropping. It is sometimes done when growing flowers, too.

When growing selected fruits and vegetables and even spices or tea, you can have a canopy installed between wood posts, but water from rain is good for all plantings so a canopy has disadvantages. Water always has to get down to plant roots so keep that in mind, relative to watering. Some canopies can be rolled back and forth, though. You want to take advantage of rainwater whenever it rains. Usually, rainwater is better than hose water for plants, unless it is acid rain, and this has been an occasional problem for a few lawns and gardens, here and there.

You can use berries in tea, and, in some areas of the South and South-West, people can grow tea in their garden. It can be a green variety of tea. All black tea is made from green tea, only it is picked and then oxidized, by way of a special process and after the oxidation, it changes color and darkens. Research the varieties of green tea. Learn what tea can grow in your area, and, how to go about growing it. Learn how to oxidate it properly, if you want to drink black tea. Tea comes from the leaves. The leaves can be brewed whole, or they can be broken up into bits. You can easily grow mint for your tea, by planting a few mint plants. Break off a small portion or a sprig from the mint plant and put it in the tea. The mint will flavor the tea.

Start with vegetables and fruit that are easy to grow; plan out your garden, leaving enough room between plants to allow for full growth of each plant. Children and teenagers can pitch in with gardening tasks and projects and a vegetable and fruit garden usually interests them a great deal. You always have to help them along, and will sometimes have to demonstrate how something should be done.

A flower garden plot is also possible on small lots, whether in the front area, or the side or the back. Vegetable and fruit gardens should probably go in the back area. That is where they're usually found. If they are in the front area of the home, you might be vulnerable to garden raiders. The same principles apply to flower gardens as they do to vegetable and fruit gardens, for the most part. In other words, flower gardens should also be planned out. Flowers can be cut from the flower garden, brought into the home, and put into a vase. They can be given to others, as might relate to a specific occasion. There is more about flowers in subsequent chapters.

Even though you don't usually find poetry in your average landscaping book, I thought I'd insert one of my poems here—titled *Flowers*. This poem is in my first poems and short works book, titled *Going through Life*. I write Introductions for all my poems so this poem has an Introduction, which I am including. I hope it will give you more incentive to grow flowers because flowers are lovely. I believe they can cause people to appreciate the world more, and to appreciate just being alive. They bring some people closer to God. They add beauty to many areas and do so, often. They cost so little when planted or seeded in a garden or around a property. Here is the Introduction, and the Poem.

Flowers—the Introduction

Flowers is a poem I love because I love flowers. It's as simple as that. Everyone loves flowers. Growing and caring for flowers can be more work than people realize. I wanted to cover the subject of flowers as well as possible and so this is a well thought-through poem. It's a poem I could read more than once. (Most poems I like to read more than once.) When I read the poem, I imagine these flowers, in my mind's eye, and that is why I enjoy reading the poem. I hope to do more gardening with flowers. I have grown some flowers and I quickly learned that growing flowers takes preparation, work, time, and some money (but not that much). You must be dedicated to any gardening endeavor if you want to succeed at gardening and you must be available to regularly tend to anything that you grow, including flowers. To achieve good gardening results is sometimes harder than it looks. In my book about landscaping and gardening, I cover some subjects more than I do others.

One part of landscaping is essentially gardening, assuming you are working with trees, bushes, vines, shrubs, vegetables, fruit, and flowers. I do not go into any specifics about flowers in the landscaping book, per se. I cover more about plants and trees. Because I am presently in the South-Western part of the United States, I make note of cactus and succulent gardening in the book. These hardy plants can put out some really beautiful blooms, but the blooms don't last all that long. I've never had a cactus that blooms for very long. Their blooms stay around for anywhere from four days to a week; the heat seems to wilt their blooms.

Only some actual flowers (from the ground) can grow in desert climates. Climate, of course, matters with all flowers. What is nice about flowers is that they can be brought inside, as a potted plant or they can be put in a vase. Some people make garlands and wreaths with the flowers they grow. We're living during a time of Climate Change so we are more concerned about everything that grows now. I cover Climate Change in the landscaping book but much more so in my Global Warming book. Carefully planned soil enrichment is important when it comes to planting flowers and anything that produces fruit or vegetables. Good organic soil is important. Flowers have to regularly be observed, as well as watered. Some of them are very fragile. They are vulnerable to excess heat, and to insects, as a general rule. They need some nurturing. Try growing some new and different ones, from time to time.

Flowers—the Poem

Lovely flowers in a bouquet–
Each type's unlike the others.
All have a different shape and size–
They're cousins, sisters, and brothers.

Red and pink, and blue and purple,
And white, orange, yellow, and gold–
Their stems get placed inside paper
So that they can be sold.

They share importance on the stage.
Together they're a winner.
They look so nice in center place
When at a family dinner.

Special occasions they adorn–
At gatherings where there's sharing.
People breathe in nice fragrances.
At funerals they show caring.

It's fun to find a flower vase
To put some flowers in.
There are some interesting styles,
So where does one begin?

Flowers bring joy and happiness
Because of collective beauty.
Buttercups, Pansies, Violets–
They're small–each is a cutey.

Chrysanthemums look similar
To fireworks in the sky
That open, fast, in front of us
And flare out, up so high.

Tall flowers, regal, in their look
Give strength to those who see.
Some are gorgeous, some are plain,
But all have majesty.

There's Hyacinths, and Carnations,
Marigolds, Roses, and Daisies,
Orchids, Dahlias, and Lilacs,
Petunias, and Morning Glories.

There's Rhododendrons, Begonias,
Vincas, Sweet Peas, Geraniums,
Camellias, Magnolias, Impatiens,
Daffodils, and Delphiniums.

There's Sunflowers and Snapdragons,
Hibiscuses, Asters, and Poppies,
Zinnias, Lilies, and Tulips,
Gladiolas, and Peonies.

There are many other flowers;
All deserve equal honor.
To achieve an eye-catching garden
Will require ample labor.

We plant flowers in a garden,
From plantlets or from seeds.
We're happy when they are mature–
This does fulfill some needs.

Rain helps to keep flowers alive.
They grow because of the sun.
A plant can give quite a few blooms,
Or a stem may just have one.

We weed and spray flower gardens,
Trim and prune, here and there.
The results are well worth the wait
When flowers cause a stare.

If I could be a special flower
I'd likely choose the rose.
They come in various colors.
I'd select red, I suppose.

We should decide our favorites
And buy them when we're down.
When we receive the ones we like,
We'll smile and we won't frown.

All flowers are God's creation.
In nature they belong,
And wildflowers grow out of doors
So is picking them wrong?

It's likely that flowers please God,
He sees them from on high.
He's happy that He made each one.
The wind reflects His sigh.

Bunches in bouquets and gardens,
And in places on the ground–
We like seeing lovely flowers
Wherever they are found.

Some people wish to grow spices, so they grow spice-related plants. They will use the spices for cooking and for tea, mainly. Before the plant dies, or even if it still has some time to go, they will dry the plant parts and leave them whole or crumple them up, to use as a spice. Certain spices are medicinal, too, and some people will only grow the medicinal spices, along with other plantings that are medicinal, of which quite a few are, including marijuana, but that would be the marijuana plant that has a low THC (the THC is responsible for the highs).

It's the CBD part of marijuana that is medicinal, not the THC. For medicinal marijuana, the THC should be very low, and it is hard to find any marijuana plants with such low THC and high CBD, but, it's around. You can't get high on it, though. Then, it is hard to sell it because some states will say no to that. Patients who use medicinal marijuana do not use it to get high. They use it to get better. There are only certain ailments or disorders that it helps, too. There are not that many of them. In today's society, ailments and disorders can be exaggerated just so some people can use marijuana legally and so people go out and get the marijuana with the high THC and hope they won't get detected and arrested. They may not even get any of the medical marijuana. Only some do this and those people are not only breaking the law but they are also abusing the law.

Recreational marijuana today generally has much higher THC than it did in the 1960s through to the 1990s, when marijuana plants started to be grown to have a higher THC. Whereas it was 1 to 2% THC, it is now up to 13% THC, on average. Presently, recreational marijuana is legal in certain places. It is grown, by some, to have as high a THC as 21-35%, which will have quite an effect on a person. Again, it is not the THC part that is medicinal, it is the CBD. You cannot make a case for legalizing recreational marijuana based on the fact that it is medicinal because it will be low in CBD. Law authorities don't always know how high the THC is when they haul in a user. Marijuana with real high THC can be dangerous to the user and to the public. Still, where marijuana is now legal, some people will put marijuana in their garden—not too many do, though. When recreational marijuana becomes legal anywhere, it is always limited as to the THC amount. Marijuana has become legal in many states, especially medicinal, now but more states are voting in recreational marijuana. In some places, people can even grow marihuana on their own lot, but it has to be cleared with certain agencies, first.

There are many medicinal herbs that can be grown. Some are used as actual medicine and some are used as foods or to enhance foods. Anyone who takes or eats this medicine or these foods must be very careful. Read up on each one before even growing them and I will list some but these are but a few. Again, go carefully into this. Also, some herbs and spices (and oils from these) are used for aromatherapy and for fragrances in general. Floral blossoms are used more for flavoring or for fragrances. Here are a few herbs and spices that can have medicinal or health value—garlic, thyme, cumin, dill, tarragon, basil, oregano, turmeric, parsley, nutmeg, coriander, cinnamon, anise, mandrake, myrrh, dahlia, clove, caraway, cinchona, senna, sandalwood, rhubarb, dandelion, chamomile, aloe, chervil, hyssop, coneflower, Indian Paint Brush, foxglove, juniper, castor bean, poppy, and cannabis (marijuana).

Spices are also used, abundantly, in cooking. We couldn't do without them because they put so much flavor into our foods. We are now quite dependent on spices. All countries cook and bake, using them. Spices are exported and imported, which gives the people of the world a variety of spices, and flavors.

Spice-giving plants could be invasive species ones so check any out if you want to grow and have ready-spices for your foods or beverages, which many people do want to have. People might even just grow one plant that is a spice, like a mint plant. If it grows large enough, that might be enough for a person's food and beverage use for a season or even for a year. For example, people use mint in their tea, and it goes into certain recipes, like other spices do. Many people grow mint plants, but they are but one example of spice-giving plants. Some people grow several different spice plants.

It's one thing to grow spices in your garden for cooking. It's another thing to consider yourself to be an herbalist. Most people would be novice herbalists at best, until they did an abundant amount of reading and got some experience behind them—experience that was legal, that is. The fines for growing anything illegal, which would include certain invasive species, are very high. You must always know if what you plan to grow or are already growing is legal. If you don't, it can cost you (and your family, if you have one).

Folk Medicine is not around anymore, on some levels. The pharmaceutical companies have researched these plantings by now and have come up with actual medicines with some of these. A number of these have become components in medicines like morphine, codeine, digoxin, quinine, and many others. A person who gardens may not know what they're doing or are getting into, were they to become an herbalist, from scratch. Roots, leaves, stems, and the blossoms or flowers of certain plantings are edible, and can even be smoked. It's just that some of them, especially in certain quantities or amounts, can be harmful or even dangerous, including when they are mixed in with anything else, as they often are, and also, it will depend on what they get mixed in with and in what amounts they are mixed in with.

As an aside, can you consider the task of bringing a number of plants into your home as being related to actual gardening? Up to a point, yes you can because you would be tending to a number of plants, of any type. Some people have as many as twenty plants in their home. A few people have even more than that. Some people do not have adequate yard space for gardening, especially apartment dwellers. Many like to nurture and take care of indoor plants. There is a bit of a trick to being successful. Plants have to get light. They would not do well in a cave. If light is not enough for them, they will die. They need just enough water—not too little or too much. Some indoor plants can be temperamental. Some aren't but can die if their care is not carried out just so.

All kinds of plants can do all-right indoors if they are cared for properly. Some may not make it, though, even with good care. Many indoor plants end out going outside and some are even planted in the ground. People buy nice pots for indoor plants, usually. Some will pick the more indoor-adaptive plants. Cactus is often selected. Pets could have a problem with that, and also, some plants are toxic to pets so don't bring any of those ones in if you have pets. Having a number of indoor plants will require actual gardening skills. This is the point to be made. They bring nature indoors, which is why people love to have them around. Indoor plants need regular care and may need re-potting. Indoor plants can be taken outside and planted at any time, and they would, then, add to the outdoor landscaping.

This concludes the part about actual gardening in the book, for the most part, although there are points about gardening in other parts of the book, too. The rest of the book mostly relates to actual landscaping . . . but a garden can be a part of the landscaping, so I am including some gardening aspects in the landscaping parts. To conclude this part about gardening, I've written another poem, similar to the *Flowers* poem that was noted earlier. This poem is titled *Gardening*. (It is in with my latter poems.) I am including its Introduction since, again, I write an Introduction for all my poems. Here is the poem.

Gardening—the Introduction

I wrote a book titled *Landscaping a Small Lot* and preparing and choosing garden plantings are covered in the book. Over the course of my life, I've done considerable gardening and learned how to both landscape and garden, somewhat by winging it. I also did some planning. I learned as I went along but I did enough planning out that I didn't make too many mistakes. It can all be in the planning, but you have to know enough about this and that, as concerns gardening, before you even plan out your garden . . . or, the landscape that is on your lot. You can bumble along a little, but not too much.

Gardening is fun. It gets people outside in the fresh air and sunshine. People are able to work with their hands to produce something practical, like extra food, or something beautiful, like flowers. I wrote the poem titled *Flowers* on 5/13/96 (again, it is in my first poems and shorts works book titled *Going through Life*). This poem was written twenty-four years later. You can, of course, grow both vegetables and flowers in your garden. You can grow spices, or any kind of plant. You can grow bushes, and trees. The sky's the limit, or the ground's the limit.

Whenever possible, everyone should try their hand at gardening. The soil has to be well prepared. A mulch combo works great. And every planting put in the soil has to be set down in it just right. Enough watering has to be done but too much watering or the plantings will become water-logged. Consider reading key related writings before you start to garden.

When you garden, you learn so much—before and after having decided this, and decided that. Plants usually have instructions on them when you buy them, which helps considerably; plus, you can look up different plants on the Internet. Many books and magazines are out about these subjects, too. Gardening is considerable work, at times; at other times, it is breezy easy.

Gardening—the Poem

Food can come from a garden.
Bad food, you don't want to eat.
Grow whatever's nutritious.
Gardening can be a feat.

The soil has to be prepared
Before you can have a garden.
The soil has to be enriched.
Its condition should be a ten.

A garden can produce some fruit
As well as certain vegetables.
You can produce what is useful.
You can stick to basic staples.

You have to tend to your garden.
You might have to pull some weeds.
You can put in bulbs and plantlets.
You can also plant some seeds.

Before you plant, cultivate,
So that the soil will be primed.
You want the roots to grow well,
And everything should be timed.

You hope you'll have lots of rain.
Rain helps everything to grow.
Again, soil must be prepared
Before you are able to sow.

You could choose to grow flowers.
They are always so lovely.
You must still have decent soil.
Flowers are always nice to see.

You have to use special tools
Like a shovel, and spade, and rake.
They will make your work easier
And so, less time, you'll have to take.

You'll need a group of arm tools,
And hand tools, you'll also use.
Keep track of them when you work.
Tools tend to be easy to lose.

You'll also need some clippers.
You may need to use a hoe.
You have to prepare straight lines
So plantings can be in a row.

Some people might plant lettuce.
Others might plant tomatoes.
Some might plant cauliflower,
Or sweet, or brown potatoes.

You could perhaps grow carrots
Or plants that produce the pea.
If what you're planting is food,
What grows will be food that's free.

A few will choose to plant trees,
Like trees that will, olives, yield,
Or ones with avocados.
With trees, you might need a field.

There's some who will grow fruit trees–
Like apple, plum, pear, or peach.
Make sure you have a ladder.
Sometimes fruit is hard to reach.

Some want to have an orange grove.
Some want to grow limes, or lemons.
Some choose to grow trees with nuts,
Like almonds, cashews, or pecans.

How big will your garden be?
A large patch of land, or small?
Some plantings are very short
But some, clearly, can be tall.

You can keep your garden small.
You can expand it, at will.
You can grow more edibles
And have less of a grocery bill.

You'll worry about watering.
Enough rain is so welcome.
Count the number of inches.
With rain, you always want some.

If it is too hot or cold,
Perhaps cover certain plants
And watch out for insect pests
Of all kinds, including ants.

Some sprays can be too toxic.
You may have to make your own.
Some people don't like bug spray;
Some sprays they cannot condone.

There'll also be certain weeds
That sprout up in your garden.
You'll spray them or pull them out.
You'll become a weed warden.

You want all plantings to grow.
You'll hope that each planting thrives.
As you observe your garden,
Look for wasp nests and beehives.

Gardening can be special
When it's a family project.
When choosing all your plantings,
Just certain ones, you'll accept.

What is life without pleasure?
That is what a garden is,
But working on a garden
Can become a worthwhile biz.

You can plan to earn money,
And you can go organic.
About finding some markets,
You can, perhaps, take your pick.

You may need to hire help
If you can't manage your garden.
It could take up too much time.
You might be busy, too often.

You can choose to be versatile.
You can plant what's new, next year.
If your garden grows at home,
You'll always know it is near.

You just have to go outside
To maintain what you've started.
After many years of use,
You'll know how long it's lasted.

You do a little at a time.
A garden can be worthwhile.
For a number of reasons,
A garden can make you smile.

What matters is preparation
When a garden is first done.
Yes there will be work and toil,
But also there will be fun.

Everyone should try to garden
And early on would be best.
Once there is adequate yield,
You will, then, be able to rest.

There are many ways to design a lot from the get go. It is good to
plan out a garden area from the get go. You can angle or position it
a certain way, to the sun. You can prepare a garden area, early on,
and do any gardening later on or after much or all of your actual

landscaping has been done. You can prepare a timetable for your planning and arrange some kind of sequence. Possibly, make the planning be tentative because there can be unexpected obstacles or glitches.

Early on, you certainly can lay grass down or plant it from seed (if there is to be grass). Laying down pre-grown grass squares or long rolls of grass seems to work quite well but you should prepare the soil and layout first. Grass is hard work once it is grown. It dies easily in hot, dry areas, and it takes a good amount of water to keep it up. Water costs money, we all know. It can add up. This is why people use landscape rocks or even gravel in lieu of grass. Some people lay down a layer of flat rocks or stones or put down bricks to cover a space, and to also use for walkways. Doing this can still make a space look barren and certainly minimal and so you will need some interruptions that break up the barren monotony.

A landscape or garden interruption is something that stands out because of color, dimension, scale, and definition. Any interruption is fine, in its place. You want to have certain interruptions. An interruption is usually something positive and good, unless it is in poor taste, an eyesore, or unneeded clutter, like something that needs to be sold or put in storage. An interruption can be fixed or moveable, like a trampoline or a swing set. An interruption can be non-living or living. Plantings, because of height and width and sometimes color, are interruptions. An interruption can be solo, as a single planting, or multiple, as a row of bushes. Interruptions have height, though—a little or a lot. Heightened stonework can be an interruption. Anything flat is not an interruption, unless there is very strong and noticeable color or unless what is related to that which is flat is something that comes out of the ground or juts up from the ground. Use of small turquoise rocks in a garden bed, for example, can be an interruption because the turquoise color stands out so much. If rocks or stones surround or frame those turquoise rocks so there is a bed set up for any planting or plantings, the framing rocks or stones are more the interruption than the small turquoise rocks are, which are inside of the bed. Something that has dimension—also as interruptions—can be an item or items of art (usually ceramic or metal), certain pottery, and even outdoor furniture. An interruption can also be a shed, a greenhouse, or a vegetable and fruit garden. It can certainly be a swimming pool of any kind, or a hot tub. Mobile homes on their own land, which is considered real property if the home is permanently affixed to the land, sometimes have a hot tub or a pool, especially if the land lot is fairly good-sized. Again, an interruption can be positive, or negative.

Water somewhere on a lot is always nice. A small fountain area would be a positive interruption. A small pond could work as long as the water did not become stagnant. Many people will put in a bird-bath and keep it full with clean water. If a fountain is to be put in, you do not want to waste any water. The water should keep recycling when a fountain is installed. A swimming pool (yet another interruption) will add water to an area, certainly. Some areas may, in time, experience water shortages and there could be water rationing. Some areas are more vulnerable to this occurring than other areas are, which is good to keep in mind. Check to see if you live in such an area. Global Warming seems to be causing what is erratic.

Again, that which stands out or juts up, be it large or small or if it has distinctive, noticeable color, is an interruption. Many swimming pools have tubular side stairs or a diving board. Both are higher up from the ground so the pool is not entirely flat. Anything flat is not usually an interruption, per se, but it can be. The sides of swimming pools may be at a slight incline, which also causes the pool to not be entirely flat so that can be considered to be an interruption, too. Many houses, of course, have swimming pools, and hot tubs. Some pools can be on fairly small lots, too.

More and more homes are putting in the above-ground swimming pools. When the coronavirus hit and everyone was in quarantine or semi-quarantine, there was a fast increase of sales for above-ground pools because it was spring and then summer when COVID-19 was initially of impact. Sales for plants, trees, bushes, flowers, and gardening supplies also went up because people were home so much and they needed to keep busy. Above-ground pools can take up a lot of space if they are the larger ones. They, very definitely vary in size. Some are made better than others are. Some are higher or taller, too. Because they are so large, they can detract from a landscape and take space away from outdoor barbecuing and eating unless there is a fair-sized patio, which can also be used for sunbathing or lounging. When such pools are set up, will there be room for a garden? Perhaps.

If an above-ground or below-ground pool goes in, some re-organizing of the yard might be needed. Non-affixed interruptions can always be re-arranged on a lot. Only certain ones could be taken to the front yard area, depending on what they are. Landscaping and gardening, in general, can require some improvising.

An interruption, by the way, is considered to be a positive, and not a negative (unless the interruption is in really poor taste or is in some way hazardous or dangerous. It is only called an interruption because it tends to be more noticed, since it is not totally flat and level or drab and in conspicuous.

You can add more interruptions as the years roll on. An interruption is merely something that stands out and is noticeable; it will usually be considered a positive unless there are too many of them and there is clutter and some crowding out. Of course, some interruptions can be eyesores and more negative and they could generate neighborhood complaints. For example, is a chicken coop an enhancement or an eyesore? Also, some lawn art may not look so enhancing. For example, I've seen large metal outdoor art on rather small lots, and the art stands out way too much. For the most part, exaggerated interruptions should be avoided, but we all know that they won't always be. Christmas lights and displays are an entirely different thing, though; they come around once a year and most everyone likes Christmas lights and displays. Some people plan out their plantings so they will accommodate outdoor Christmas lights and decorations and that is something to think about, early on.

Landscaping almost always includes plantings. Basically, a planting is that which grows out of the ground after being put into the ground. A planting is any organic growth that has roots or the potential to have roots and that has been or will be secured in the ground. Plantings can be flowers, shrubs, bushes, trees, succulents, cacti, and miscellaneous other plants. Plantings can include vegetables and fruit. There are many kinds of available plantings so it's easy and fun to shop around. A planting is still a planting if it is in a pot and you intend to put it into the ground. If you intend to plant it, it is a planting. Otherwise, it is a plant in a pot with the potential to be a planting.

Something that's important to keep coming back to is that landscaping should be planned out in a specific way. Planning can be loose or strict, but there should be some forethought. When to plant what and in what order is a consideration. Knowing what size the different plantings will max out at is also a consideration. You have to be concerned about certain issues. Plantings have to be carefully fitted in to spaces, according to their maximum-growth size. How tall and wide will plantings grow and get to be? What would look best in what areas around the lot? What should be planted first? What should be planted last? Relative to both time and money, how can the budget for landscaping and plantings be met? For me, I kept it simple and did a little at a time, all along the way, until finally, the lot was finished and all I had to do, in the main, was maintain it. I tended to do more, faster, at the beginning. Eventually, everything was done to my satisfaction and I had a nice, low-maintenance landscape that I enjoyed looking at and being around. It got to be a real pleasure— going outside did. I even enjoyed the maintenance part.

It's good to get general accord from other members of the family about what plantings are to go in, and where. It makes it nicer if all family members have at least some say in what plantings are to be selected. For any couple that selects a home that has any-sized lot, they may want to go shopping together to select potential plantings. Both should have a say in how their prospective landscape and garden will turn out. One spouse should not steamroll the other, even if they may be doing most of the work. It should be a joint project so it will be jointly enjoyed. There should be general agreement about what is being done, all along the way.

Quite a few people have lots that have that Spartan look. They plant some greenery here and there, but the plants are few and far between. Frankly, some people can't afford to have a lavish or even semi-lavish yard, so they plant very little. Others just don't want to be bothered. They just don't care, and they have a very pale green thumb instead of a darker green thumb. Therefore, they do the very minimum, if even that, and then they leave it at that. For example, you can drive through a mobile home park, of almost any rating, and see all kinds of yards. The park I lived in when I wrote this book had an average rating when I first moved in, but it eventually got a higher rating. Then, it went down again, but that was after I had finished with my landscaping and gardening. I like to think that the hard work I put in to my lot had something to do with the park's improved rating, before it started to go down.

It truly is relative, as to the time and money that residents put in to their lots. Some landscaping and gardening on some lots is still in process so you can't necessarily judge a book by its cover (until later on). In my own case, I essentially did a little at a time over a period of years. I'd do one big project, every year. This worked best for me. Some people will try to get most of their landscaping done quickly. They put considerable time and money into landscaping from the get go. Some people hire out, to have some or all of their landscaping done. I enjoy planning out and doing my own landscaping. I generally knew what needed doing but if I didn't, I learned and applied what I learned as I was going along. My yard and landscaping was in process for some time before it finally got finished. (Of course, it still required general maintenance.) Little by little, all the areas were filled in to my satisfaction. I had to do at least some revision from time to time, but it finally all got done. Now, with all I know, were I to start a yard somewhere else, there would be little to no revision over a period of time because I have accumulated experience. I could probably get it all done a little faster the next time around, too. A well-landscaped lot will help you get a better price for your house or mobile home. I have always had to tell myself that. Also, when you relocate, you may be able to take some plantings and materials with you. Bricks, pavers, stones, and blocks can go to the new place, and some plants can even be dug up and relocated. But, you don't want to offend any buyers about that; you may want to leave everything intact.

Before you get too much of a start with your landscaping, decide if you want to grade any area on your lot. Grading can create a more interesting landscape and cause the landscape to lose that common look. Grading areas of a lot is somewhat scientific because you must be concerned with the soil condition and especially drainage. It is advisable to hire out for this job because heavy equipment may be needed. Plus, to emphasize, any soil removal or disturbance will need professional attention, especially if you plan to use any graded areas for plantings. Grading has advantages, but if you plant anything on an incline, there will be water runoff and any plantings on the grade and even on top of the grade will get less water and will grow slower than had they been on level ground. You may also need to flat grade for a garage or carport, if one is not yet on the lot. You may need to hire the same company for both jobs.

Most mobile home lots are flat unless the land and the home are owned by one person or a couple. Mobile homes found in more rural areas, for example, may have uneven grading that surrounds the home. The home will be on level grading, though. It has to be. On such lots, some grading could be done. It's important to do any grading before anything else gets done. Less of an angle can be done, as can some leveling. Keep in mind that if any grading is to be done, you should first learn where any utility lines and pipes are, before any digging or re-arranging of dirt is done. Utility companies have to come out and map everything out for you before there's to be any digging or dirt re-arranging. They use color-coded chalk-like paint that eventually dissolves. Again, plantings will get more water when they're in and around the lower graded areas so consider that, relative to any grading.

To emphasize, you always have to be careful about underground cords and pipes whenever you dig. (A cord is the same as a wire.) <u>You may have to get one or more city permits before you do any digging, in certain areas.</u> It is wise to have city and/or county workers to come out and spray thin, colored lines on your lot first, before you dig very deep and dig where underground cords or pipes may be. This service is something your tax dollars may or may not pay for (but they probably do). The different cords or pipes, wherever they are, will be noted by paint color, on top of the ground—per utility. The paint lines run all along where the utility cord or pipe is likely to be. Gradually, this paint disappears and goes away, but it takes a while so you'll have to have it re-done if you want to dig, again, later on, unless you photographed the previous painted areas and spots, which I suggest you do.

At the very least, make some good notes about where everything underground is. Do a picture map, too. Sewer and plumbing lines are down fairly deep. Cable lines don't go down so far. Some gas lines may not, either (but they usually do). Occasionally, a tree root will crack and split a pipe. This will eventually be problematic; if the root obstructs flow in any way at all, it can become a real problem. Gas lines can be quite dangerous if they get cracked or broken. Gas lines can be metal but some places may have changed that. Any time a fence goes in, all these city inspections must be done and perhaps especially be done because so many posts must go in. Not all cords and pipes end out being on outside perimeters of lots and this is important to keep in mind. The sewer lines can be anywhere, but they're usually down deep (but may not be). Other lines (pipes/cables) can be anywhere, too.

Most people just go ahead and plant whatever they want whenever they want. If they mess up a cord or pipe, they must call the City, or in some cases, the County. Roots will often curve around a pipe (go over or under), but it is good to take note of where underground pipes are before you plant something that will have big roots. If you know where wires and pipes are, keep in mind that certain trees, especially, will eventually grow large roots. So, don't plant the tree very close to the wires but especially the pipes. A pipe can enclose a wire, too, in some cases. Some electrical wires are buried underground and there are no telephone poles around.

Cords and wires are a little different. They curve and bend pretty well around roots. The danger with cords and wires is that cords and wires can be easily cut or damaged by gardening tools—usually, shovels. Always, when you dig, be on the lookout for anything that is buried underground. Don't take your eyes off the ball. Look very closely, and sometimes do not thrust a sharp shovel into the dirt until you've double-checked the spot and you know where cords and pipes are placed. You may want to slow dig, not fast dig. It's when a shovel is thrust in forcefully that a cord or wire can be cut. Vinyl or plastic around a wire can be cut. Even if a cord or wire is partly damaged and not cut all the way through, it is considered damaged and an official must come out to repair it. It could be dangerous.

Generally, utility lines tend to be down fairly deep, but you should ask the city workers how far down the different lines go (if you can catch them when they come out to mark your lot). It may not be enough just to know where they are. Take good notes about both issues so you don't get confused. Call the City (or County) people up on the phone. Because it is understood that people will be landscaping around their homes, cords and pipes have to be laid down fairly deep into the ground. The cable TV lines are a different matter. Sometimes, these are buried very close to the ground surface, if they are buried at all. Telephone lines are not buried real deep, but they're usually down deeper than cable TV lines are, on the whole. This could vary, though, from place to place, as can the other cords and pipes vary as to the depth they are buried. Get your information from the experts.

When you shovel out first dirt, be very careful. After the ground has been well watered and saturated, and somewhat dug out, I get down on my knees, use a hand spade, and dig out only a little dirt at a time. Once I dig past a certain point and see no cords and pipes, I relax a little, and keep digging. I still keep watch for any cords and pipes, though, because I know they have to be somewhere. In certain cases but not all cases, you will need to get a special permit to dig anywhere, even on your own lot or property. People who own property do not always have a map at-the-ready, of where all the utility lines are, but, again, it is something they should have, even if they end out mapping it all out for themselves. (And, if the place is sold, it would be a courtesy to hand that map over to the new owners.) If you come across any kind of cord or pipe, you, of course, always have to work around it or figure out another area for what you want to plant. Knowing where all the wires and pipes are will prevent hit-and-miss digging. It will be extremely helpful relative to your landscape planning to be in the know. However, even when you have such a map in hand, you should still dig really carefully all the time. Always be looking for anything, when you are digging; keep your eyes wide open. The ends of shovels are sharp.

Something else you may wish to put in, early on, is a water pond, if a water pond is viable. Some make a water pond the central focal point, and there is normally some kind of stonework involved. For example, stones that are mixed in with concrete and that encircle the water area is popular. This kind of stonework can be done to establish plant enclosures, too. Dirt goes in the center area instead of water. With water ponds, decide in advance where the water for the pond is going to come from, and also how the water can be drained so that fresh water can be put in from time to time. Also, some water ponds may need to have a liner. If fish are to be put in the water pond, there is some science to that and so do some research and confer with the experts.

For people who enjoy barbecuing and eating outside, their yard is considerably important to them. Also, many people enjoy lounging outside, and when they are outside, they take note of the yard and landscaping. Sometimes, parties, ceremonies, and gatherings take place in nice yards, too. People who enjoy being outside tend to want to have a nice yard and to enjoy looking at certain eye-catching landscape areas. Planning, preparing, developing, and maintaining a respectable-looking yard and landscaping gets people outside. The more work that people put in to their yard and landscaping, the more they tend to enjoy being outside. Going outside and sprucing everything up and watering various areas gives a resident a reason for going outside and getting some fresh air and sunshine, and this can be good for the soul. Doing yard work is invigorating, and it gets those endorphins going. Most of this kind of work is light work, but some of it may require considerable exertion.

Any lot can be fair-sized. Of course, some lots are larger than others. The width of the home that is on a lot will determine how much yard space there is going to be but this can also be determined by the length because the length of homes vary. A patio or deck can vary in size, too. Some homes do not have a patio or deck, though—only some stairs. In any event, residents of any home can look over the lot area, and figure out what can or can't be done, relative to their landscaping and gardening. Like with the mobile homes, some houses have limited land area, but even where there isn't very much area, a nice yard can still be planned and completed.

Some residents want to put a shed on the lot from the get go, and do so. Even if people have a garage on their overall lot, they may still want at least one shed. A shed is a good place to put garden-related items and all kinds of other items. A garage is a good place for such items, too. It is good to have both if you can. Shelving in either area is useful and should go in, early on. Put a good lock on the shed, though, and these days people lock their garages, all the time. On occasion, two sheds are put up—generally, a larger one and a smaller one. A shed can be quite large or quite small, frankly. It all depends on what a resident wants and can afford. If there is no shed on the lot yet, it is a good idea to plan the landscaping around where a shed could eventually go, assuming one can be added later on.

Sheds are great for storing landscaping and gardening tools and items, and, in fact, this is sometimes the principle reason why people even put a shed up in the first place. It also stores all equipment and Christmas decorations and God knows what all. Some people use it to store old business-type records and files. Buckets, planters, clothes, auto supplies, hand tools, home maintenance supplies—all can go in a shed. Bicycles can go in, too, but they take up considerable space. Mainly, all the garden tools should be easy to get to. All gardening supplies should be, too.

Concrete or paver floors are best for sheds. The wood floors eventually rot out and need to be replaced and they may sag in spots if they are made of wood that is raised up. Water, if it gets in, and it sometimes does, will collect and cause wood sag and damage. If a concrete floor is poured, you may as well have a pathway to the shed poured at the same time. Again, vinyl-coated steel cables can be put over the top of a shed, whether the shed has a rounded top or a flat top, and the cables can be attached to metal stakes that are hammered into the ground at an angle. If there are high winds, the shed will then be much more secure. No shed should be unsecured. Unwanted high winds always come, no matter where you live. A concrete floor for a shed should be put in before the shed gets secured. If there is already a shed, it may need to be picked up and put in a different spot, temporarily, right before the concrete floor is put down (poured in). Once the concrete dries, the shed, then, goes back over the now-concreted flooring. Then, the tie-downs have to be done.

Some people like to put plantings near or next to a shed so that less attention is drawn to the shed itself. Plantings near and along the path to the shed are nice because the resident would be able to enjoy the plantings every time they went out to the shed. I personally had plantings near my shed but not right next to my shed, except for an Oleander, which needed little to no water other than the water from rains. I didn't want to have to hand water too much right next to the shed because the watering could have affected the shed floor if I left the tap on too long.

Only plantings that require very little water should be next to a shed. Flowers, there, are not a good idea. They need more watering than Oleanders, for example. This principle can apply to homes, too, depending on the situation. If a home is on the slab (on concrete), be concerned about watering nearby plants (too long, especially), but be concerned, as well, if the home has a raised foundation. Too much watering right next to either type of construct can gradually do some damage. With a mobile home, the home is on top of a number of concrete blocks. The blocks are in stacks and are placed at different points underneath the home. Watering plantings usually does not affect dirt under these stacks of blocks, even if you occasionally leave the hose on for a little too long. Still, excess water is something to consider. You do not want it. Usually, mobile homes sink a little after a while, anyway, because of water saturation of the ground, but they sink so slightly that no one hardly notices it. This can vary from place to place, though, because of soil composition and rain amount. Rain gets down underneath a structure, way more than water from a hose usually does. Leaving a hose going for days, though, is not a very good idea, especially if it is right next to a concrete slab or concrete blocks. It's easy to forget that the hose is running. Timers can serve as reminders.

Realize that whenever you plant anything, anywhere, that there is what is known as a growing season. The growing season is spring and summer, as a general rule, but exact dates will vary, according to the area. It is more ideal to plant new plantings somewhere around the beginning of a growing season because weather and rainfall will be more ideal, as a general rule. If a planting will yield fruit or vegetables, though, you would plant it at the start of the growing season, as a general rule. However, some plantings can go in, in the middle of the growing season and it's not going to matter. Some can even go in towards the end of the season, but not too close to the end because the roots of any planting have to get established by watering and if it is colder outside, you have to be very careful about watering.

In many cases, once it gets cold outside, you cannot water any plant and the best guide is 'how cold does it get at night'? It may be warm and sunny during the day but if it gets chilly at night and water in the ground gets cold and water the planting has just taken in gets cold, the plant can go into shock and can end out taking on a different color (on some or all of the plant). The plant might come back to health to its usual color in the spring, but in the meantime, it will not look so great. The plant can do other things besides changing color because of the cold, and because of the water during cold nights. For example, some of the plant can turn brown, some or all of it can get a wrinkly look, and a number of leaves can be shed. Too many assume that if it is warm during the day that the nights will be warm, so they water some plants. Then, it gets real cold for them, at night, which is not good for any planting. You must focus in on both day and night temperatures, when gardening.

You can actually do some winter gardening in the more southern areas of the United States. If the sun is out, once the outside gets warmed up, you can do some shaping and trimming of bushes and trees. You can remove anything that is dead, and you can also remove leaves. Some leaves you may have to remove by hand because raking can break dried leaves up into small bits and you don't want all those small bits all over the ground. Walking on top of dried leaves does this, too, so you always have to be careful where you step whenever dried leaves are around. Also, the gentler you are when you rake and pick up dried leaves, the less apt they are to break up into small bits. They break up into bits on grass, but they especially break up on landscape rocks.

It's good to gently scoop up leaves and pick up bunches with your fingers if the leaves are inside of actual beds that have been set aside for specific plantings. I get down on my knees with an old pillow I use for my knees. I put the leaves into a flat box with about a 3" to 4" edge, and dump them into a larger box when the flat box gets filled. The larger box is right by me, too, so I don't have to get up all that many times. To each his or her own, though, as to how anyone goes about doing such work, if you can consider gardening to be work. Many people feel that gardening is fun and creative. To them, gardening is a hobby. It is recreational and it isn't work, not in the main. It isn't exactly fun, but it is a creative and interesting hobby. It is an enjoyable enterprise.

Always know the approximate dates of the growing season for your particular area so you will realize, more exactly, when you can do what, relative to your lot care. You might even want to mark your calendar so when the season starts, you are ready for it. The best time to work on the lot will be earlier in the growing season because the weather is usually wonderful. Still, lots have to be maintained year-round and, unless there is snow, there are always projects you can be doing throughout the year. In areas where the weather is generally nice year-round, you not only can work the lot all year, but you should work the lot all year whenever there is work to do. In the southern half of the United States, year-round lot care is more feasible.

Many people tend to do much more work on their lot at the beginning of the growing season and, then, at the end of it, in preparation for winter. Still, different projects can be done at other times, as might be necessary. It's a good idea to make up a task calendar for all the year-round projects you will have to do. You can hand the calendar and notes over to any buyer, later on, if you ever move, although, some people stay in one home all their life. When you landscape a home and fix up a yard and are happy with it, you may never end out moving. You might think you will, but then, you may end out staying. This happens a lot.

It really is smart to at least keep notes on what to do and when to do what, relative to year-round gardening. If you can, set up that yearly work calendar early on. Each month you'll need to make note of specific tasks that will need doing next year at around the same time. There are always specific tasks to complete each month, or certainly each season. You can sometimes defer some tasks and projects on your calendar but sometimes, not for very long because there could be task and project deadlines. You can maybe juggle some things around, but in some areas (especially the more northern areas where there are colder winters) weather will always dictate what needs to be done and there can be priorities and deadlines. There will always be a general schedule for every yard; some things have to be done by a certain time. Gradually, you figure out priorities and timetables for the seasons, regardless of where you live.

Florida has many mobile home parks. Much of the South-East does. A number of the parks are retirement communities. Florida has many retirees. Florida is known for their diverse plant life and foliage, in large part because it is a humid state and foliage thrives in humid weather. Bushes, shrubs, and hedges are particularly noticed in the State of Florida. They're generally very healthy looking. So are flowers. Orange trees grow in Florida. But just about anything can grow in Florida, even certain African Violets, because of the high humidity. You can bring practically anything into the State of Florida (if it clears their customs) and it will have growth success. People who live in any kind of home have a field day trying to decide what to plant, since there are such a number of options. Even cacti and succulents are abundant in Florida because they do well in the sun. Most of them don't need the humidity, but it provides them with more moisture.

Like Florida, California has diverse vegetation. But California has less humidity, overall, when compared with Florida, which is why they get more wildfires. California gets a great deal of rain in some areas, and, ocean breezes bring ample humidity into parts of the State—mainly around coastal areas—which is similar to what you find in the State of Florida. Mobile homes are popular all over the Sun Belt sector, in general. The Sun Belt is the whole southern part of the United States. The Sun Belt goes from California to Florida (but Florida is surrounded with water, except for way north). It isn't that hard finding a decent mobile home in a Sun Belt state. They are all over the place . . . and on the increase.

Mobile homes are all priced differently, but there's so many around that it's usually a buyer's market. They keep making them, too, even though they don't last as long as a house does, or hold up as well. They can certainly last a lifetime, barring something unforeseen. There are some mobile homes that are very elaborate and more like houses. You can find the plain, the average, and the fancy. You can find different floor plans and styles. You can find the small, the medium, and the large. You can find the old, the middle-aged, and the new. The sky's the limit. Again, and to emphasize, this book is for mobile home owners and mobile home renters. It is for house owners and house renters. It is for building owners and building renters. It is for anyone who needs to, or wants to create and establish landscaping on any lot. Some mobile home parks are quite old, but they must all be parks that are kept up, to a certain standard. They get a rating, regardless of their age. A lot is a lot is a lot, wherever it is. Mobile home owners must abide by standards and regulations.

Even though mobile home lots are usually rectangular in shape, you can do some nice landscaping and gardening on those lots. You can find mobile homes on separate land (you buy the land and the mobile home), in mobile home parks, where rent is paid for the lot and you own the mobile home, and in mobile home parks where both the land and the mobile home can be purchased at the same time. All of these lots or land areas need landscaping and gardening because people want their residence to look nice and to enjoy their home and enjoy life. A home is a castle—yard and all.

Mobile homes can be sold when the land is not part of the sale. In many mobile home parks, the land is not owned by the mobile home owner, who is renting the land that is owned by someone else. Sometimes, a big company owns the mobile-home park, and this would include the land. Lot sizes vary from park to park, and they can vary a little just in one park, even if the park were to only have lots for singlewides. Some people will put a mobile home on their own land, either within a town or city of outside of a town or city. Those kind of lots tend to be fair-sized, but they can be smaller, too. In such cases, the landowner has to see to getting all utilities installed and hooked up and when they are being buried or installed, it is good to map out where any pipes or encasings are, underground, so when you plan out landscaping, there won't be any problems if you do any diffing. There are mobile home parks where the land is sold and if there is already s mobile home on the land, you buy the home and the land. Otherwise, you have to bring a home in and put it on the land. There may still be some community codes in place that relate to homeowners and some of those regulations could relate to landscaping issues so be sure to learn what they are. Sometimes certain trees or bushes can't be planted, but there are many other possible restrictions.

Whether a mobile home is a newer or older model, fixing up the lot is important to most residents. There's just something inside people that makes them want to improve their lot. (Just in case you didn't get it, that is a pun.) Sometimes, they want to do some landscaping and gardening for investment reasons—to make an eventual profit—but sometimes, they just want to make things look nice, for themselves, and those they love. There's something inside people that makes them want to create and to make right or best. They want things finished. Fixing up a mobile home lot fulfills the need to create—to become an artisan of sorts.

See the vision of a beautiful and completed yard or lot, but allow yourself some time to reach that destination. It may take you twenty some projects (give or take) to accomplish the overall goal—of which each completed project will be a small goal met—but as noted earlier, the day will come when the last project is finished if you just keep pressing on and finish the race. It can be a marathon, quite frankly. Even if you only live in the home five years, you can still get a lot done. Of course, you can get even more done if you live in the home ten years or more.

If you are considering living in a mobile home, again, there are singlewides, doublewides, and triplewides. Always consider size and dimension because all three come in varying sizes or dimensions. Some mobile homes have add-on rooms. Mobile homes are now called manufactured housing (by some people) because the term gives the image of such homes more class, but also because the materials used for manufacturing are different. I tend to use the word mobile homes for all of them because they can all be moved or re-located but realize that mobile homes, in general, tend to be older while manufactured housing came in after mobile homes did. Manufactured housing has different siding. The older mobile homes have metal siding. Those ones are true mobile homes (as opposed to manufactured housing). When the siding isn't metal on homes, the homes tend to be manufactured housing. Some mobile home parks will not allow in the older models. As time goes by, mobile homes with metal siding will become fewer and fewer. Older parks still have them. They cost less, initially, because they are older. Some are still in very good shape and keep holding up so why not put a nice landscaping on them? Such homes can last quite a long time but like with houses, they require routine maintenance.

In a sense, the doublewide and triplewide mobile homes are modular homes because the two, or three, components have to be put together, but modular homes are different from mobile homes. They are homes put together by several pre-made parts or components, and not just two, or three parts. They have a totally different look to them and they are assembled differently. They aren't elongated like mobile homes are. Europe has quite a few of these modular homes but they are in America, too. Modular homes are pre-fab homes (i.e. pre-fabricated ones). Mobile homes (manufactured housing) and modular and pre-fab homes are found in areas with both warm and cold climates (and whatever is in-between), but if areas are really cold, they are not so practical as a general rule. How much insulation is in them is important. Also, how good is the heating? They work well in warm climates.

The shape and dimensions of a lot will be different, depending on the type of home one gets in to. Obviously, the singlewide mobile homes are going to be on a more rectangular-shaped lot. I called the mobile home that I lived in 'the comfy shoebox' because it was shaped like a shoebox. There may or may not be much excess land for a yard on the lot of a doublewide or a triplewide, it just all depends. Generally, there's not too much land to the sides of wider mobile homes. Mobile home parks are not all partitioned the same way, though, and some have larger lots than other parks have. Some parks have more curves to their streets and the lots are not so rectangular.

Be it known that mobile home parks are not trailer parks. That is a misnomer and it can be insulting to hear for those who live in mobile home parks to have to hear that. Trailer parks are places where actual trailers are situated. They're better known as travel trailers. Some trailers are fairly large, and can be slept in. Larger trailers are hauled behind a heavier vehicle, of some sort, and they're less wide than mobile homes are, by quite a bit. They're also not as long. Some of them are used for camping. A mobile home is also not a recreational vehicle (an RV). RVs have their own front motors or engines, and people can live in them as they travel around, or stay in one place. RVs are not as big as the customary mobile home is, but they are larger than trailers. Trailers are usually used for camping. You can pull trailers if you have a heavy enough truck.

There's the type of trailers you can stand up and move around in, with a bed, and there are camping trailers that really just haul camping items. No one can live in those. Some people have been known to sleep in them, when camping, but these days, you'd better have a gun if you do that because of hungry animals and certain people. The larger pull-trailers that are enclosed and you can stand up in may or may not have a small cooking area in them, or a commode. The only type you want to live in and also fix up the surrounding lot for is the permanently implanted manufactured house type (that are no longer called trailers, though you could move these to another land lot, somewhere, at a cost). These larger, nicer mobile/manufactured homes are in mobile home parks and communities or on separate land, with all hook-ups working. Again, these are <u>not</u> trailers, but once upon a time, they were called that. Some of these parks and communities are quite nice—even classy. The ratings for them are relative.

Many trailer parks (versus mobile home parks) can be nice and decent, but there's not too much landscaping around trailer parks (if there is any at all), in part because hitches stay on trailers so people can come and go. People don't usually stay. It is the same with RV parks in that they come and go on a regular basis, too. At mobile home parks, hitches (sometimes called tongues) are often required to be removed (cut off or disassembled) or they must be covered up and enclosed by metal or plastic skirting. If they are cut off or disassembled, they are sometimes pushed underneath the mobile home, for storage. In other words, mobile homes tend to be permanent, compared with trailers and RVs. Plus, again, they're larger, over all, and they serve as decent-sized homes, even for families. Mobile homes do not have motors or engines. Some mobile homes are affixed—concreted in—and can then become real property (like a house is) if the land is owned by the home resident or even by someone else who rents out the home. The taxes won't be all that bad if it becomes real property. Mobile homes tend to stay in one place. Whereas mobile homes might be surrounded by a fence, trailers and RVs usually are not, except to be stored, perhaps.

Actually, mobile homes are sometimes referred to as manufactured housing, which is a more elevated ascription than mobile homes is. Some mobile homes have a metal exterior and these tend to be the older ones. Today, manufactured housing tends doesn't have the metal exterior; rather, these homes have a plastic resin/polymer type of exterior. They look more posh than the older ones with the metal siding look. These homes are all newer than the metal ones are. Still, they are generally referred to as mobile homes and for purposes of this book, mobile homes is the catchall ascription for the kind of home that is found in a mobile home park. Unfortunately, mobile homes are still referred to as trailers, by some, so, mobile home can be trailers (if they're big enough to live in), homes with metal siding, and homes with plastic resin/polymer siding. People don't like the word, trailer, compared with the term, manufactured housing. People do not travel around in the large mobile homes that get termed 'manufactured housing'. They do travel around in trailers, though, and RVs.

Once a 'mobile' home is set up in a park, it ceases to be mobile, but it could become mobile later on since it could be moved. The ascription, mobile home, merely means that the home can be moved from one place to another. They could be transported to another place later, but they likely won't be—not for some time, if ever. They become 'rooted' homes. Homeowners or tenants establish roots, then, and while they are doing this, many will want to create and establish a favorable landscaping around their lot.

People like mobile homes for different reasons. There are few to no insects in the home (including termites), since the home is up on blocks and is higher up. There are rarely any rodents. Furthermore, there is 'enough' distance from neighbors so there's privacy. And, there is a fair-sized land area to take care of and to, therefore, enjoy. Mobile homes are often placed in a particular location and many times, stores, a school, and a park is nearby. There are often some park amenities, too. There's also low taxes, a low price for the home (compared with for a house), low taxes, lower insurance rates, and on and on it can go. Often, because people living in mobile homes save money by living in a mobile home, they can afford to put money into their yards and the landscaping. People buy houses with small lots too, for different reasons. Sometimes, they have little choice in the matter but sometimes, they simply prefer a smaller home that has a smaller lot. Again, this book is for anyone who has a lot to landscape—be the lot small, medium, or large, and regardless of how the home and lot is laid out.

Many mobile homes are found in desert areas. They hold up well in that climate and provide affordable housing. Amazingly, though, mobile homes are also sold in northern areas and even upper northern areas. Those mobile homes generally have thicker insulation, or they should. There are mobile homes as far north as Montana and Minnesota (they're even all the way up in Canada), but, mobile homes and mobile home parks increase in number the more south you go. However, keep in mind that this book is for a mobile home lot as well as for any other type of lot. Anyone can apply the points that are made in the book to even a very large lot.

A mobile home community is a park that houses a number of mobile homes, and a space number is assigned to each mobile home lot. (Less often there are street names and addresses.) The lot number becomes part of the address. These communities sometimes provide amenities, as, one or more pools, a sauna or Jacuzzi, a recreation center, a reading room, tennis courts, a basketball court, a shuffleboard area, some children's play equipment and play yard, and a grassed-over park area. Some mobile home parks have security of some type. At mobile home communities, residents may own the land their mobile home is on, or, the park may be owned by a person, a partnership, or a group of people. If the owner or owners live in the park, they are tenants and must pay lot rent, every month. Often water, garbage pick-up, and electricity are included in that rent bill. Some people who have lots of money do little with their lot.

At the other end, some people who have little money put a good deal into their lot. It's all relative.

Most managers and owners of mobile home parks like it when there are plantings all over the park because it makes the mobile home park look more attractive to renters and outsiders. They cause different mobile home to appear to be more valuable. The park will have a more established look. Managers and owners tend to give carte blanche to tenants when it comes to plantings and landscaping, as long as anything done is within reason and generally standard, compared to what could be excessive, unsightly, or oddball. People are more apt to want to move in, and not move out, when yards look normal and nice. As noted earlier and to emphasize, if a yard looks nice, the mobile home will sell better and for more money when it comes time to sell. Many mobile homes are available to buy but again, they're especially found in more southern areas and the Sun Belt. Again, there are mobile homes in northern areas, too, but mobile homes abound in warmer climates.

Many people in the north buy a mobile home in the south to serve as a second residence. They become snowbirds. Some northerners will buy a real nice mobile home in the south and then retire in it. Many people don't quite know how to go about landscaping their mobile home lot. Some may move into a mobile home and not like how it's landscaped and will want to re-do it. People are grabbing up mobile homes, right and left. More mobile-home parks are being set up. Owners want to keep them well maintained. Again, more people are wanting to live in a mobile home, these days. Some are similar to houses. Perhaps they all are.

Some people take time out to plan out how they're going to do their landscaping and plantings. It will take time and some thought. Some people don't care to do any initial planning. They think about things as they go along. Even if people move in to a place that already has some landscaping and plantings, they will still decide on an approach and a plan for what they want to do; they'll determine what they want to remove, re-do, do better, replace, leave alone, or add. Some people are organized enough to actually put their plans on paper. They draft what they want to do and may even do one or more drawings. This is usually done after soil samples of the area have been done, and any grading of the area has been determined. Soil samples can sometimes be done just by looking at the soil.

Grading can be ascertained just by looking, too, but some people use science and math to figure it all out. They want everything to be precise and exact. Some lots have to stay like they are and no grading is needed. It wouldn't work to do any grading. When cumulative costs are factored in, some costs may not relate to landscaping and gardening. Grading could be one of these costs, if any grading is wanted. Grading can relate to leveling. It may be needed to prevent flooding.

PLANTING AND TRANSPLANTING

Because trees take a while to get growing, they should be planted on the lot first. There are so many kinds of trees available for planting, but one must choose trees that will thrive in the locality. Drive around the area and take note of the trees that are growing well. Look at their size and shape. Some tree types do better than others do, in certain areas, and weather is the principal reason why they do. If you need shade trees, and don't mind the birds, figure out where they need to be on the lot. Figure out how tall and wide the tree will end out. Trees can't be too close to a residence, or too close to a border or boundary because branches hang over a neighbor's lot and property. They may not mind this but then again, they may. Trace the movement of the sun in relation to how the home sets on the lot. Late afternoon sun is the hottest so you want to place a taller shade tree in the spot that is best for blocking out the afternoon sun that hits the residence full force. Where you want sun blockage on the home is important to figure out, early on. You may want to plant more than one taller shade tree. You may not want one that grows exceedingly tall, just tall enough to shade the side and top area of the home.

Don't plant some tree types too close to the home, itself. If the tree branches out too wide. Over the years you'll have to do a lot of tree trimming. Besides, wind or lightning damage can affect a tree and cause the tree to damage a home, or even a car. It is the less dense-wood trees that tend to snap during high winds. Some trees fall down at the base around the ground, when winds are intense. They literally get blown over. For this reason, any tree you plant must be carefully planted. You want to spread the roots a little outward and situate some of the roots a little more downward, but still, this may not guarantee that the tree won't topple over if the wind blows hard enough. The roots of trees will try to grow downward, but they have to be pointed a little downward from the start. Again, you want some roots to be spread out. Roots that go to the outer edge of the root grouping should be placed outward and pointed downward a little. The other roots—the middle ones—will naturally go downward, since they are in the middle and are already going downward. If the roots are too close to the top of the ground, you will eventually get root bumps at the top, ground areas. You can trip over these, and they're just not ideal to be showing around the ground area of your tree or trees. When planting a tree, the dug-out hole should be large and wide so the roots will go in nicely and can be placed in correctly.

You may also want one or more aesthetic trees or cosmetic trees. They provide little to no upper shade (over a home), but they will provide shade underneath the tree. They can be pretty to look at. (They will certainly shade a pet, though.) Usually, these types don't grow too tall, and they tend to be full. Some of them you cannot walk under (if the branches are quite low) so keep that in mind. On occasion, you can find one that doesn't shed leaves or needles. If they'll thrive in the area you are in, these types of trees are practical because they are little to no work, assuming you choose them well. Some of these types don't even require trimming. The Arborvitae tree is one example. Certain Evergreen types work well as aesthetic or cosmetic trees. In fact, the Joshua tree, found in desert areas, is actually an evergreen and it adapts well to dry climates. (It won't shade a pet very well, though.) The Joshua tree is one of the largest Yucca plants. Yuccas are evergreen shrubs and trees. You see a number of Joshua trees in California. In their own way, they're as eye-catching as the Saguaros. They aren't so dangerous to brush up against, though. The tree is quite cosmetic and aesthetic, and it well contributes to the ambiance of a lot, just like Saguaros do, but they are only found in certain South-West area. The Arborvitae tree, you cannot walk under. It is full at the base. You have to decide if you want to walk under a tree, early on.

Half the challenge of landscaping is finding the right plantings for the lot and the area. Do some studying, see some pictures, talk to locals, gather some facts, and get the scoop about which plantings are best and available. Think about it all, for a while. Keep in mind that some plantings can be special-ordered, and also that some plantings are available only during certain seasons. Keep in mind that one nursery will have plantings that others won't have. You may want to visit more than one nursery or plant shop. Getting a variety of plantings to go on your lot can be somewhat fun (and a challenge).

One tall, thin tree that grows well in many areas is the Italian Cypress tree. There are other kinds of Cypress trees, too, and they all look very similar. It is sometimes referred to as Blue Italian Cypress, but it doesn't really have a blue cast to it—it's pretty green. The Italian Cypress is stately looking and they look good in front of a lot or along the outside edges of a lot. They also look good to each side of a doorway, as a pair. They are very tall and very slender and come to a point on the top. They seem like they are Evergreens because of their foliage. They look very stately. Once the roots get established, they require little water. (Still, you have to monitor their external appearance because they can begin to look too dried out, and they certainly can die, from lack of water.) I have six of these trees on my lot. They shed no needles and usually only one bird makes a nest in the larger ones each year. The tree has to be sturdy and full grown before they'll nest. Any stray cats cannot get to the birds, in part because the tree is full all the way around and down to close to the ground. They cannot grip any trunk area.

You have to keep close tabs on Cypress trees, with regards to watering if it hasn't rained for a while. Most people believe Global Warming has set in, and as a result, all plantings must be more carefully monitored and some plantings are going to need more occasional watering (unless you get enough rain). Any planting can dry up, become only partly green, and can then be on its way to dying. Observing browning, drying, brittleness, and loss of leaves or needles should be cause for concern. If you don't catch a downturn in time, and put the planting on a long, slow drip so the plant will get moisture into every root and area, you can easily lose the planting. Every so often, walk around your lot or property and check every planting for general appearance and health. The best time to do slow-drip watering is after the sun goes down. I often leave a slow drip going on all night long and then turn the faucet off in the morning.

Don't assume that any of the established trees on your lot will live a long time. With larger, taller trees, roots can go way down and be near or at the underground water table, deriving ample moisture, but an underground water table can change and there could suddenly be no water, down deeper. Many underground water table areas have been going down, as to level, all over the world, in large part because much of the underground water has been used up because of wells and irrigation usage. Roots of some trees may not be near such underground moisture, and if there is a dry spell, you'll have to well water that tree. Always consider recent, past weather, including rain amounts, if you are responsible for caring for trees, or for any other plantings on a lot. When you put a number of plantings on your lot, you have to become a supervisor, of sorts. If you lose a magnificent tree, it will be quite a loss.

Whenever you see yellow leaves, and drooping leaves, a tree or planting will need water. Put the tree or planting on a slow drip, and let it soak in as much water as it seems to need. Periodically check any trees or other plantings on your lot and if any of them look particularly 'thirsty' (based on the signs), water the tree or planting well but if the days and nights are starting to get too cold, you may have to wait for the weather to warm up before you water it. If the day is warm and sunny but the nights are cold, only water the planting early in the morning and just give it a little water so all will be dry by nightfall. You want to catch any drooping, etc., <u>before</u> it gets cold. Keep in mind, too, that some leaves—mostly on trees—will droop and fall off in autumn, no matter what, and certain ones will have leaves that change color. If something is normal, don't be concerned.

If the weather has been warm and you sense a danger (of possible loss), you may have to go around and slow drip a number of trees and other plantings, and give a couple of hose douses to a number of the plants. With slow dripping and with some plantings, you may have to let the hose drip for several hours. It depends on how slow the slow dripping is. If you have too much water velocity going through the hose, it won't absorb in the concentrated area as well as you think because likely there will be water runoff. Water will trail somewhere away from the planting's center area. If the water velocity is too little, not much water will go down deep, to get to all the roots. In time, you will know how much water to give to each planting and how much water velocity is best. You have to be consciously assessing water amounts as you go along and water. It will take focus.

Some plantings require little water. Cactus is big in the South-West. The Saguaro, or the Carnegiea gigantea, only grows in a few areas of the United States. It particularly grows on the Sonoran Desert that is on both sides of the Mexico/United States border. Some Saguaros are, however, found in other Arizonan areas and in a few spots in California and Texas. A Saguaro cactus is classified as a tree, by some Dendrologists. The Saguaro grows very tall, and it eventually grows arms, which could be called branches. A Saguaro at fifty years can be approximately thirteen feet tall and have several arms or branches.

I don't mind nests in trees at all, but a giant Saguaro can end out with a dozen round entry holes in it that birds have pecked out in an effort to create a safe nesting place. No resident really prefers this, even if they care about mother birds and their babies. Most people would rather they nest somewhere else. With my large Saguaro, all the holes ended out being on the side where the sun hits in the morning, which was not the side facing the home. It was the side facing the street. I think that peckers choose a spot that relates to amount of sun, intensity of sun, and perhaps wind flow. The areas with the holes in them did not get the hotter afternoon sun, just the morning sun. Rain can get inside and drench a nest, if winds are high during the rains, but that is a chance a mother bird has to take. They aren't too keen on traffic being too close by, or too many pedestrians walking by, but they, absolutely do not like the hot afternoon sun shining into the nest hole.

Some say the bird-pecked holes in Saguaros add to the charm or ambiance of the South-West. I 'try' to look at the marred Saguaros around town that way, and at my own Saguaro that way, too. In Arizona, the Picoides Arizonae is the culprit woodpecker that usually does all that pecking. The bird is also found in New Mexico, Western Mexico, and Southern Mexico, and it is a sub-species of the Strickland woodpecker. It's a prolific bird. Other birds, as the owl and the Cactus Wren, will take advantage of these pecked-out holes during subsequent years. It is first come first served with these birds. Strong-minded, determined woodpeckers will try to peck holes in mobile homes, too, so in the newer ones that have the pervious siding, you'll see occasional woodpecker holes, which residents have to fill in. These holes can't go deep enough for a woodpecker to be able to go in and make a home of it, but they can get to be good-sized holes once they are pecked at. They're always round. Once the woodpecker realizes it can't go into the hole it has been pecking out, it leaves and tries its luck elsewhere. You feel a little sorry for the woodpecker.

People put up large plastic realistic-looking owls in an effort to keep woodpeckers away, but this doesn't always deter them unless the owls are battery-controlled or electrical. Occasionally I heard some pecks on my mobile home exterior. The woodpeckers gave it a couple of goes and then suddenly left because of the metal siding. These loveable pecker pests don't like the metal siding, and they very soon realize that their beaks aren't making much progress so they leave to try to find greener pastures, or greener something, like a Saguaro. They have to nest somewhere safe and no predator will climb up a Saguaro. And, generally, the holes they peck are too small for larger birds to enter, as hawks, ospreys, and eagles. Those kinds of birds are perch birds. They likely aren't able to land sideways on a Saguaro. They would get a very thorny welcome.

Every spring, different birds came to nest in my Saguaro and they are not, necessarily, the woodpeckers, even though they were the birds that did all the initial work. None of these nesting birds are very big, not even the woodpeckers. Too bad I couldn't have charged rent for holes in my Saguaro. Several tenants occupy just one Saguaro at one time. When you walk by a Saguaro with nests you can hear the babies chirping away, inside of the holes. If you get too close and stay too close, the mother will start to scold you, hoping you will take the hint and leave. I call the noise she makes scirping because it's chirping with intent to scold.

Saguaros can be fun, because of the birds and their nesting. They tend to select the bigger, older ones, even when they choose to peck out the holes. Birds build nests at Saguaro arm joints too, out in the open. The thorns hold the nest in. Saguaros are stately looking and can grow to be very tall and broad. Some of them grow lots of arms. Saguaros can remind you of people, and when they get one or two arms, they especially remind you of people. Saguaros grow very slowly, though. The arms seem to grow a little faster. The real large ones can be one to two hundred years old. It's expensive to buy larger Saguaros. They are very hard to move. They're dangerous to move, too, and a permit is required before one is taken out of the ground. Government fines are extremely steep if a permit is not first obtained. Saguaros are sold by the foot, and sometimes by the inch. A two-foot one can cost forty dollars or more. A two-inch one is only three or four dollars, so small ones are good to buy.

If you give Saguaros a little watering, they'll grow taller faster than if you give them no watering. You don't really need to water Saguaros and you don't really need to fertilize them, either, but if you water them once a week or every two weeks and fertilize them once a month (mix the fertilizer compound with water and pour it around the cactus), they will grow better and faster. Like the Desert Palm Tree, the Saguaro has a mass of roots—a very thick grouping. Because there are so many of them packed in together, the Saguaro (and the Desert Palm Tree) is held up very well. The Saguaro's root base goes downward and outward, but is fairly shallow, except for a taproot, that usually goes down fairly deep and so it better secures the potentially-tall cactus, to the ground. Saguaros don't take up much space on your lot because they grow upright, and any arms they grow are way up high. They also have a thin base.

Saguaros can get to be up to forty feet tall but the Mexican Cardon can get to be up to fifty feet tall. Both of these cacti are thick columnar ones, but the Cardon has several branches close to the ground that are upright. The Mexican Cardon, also known as the Pachycereus pringlei, produces tasty and edible fruit. There is an Argentine Cardon, the Trichocereus pasacana, which is conspicuously different from the Mexico one, but both of these can be used to make furniture. They can be made into long pieces of lumber. These very tall cacti will only grow in certain deserts and climates. If you grow any, they'll take a long time to get tall but you'll enjoy the fruit along the way.

If you like cactus, consider planting the ones that produce fruit. With some, there is a knack to removing the spines or the outer part of the fruit. There are recipes you can find that relate to using cactus fruit. If you have room for several of these fruit-type cacti, you can harvest the fruit at the same time. Jam, preserves, syrup, sweet relish, other relish, desserts, candy, et al. can be made from cactus fruit. It can also be put in salads.

The Mexican Cardon is less resistant to frost than both the Saguaro and the Argentine Cardon. They all require lots of sun, and snow and ice, depending on the amount and temperatures, can kill them all. Each cacti type has a range of temperature that they can live in. Before you invest in any, and this would relate to any and all types of plantings, know in advance what the range of temperature is for each cactus, and decide if the plant will be safe in your locale and in the spot where you want to plant it. Keep in mind that Global Warming has increased temperatures by a degree or two around the world. Some areas have been more affected by Global Warming than other areas. I make note of many details in by Global Warming book. Even with Global Warming being present, people should still be landscaping and gardening. There are still year-round seasons (and related growing seasons).

Many Killer Bee colonies (hundreds of them) have moved into Saguaro National Park in Tucson, Arizona. They started out in Africa, were 'let loose' in Brazil and went to Argentina and then headed northerly, all the way through Central America and then finally on up to Arizona and other states, where they like the dryness. There are still plenty of blossoms in dry areas. Not everything blooms and blossoms at the same time in dryer areas but something is usually available to them and so bees can make honey when and as they need to. There is enough rain, and flash rains come about a couple of times a year (or more), which sometimes causes flooding in spots but the flooding doesn't seem to hurt the plantings and vegetation and, in fact, it seems to help every growth. The flooding is usually not all that bad and it is short-term. Killer Bees keep increasing. Killer Bees continue to kill people and animals. More people should go into the pest-rid business around a number of states just because of the Killer Bees. That's my view.

Are some of the Killer Bees setting up hives in any of the holes in Saguaros—the ones that the birds have pecked out for their nesting? Yes. They are, which means that they could conceivably do the same on people's property, when there are Saguaros. They can also colonize underground, and in trees and in building structures. Bee hives can be inside of tree hollows. Abandoned or rarely-used buildings seem to be preferred by bees, too. They'll use any private hole, burrow, or cavity.

What I find interesting about Killer Bees is that if someone is approaching a hive or standing close to a hive, two or three of them will bump the intruder, as a warning for them to go the other way. That would be the time for the intruder to be very focused and alert and get considerably out of range, really quickly. Sadly, approaching animals don't know what to make of this bumping so they proceed as they had been and then end out getting stung, often to death. These killings would include beloved pets. Many horses have been killed. Usually, smaller animals are goners. Well, so are really large animals because there can be hundreds of stings. The heart goes, or breathing can stop so again, we need more laborers in pest control to hunt down and kill these Killer Bees. Killer Bees have become more than just a nuisance. They are a threat and they bring about death.

All children are in considerable jeopardy and should be profusely warned about Killer Bees and given adequate education about their habits and ways. Running fast and far away can save a life but even so, there could still end out being many bee stings and the person stung will have to get to emergency care, fast. The shock itself may require medical treatment, depending on the number of stings, and the patient.

If Killer Bees swarm and start to sting, run in a straight line, pull your shirt or blouse over your head to protect your face and neck (because those areas are what the bees are really going after) and get to somewhere where you can close a door. Run against the wind if you can as the bees will then be delayed. You might have to flail your hands around your eyes as you are running so they won't get your eye areas. If you live in an area where these insane bees tend to live, always be alert to begin with when you are out of doors at any time. They can even be in a populated area, assuming they find a place they consider to be safe for installing a hive. Hives are not always rounded and shaped. Everyone should know this. Hives can be packed in to some kind of irregular type of space—in the ground, in a log, up around the eaves of a building, packed in to a tree hole—and so it can go. That's what I mean—teach all children these facts. Killer Bees can live anywhere, and sometimes in the least expected areas.

<u>Humans really need to go on the warpath against these particular bees, literally, and exterminate Killer Bees and every year and all year wherever they are habituating around humans</u>. The Federal Government or the State needs to set up a program, just for year-round extermination. They could start at Saguaro National Park in Tucson, Arizona. Mexico should also set up such a program. <u>Do not let these bees increase any more than they already have. These Killer Bees are not needed but the Honey Bees are</u>. Preview an area first, every time, if you are going to do any yard or landscaping work. Check the whole area out real well. Keep in mind that all bee types can build up a colony fast, so check <u>every</u> time.

We also need to get rid of the Giant Hornets—now, and before they multiply. They are in the State of Washington and they came in from Asia. (A hornet is a type of wasp.) They are very aggressive and will attack people and animals, and other bees. They're going to try to get rid of them but who knows if they'll be able to prevent their spread?

The Giant Hornets started in western British Columbia, Canada, and somehow got down to Washington State from Vancouver Island. They don't attack people and pets unless they feel the nest is being threatened. They aren't the attackers that the Killer Bees are. Both Killer Bees and Giant Hornets kill Honey Bees, though, so both stinging insects should be eradicated. If they got over to the rest of British Columbia (the mainland), they could be spreading eastward from west-coast Canadian areas, and then they would go southward into other USA states besides Washington, if they can handle the cold. They are abundant in Manchuria, China. They are believed to have come in from China. How <u>enough</u> of them got on Vancouver Island to start spreading is anyone's guess. There would have had to have been one or more queens and that, alone, can be telling. In other words, somebody had to have purposely brought one or more groups of them over, for some reason or another. Perhaps they thought they'd get rid of certain insects for them? And so, their getting into Vancouver Island may not be so accidental. From Manchuria, China (Dongbei), you'd think they would be in North and South Korea by now.

These hornets are not hive-making insects, but their nests have chambers, like beehives have. Some hornets build their nests close to, or under the ground; other wasps build nests in trees and vines. These Giant Hornets build their nests so eggs can be placed in the chambers by any queens. Nests are paper-like but durable. Plants these flying insects eat are turned into this papery material as they are making their nests.

Bees like being out of the rain as much as possible so they like to be enclosed in a hole or cavity, or well covered, but they like their privacy and usually won't start building a hive if human or vehicle traffic is steady in an area. It is the same with the birds that peck holes in Saguaros. Saguaros add something special to a lot, though. They tend to be the first-noticed planting on a lot. They're stately and add a South-Western ambiance.

A strange phenomenon occurs with the Saguaro that no one can figure out and that seems to relate to arm growths. What is known as a Crested Saguaro crops up, but it is not at all common. Some have said that perhaps five in a million will crest, but others say there are a lot more than that. You can't miss these enigmas. They crest at the top, or can flare out. These anomalies look like they've been grafted but they haven't been. There is now a Crested Saguaro Society that retrieves photos of these odd cacti. The crested area ends out with several flowers when the cactus blooms. The cactus is apt to have some normal arms, and the cresting usually only happens on top. (In a few cases, it has occurred on the arms, too, though.) No one, yet, knows why they crest. It's some kind of mutation. The top can actually take on a number of looks. They don't all look flared. There is a good deal of growth activity at the very top—this is the point—and it tends to look stunted and all jammed in because there are always several outgrowths.

On occasion, but really rare, there are such outgrowths on the side arms (on one or more than one of the arms). The arm ends may look different from how the top of the Saguaro does but you know when there is an anomaly because there won't be a smooth rounded look at the ends. When top areas look odd, it looks like the Saguaro has had a bad-hair day. Yet these odd-looking cacti seem to endure.

Some have said the condition relates to a hormone in the plant. Others think it relates to their blooms, and to pollination that is done to the blooms. Some believe the condition cause relates to lightning. Many would love to have one grow on their lot but that probably will never happen. Something in their growth pattern gets interrupted and if the cause could be determined, and such a condition could be replicated by man, people all over the world would grow them and do we really want that to happen? It makes me think of Bonsai Trees, somewhat. They are made to grow small. Many like Bonsai Trees. They are curiosities, but do we really need stunted-dwarf trees? Some think they aren't natural because they've been tampered with. Bonsai Trees can be outside, but they tend to be put inside. Often, they are in a large pot.

The Crested Saguaro is a curiosity, for sure. People like to buy what is different, which is a subject all in itself. I have my own belief about the cause but who knows if it's right or not. It has to do with snow and freeze and it is this—if a cactus, when it is younger, has to endure snow and freeze on its top and has not yet grown to a certain height and thickness, the cells at the top get damaged. Have you ever seen what happens to a watermelon after it's been frozen? Check out the rind. It's damaged—seriously. Like a watermelon, a saguaro is loaded with liquid. After so many years, the top will, consequently, grow in odd ways. Even arms can get overly frozen at their top because they curve up. Snow can settle on top and be there long enough to freeze and damage the cells. That area is then doomed to grow in strange ways. Growth gets interrupted and the damaged cells disrupt the subsequent growth pattern. Yet, there is still growth. Saguaros have what is known as pleats all around the cacti. You will still be able to ascertain pleats when these Saguaros crest in irregular ways. The pleats will look odd and will seem to lack a pattern because of the interrupted growth. Again, this is my own personal, possibly new view.

When I was younger, I owned a home, then a condominium, but I never did much, if any yardwork and I always wanted a garden. I owned a house, subsequently, but didn't live in it very long so I did little yard work. I maintained what was there. It had a lawn. I bought a mobile home and got my chance—a lot of gardening was ahead of me. When I first moved into my singlewide mobile home, I had to get rid of most of what had been planted. There were two large Prickly Pear cactus plants that had grown way out, to excess—Opuntia engelmannii (Engelman prickly pear). There are actually around twenty-five species of this genus, but certain areas will get certain ones, more prevalently. I called them yard huggers because they took so much area and space. The 'pears' looked like thick green 'pancakes' all piled up and placed around together, but they had quills all over them so they weren't like pancakes at all. In fact, they must have had thousands of quills on them. Quite a few refer to these pancakes as pads. I had to clip each piece off with a long-handled pruner and pick the pieces up with large tongs. Some people use a pitchfork. (I got one later.) As each piece was picked up with the tongs, it then had to be put into a tall box so it could later be carried away.

Anytime you remove a cactus or parts of a cactus, you should use a sturdy box so when the contents are picked up, no one will be hurt. The bottom of the box should first be reinforced with strong tape. I did the same with Cholla cactus (Cylindropuntia imbricate or Cylindropropuntia bigelovii), which had grown tall and full and was supra loaded with quills (even more so than the Prickly Pear ones had been). There were also two of these types of plants on my lot, and they, too, had been quite large. I just didn't want those types of cacti and quills around my lot so I cleared those plantings off. They were planted right in the middle of where you needed to walk, too. In other words, they were in the way and deterred my movement. I didn't find either type to be all that attractive, either, compared with other cactus types, but, to each his or her own. Over the years, too, these supra-thorny cacti throw thorns around the lot. Occasionally, thorns break off of cacti, for a number of reasons, and they get blown around by the wind. I had to keep my eye out for these thorns, even years after I'd already removed the cacti.

Prickly Pears (the Opuntia group) are actually a succulent because of their round pads that store water. The plant spreads out as more of these quilled 'pancakes' are added to the plant. After a certain point, they can really start increasing in number. After some rains, the plant adds quite a few of these 'pancakes'. These 'pancakes' can resemble 'pears', but they are really more rounded than pear-shaped. Some say they resemble beaver tails and yes, they do—perhaps more so than 'pancakes' and 'pears'. All the many quills that grow on these 'pears' or 'pancakes' (the quills are sometimes called spines or needles) make it so the plant loses less water than a plant with leaves would. They grow out of what is known as areoles. These surround each quill and readily absorb water. Plants with leaves lose water by the process of transpiration. This is why they end out dropping off. A baby Prickly Pear will look quite harmless and innocent, but if you plant it, it will grow wide, wide, wide, and become a yard hugger. Other cacti might do this, too, so know how big and wide they can grow before you spend any money. To emphasize, too, Prickly Pears are prickly plus.

Sometimes, a resident has no choice but to get rid of certain plantings that are already on the lot. My theory about this is, don't get rid of anything unless the planting is dangerous or impractical. If a planting is healthy, you may as well keep it. If it's a little sick, just try to nurture it back to health. Often, you can. There have been a number of times when I ended out saving a particular planting. I was always glad I held out and kept trying. At least consider keeping a planting you don't like and that was there before you moved in. You can grow to like a planting, and remember that something you don't like, neighbors or visitors might like. If you remove perfectly decent plantings that are already established and really could continue to be used, you are essentially throwing away money, and you're also harming a planting.

One planting that a neighbor of mine had, which I secretly wanted him to get rid of, was Echinocereus stramineus, aka Hedgehog cactus. A similar genus is Echinocereus engelmannii (that sounds a little like that Prickly Pear I just noted—Opuntia engelmannii). Yes, the separate Hedgehog cactus do 'hedge' forward and all around, and yes, they do 'hog' a whole area. They grow, and keep adding more to the rest of the cluster or batch, all around them. You can get a hundred of these, all growing together, and they'll all lose lots of quills. To me, it's just too much of one type all in a large area. Each cactus got to be five or six inches tall, and were columnar and they all continued to grow side-by-side, in clusters. The area was loaded with quills, or spines as they're sometimes called. Echinos means porcupines, for the record—no surprise there. You can get too much cactus, jammed in together. In my cactus bed, each cactus is put in at a distance from the other cacti. If a cactus is a cluster or add-on one, it grows within one single pre-determined area and the rocks surrounding the bed that is closing them in keeps them contained so they stay in one area only. They cannot grow beyond the edger rocks.

With those Hedgehog ones, I don't know why my neighbor didn't just start potting the majority of them, to sell, except, there are plenty of cacti you can buy that are not that thorny or spiny. There's even cluster or add-on ones that don't have nearly that many thorns or spines on them. One day, he finally got rid of them, but so many thorns were left, all over the place. He just left them all there. Many of them blew over to my lot—grumbles. Some cactus drop or lose quills easily and a' plenty. Some drop or lose very few quills. Some drop essentially none. And, of course, succulents drop no quills at all. They have no tubercles or areoles, for one thing. (Again, quills grow in or from the tubercles and areoles.) It's pretty amazing that tubercles and areoles exist, when you think about it. They are there to keep cacti alive.

People wonder why cacti even exist. What is their contribution to nature, in other words, especially since they have so many quills. We could, as humans, be eating lots of cactus fruit if we would just get rid of the quills. Maybe we could be using the cacti and flowers for different foods/medicines/endeavors/projects, especially if we had to (like certain people native to certain areas have had to do, over the years in order and to survive and have a better life). Quills can easily be removed <u>if</u> people know how to do it. There could be many uses of cacti we have yet to tap into and utilized on a mass scale. In time, perhaps we will figure out more. Already, there are jams, relishes, sauces, and candies, but more foods could be made from cactus. Some cacti are used for building material, and for basket weaving and hat making. Medicines from the different cacti haven't, perhaps, been studied enough. Could cacti be better explored in the area of cancer research, for example? What about skin diseases?

I personally don't like to harm a planting, or to discard plantings, even if they have flaws. If nothing else, I pot such plantings and put them in one section. If a cactus is scarred, in some way, I put it in that one section and turn the cactus so you can't see the scar. Of course, if any cactus ever dies and rots, it is removed and replaced with another. Sometimes gophers eat the roots, and the next thing you know a perfectly good cactus has no life. They eat most any plant roots—cactus or otherwise—so sometimes you have to trap them, and take them out to the country. Everyone should own a small animal slam trap.

Generally, the better time to plant or re-plant anything is in March (or for sure, April), after the last frost or cold spell is done and gone. May is not the best month for this because by May, blooms and blossoms come out and you will preferrably want everything settled and in the ground before May. (May can work, though, especially in some warmer areas.) Rains can come in April, too, and this will help any of the plantings that are planted before April. Keep in mind that

'April showers bring May flowers'. Focus in on how much watering any new or re-planted plants are getting, though, whether it's been raining a lot, a little, or not at all. It can be tempting to overwater new plantings. Often, it is accidental—you water them, then it rains. You can harm certain ones with overwatering. Some plants will only take in what they need, however. Keep in mind that it can also rain a lot in March, in some areas, then when April rolls around, there may be little rain. Make a note of month-to-month weather conditions and patterns, in your particular area. Write such observations down somewhere. March or April is also the best time to do any major pruning or trimming but you can do some occasional minor pruning and trimming throughout the summer, as well. Realize that some plantings can go in to the ground in autumn, but assess the situation first because you might want to wait for spring.

As for when to plant, the spring is the best time, usually, but in the southern areas, some people put some plantings down in the ground in autumn because it is still warm, but it is usually early autumn. In southern areas there is plenty of sun during fall months. The nights are not too cold in the early autumn; in the later autumn, they can be. Many plantings will need three or four weeks to get established, enough so they can withstand colder months.

If any planting is put down in the ground in autumn, and if it is planted in a shady area, it will take more time to get established. By established I am referring to the growth of the root system. The roots have to grow well enough into the dirt to be very secure and the ground dirt will have to be packed into its usual, normal density, all around the roots. The root growth has to get to a certain point for a planting to be established.

Keep in mind that shade will always change—both during the day and over the four seasons. The sun moves from side to side (essentially) and the Earth goes around and rotates. It tilts to the sun's location in space. The bottom line is this: put plantings down in the ground at a time when they will be safe from too much cold and heat all year round. Even after a planting is established, not enough sun means that a planting can get to be too cold during colder weather and too much sun means that a planting can get too hot and can even burn (or cook) during the hotter weather. Try to pay attention where shade tends to be during the day and even over the year, and keep a regular watch over all plantings relative to any and all shading and shading areas. With many plantings, in many areas, they will do well no matter where they are planted. These are good plantings to acquire.

In hot areas, some people think that practically everything has to be planted in the shade. This is not true; in fact, many plants have to be planted in spots where the sun hits. If any plants seem to be being harmed by sun contact during the hottest summer months, cover those plants with an old bed sheet or a similar cloth. The material must be a 'breathing' type of material. The use of plastic will cause plants to bake so don't use it as a cover. You can also cover plants with a piece of crisscrossed open-patterned wood or plastic (usually used for any shading). (These pieces are also used for lattice panels and you can cut them to size.) Put tall bricks to each side of the plants and lay the piece of crisscrossed open-patterned wood or plastic piece on top of the tall bricks. This will create the needed hot-weather shade. You could even use a regular piece of wood so the plant only gets some sun, some of the day. The sun will come in at an angle for a short period of time only so the plant won't get burned. Some cacti should be in the shade, at least some of the day, but some are all right if they're in full sun, and even in full sun all day long.

If you have to dig up a cactus, particularly a large one, or dig up any planting for that matter, and you want to transport it elsewhere on the lot, you should put the item in a box first. The box should be low or shallow so when you go to put the planting into its new place, all you have to do is tip the box up and the cactus will slide down into the hole that's been pre-dug. If you are transplanting a succulent, you want to try to keep it upright because they have offshoot blades or branches that encircle the plant. These blades/branches can easily break so you don't want to put the plant on its side, lest a blade/branch should break off. Some people call these blades or branches, petals, but they're really too firm to be petals. Aloes and agaves are examples of plants that have these encircling blades and branches. Such plantings you must always keep upright, when planting and transplanting. Regular, non-cacti and cacti plantings can usually be set on one side during the transplanting process. Nothing will break off. Quills or spines on a cactus usually don't break off. They are tightly attached to the cactus.

I keep two plastic/rubber-based garbage can lids around, as part of my gardening-items group. These are needed for whenever I dig dirt out of one spot. I shovel the dirt onto the upturned lid as it sets on the ground near to where I am digging. At times, too, I use these lids to hold a larger cactus I'm digging up and transporting to another part of the lot. When the cactus—usually a heavier one—is on the lid, I can carry it or pull or scoot it along to its new site. These lids are good because they're rounded a little and have an upturned edge so dirt can't spill out of them. You can carry the lid and the contents to a new area or you can pull the lid and its contents along from one place to another on your lot if you need to (even after putting in some or a lot of dirt into the lid). Of course, some people just use a wheelbarrow, to transport dirt or plantings. I never owned a wheelbarrow.

If you have a wheelbarrow, when it's not in use, turn it upside down because if rain collects in it, mosquitoes will breed there. It will also rust in the cavity. Once or twice a year, go around and screen for mosquito-breeding areas. Control such situations as best you can. If anything collects water, remove it or put it upside down. In potted plants, use porous potting soil so water won't collect for very long at the top of the pot. Mosquitoes need water to breed in. If an area dries where their eggs are, the eggs will die. Mosquito eggs hatch fairly fast, some say in a couple of days. Everyone worries about mosquito-related diseases, like malaria, West Nile Virus, Dengue fever, Chikungunya, yellow fever, encephalitis, and Zika fever, even though most of those are not in America, but, some of them have already come to North America.

You do not want pools of water collecting anywhere. You simply don't want the mosquitoes. Unfortunately, not all near-by neighbors are so conscientious, and they may routinely leave standing water around on their lot or property so you will still get the seasonal mosquitoes. Helpless dogs can get heartworms from mosquitoes, too, and they're so often outside. They can really get menaced by biting mosquitoes, too. <u>Standing water has to be removed and eliminated, everywhere it is</u>. Warmer-climate areas are vulnerable to these diseases. Mexico, Central America, and South America, the Caribbean areas, the more southern African countries, India, South-East Asia, and Indonesia are the vulnerable places for mosquito diseases. Rarely do certain of these viruses hit the United States, but knock on wood because they do and you never know when or how hard any one of them will be to contain. The coronavirus—COVID-19—came in like a flood to all countries around the planet and it came in from China, but it is not a mosquito-caused viral disease. It gets into animals. People got it from a bat from a science lab, or from a wet market that sold raw meat, in China. Some wonder if they got it from eating cats or dogs, because that is done in China. The coronavirus is aerially transferred, person to person or even from touching where the virus is and then touching the face area—the eyes, nose, or mouth. The virus can enter all three ways. Breathing it in is the more common way to get it.

With some plantings, all you need to do is hand carry them over to their new site. Before you do, a hole for the planting has to be pre-dug. If a planting tends to shoot outward, as an aloe or agave type of plant, you have to be especially careful when transporting it and when putting it into the ground because, again, the offshoot growths are easily torn or broken. If you accidentally have a blade/ branch break off, you can use scissors to clip the two sides of the blade or branch to shape it into a point so it at least looks similar to the other, longer pointed blades/branches. As the aloe or agave gets bigger, bottom blades/branches get bigger, anyway, and you can cut the lower ones off, which usually takes care of any blade/branch that was previously damaged. Over time, you can cut off one group or ring that goes around the lower blades/branches, or even more than one, depending on how low you want the existing lower ring to be when it is next to the ground.

With large agaves, some people like to cut off the lower blades/ branches at the bottom base area (at least a few times, all the way around). They may cut off a lower ring of blades after the lower blades/branches hit the ground and start decaying. They may even cut a second ring of blades/branches from the base of the planting. This way, the blades/branches won't touch the earth. After the second clipping, around the plant, some people usually leave the agave be. However, some people like to cut off several rings of blades from off the bottom. You have to use a saw if the agave is large because scissors won't work anymore. (You only use the scissors after first using a saw and the scissors can then be used to clip off any of the blade's remaining threads.) Some agaves can become really large. With agaves, you can use scissors to cut off the sharp points from the tip of their branches/blades (because they are so sharp). Therefore, there will be general safety if people or animals accidentally bump into them.

Any cutting off of those large, thick branches or blades from agaves can be tricky. A power saw tears them up and makes a stringy mess. If you have a good hand saw, cut each branch or blade with the saw blade moving towards you (and you have to carefully situate yourself to do this). If you try to cut the other way (from where you are to away from where you are so you are pushing), it doesn't work, so you have to keep raising the saw blade and cut towards you with the saw (pulling the saw) until you are almost through the whole branch/blade or are even all the way through it. If there is just a little bit left to cut through, you can cut that part of the branch/blade off with a good, sharp pair of scissors. It will be very thin there, not at all thick. You snip off any excess or strings with the scissors, and shape the cutting that you just did with the scissors so the cut is completely flat and blunt and has that finished look. With these large agaves, you don't have to do these very often. Agaves are very popular in South-Western states. I write about them more in my *Living and Travelling in the South-West* book. Other succulents and different cacti are noted, as are touring sites, food, animals, and many other subjects. Certain subjects centering on Mexico are also covered. It is fun to read.

Friends and neighbors can establish a plant-exchanging program. You can swap cuttings and baby plantings, and even larger plantings. You may have some plant types someone else can make good use of and vice versa. Doing this will, of course, save some money, and also foster good will. Find out who the gardeners are and keep in touch with them from time to time. You may want to join a local gardening club.

At times, you may have to do some revising or re-planting. The spring and early summer is a good time to do this, but if you can't get to it then, as noted before, do it in autumn, before it starts to turn cold. The plant will need to well settle in before the cold comes. One planting may grow too big for an area, or it just may not look good where it is. Or, perhaps it might be getting too much sun. Perhaps it may be in the shade more than it should be. In any event, if putting it elsewhere would be best for the plant, this is what you should consider doing. It is not hard to transplant plants unless they are fairly large. With increased size comes more difficulty so transplant plantings as early on as possible before they get bigger. You have to be able to think ahead if you are a gardener.

When you first plant a planting, you don't always know, at the time, if it should stay where it is. Generally, it will stay, but sometimes it's better for the plant if it's re-planted and put somewhere else. You may decide to remove it from the yard, in which event, perhaps someone you know might want it. You can always pot some plantings. Potted plants can decorate one or more areas around the lot. Sometimes, you may find some plantings later that you prefer over some others you've already planted. This sometimes happens in the world of gardening. This situation can be the sole cause for re-planting or potting, or for giving some of a planting to someone else. It's just not always good to mess up a perfectly good planting by uprooting it. Sometimes too many of its roots are cut or roots can be cut too short when someone is transplanting. It is never good to ruin or throw away a perfectly good planting. Be utilitarian.

Transplanting can be tricky and many plantings can die because of it, especially if they have already established an elaborate root system. Too often, roots are cut off too close in to the plant. They're chopped off too short, in other words. This is not at all good for plantings. And also, too often the taproot is cut because the digger does not put forth enough effort when digging it out, whole. You have to wet down the dirt around the roots quite well and then slowly and gently pull each root up so they don't snap and break, if you are removing a planting. The water must be allowed to soak way down deep and well so that all the roots can be loosened. You sometimes have to jiggle the roots out a little, but never too forcefully. You have to do that with the taproot. You may have to dig a little deeper to get that.

To emphasize, to remove any planting, the <u>best</u> way, you first wet the area and let that water soak in. Then, you dig out some dirt, very carefully so you don't cut any of the roots, then you re-wet that area and let that water soak in, and you keep on doing this. Remove dirt, wet down, soak, and loosen roots, in other words, until it is safe to lift all the roots up without breaking them, which would include the taproot. As you do this, gently and carefully pull out the roots, one by one. Try to keep whole as many roots as you can. Maintain a high level of patience while you are doing this. I don't know if plants feel pain or discomfort but if they do, then it is better to not break, cut, or chop off any of the plant's roots. If you get all the roots loosened, by gently and carefully pulling each one out when the dirt is totally saturated and soggy and much of the dirt has been removed, then, when you put that plant elsewhere, it has a much better chance of survival. (If only plants could talk, I'm sure they would say "thank you".

When you go to put the planting in its new site, you want all the roots to have enough room to thrive in the soil. You don't want to jam or bunch the roots up, underneath the planting. The hole you dig for it has to be wide enough for the plant and deep enough for the plant's roots. You spread the roots all around, at good angles. The ground area where you put the planting will be wet, since it is easier to dig out dirt that is wet. Hold the planting up so the roots fall down into the hole, spread most of the roots outward, somewhat, and put loose dirt all around the roots of the planting with your other hand, while you are holding up the planting. You will probably have to keep tipping the plant a little, as you put loose dirt in, all around the roots.

Once all the dirt is in and patted down as best as possible around the planting, hose down the spot a little so the dirt gently packs in all around the now-buried roots. The area around the planting should be slightly recessed and this is what you want so that water will always collect in that bowl area and the planting will be better watered over the years. Some plantings do all right with a flat top surface area, but some may need more water; therefore, a rounded, slightly dug-out dip or bowl area would be better for them.

If the planting is a small cactus, put it in a hole and tip the cactus a little as you put loose dirt around the cactus. I use a spade to do this and I don't handle the cactus. The spade does. If it is a larger cactus, you may need to put the cactus on a shovel blade and tip the cactus as you put loose dirt in, all around the roots. You always try to hold a planting up at just the right height as you are putting loose dirt all around the roots. Doing this right gets to be a skill and a gardener improves after having enough practice. If a cactus is taller and it tends to tip over after it is planted, put a wood stake up beside the cactus so it will stay upright. A stone can work, too. Get the cactus upright. Remove the stake or stone later on when the cactus is sure to stay upright.

The taproot is always a long one that usually grows downward (vertically), but it can grow over more to the side, too, depending on how the planting went into the ground and depending on other factors, as well. A taproot can look like the main roots, but it is bigger and thicker, and it grows longer. The larger roots can be growing all around the planting but a taproot is usually there. Some plants don't have a taproot. If there is a taproot, usually there's only one. For example, the carrot itself is the taproot of the carrot plant. If you envision a carrot, you can conclude how vital taproots are. The taproot is of utmost importance to any planting. A planting can go into shock, wilt, and die if its roots are chopped off too short, or if its taproot is broken off or cut off too short. The taproot can grow very deep and be very long so you have to dig all around water-saturated dirt and work hard at getting it out, in a way that won't harm it. To repeat, you have to <u>keep</u> removing dirt and adding water and carefully dig and feel around in the soggy, muddy water to get the entire taproot out. If you only get some of the taproot, it may live when you re-plant it, but it won't be the ideal situation.

You'll have to <u>use both hands</u> to ease all the roots out, slowly. Usually, when you get to the actual taproot, you know it. This method relates to the removal of any planting from the ground. To clarify further and to repeat, as you keep removing dirt, keep wetting the area with the hose and let more water soak deeper into even more of the ground so that all the roots, slowly and one by one, can end out being eased out, without breakage. If the plant doesn't have real deep roots, you can go ahead and gently pull up the whole plant, as long as the dirt is pretty soggy and you know all the roots will come up. You can shake off this muddy dirt, or gently tap the dirt off with a gardening hand tool. Frankly, there are plantings that have oodles of fibrous roots, which don't go down real far, but there are other plantings that have several thicker, single-strand roots, including one very long taproot. Certain desert plants have a large root system because they have to be able to take in more moisture. Also, roots are obviously needed, to secure a plant into the ground. Mainly, though, roots drink in water.

If you are transplanting, dirt and debris can get on the planting while you are transplanting. Gently hose this off after you've finished the transplanting. If that which was transplanted was a thorny or quilly cactus, hose off what you can, but you may need to use an old toothbrush to get between the thorns/quills and remove any dirt or debris. If tiny rocks are stuck between the quills, use a nut pick. Hosing is also needed for packing in all the dirt and evening out the top ground area, after the cactus goes into the ground.

If you ever buy terrariums, which are rounded, dish-like planters that are filled in with potting soil and a variety of small plants, eventually these small plants grow to a large enough size that they need to be re-potted or put into the ground somewhere. Terrariums are visually lovely to begin with, and it's a bit disheartening to have to take them apart, later on, but this must be done because roots will crowd in if you don't. Plus, the small plants will grow and become too big for the planter.

With terrariums, some roots grow to the side and not downward, and you want to straighten this out when you re-plant these plantings, if you can do so without breaking any roots. Usually, you can straighten out the roots, but sometimes the roots cannot be bent. Still, you point the roots downward and outward as much as you can when you plant anything. It's good to re-plant plantings in terrariums as soon as possible because the round, shallow perimeter areas of the planter cause the roots to curve and to grow that way.

There's a great deal of effort that goes into transplanting so you have to be prepared for that. Pre-plan the work and projects. You can't do it right if you're impulsive and impatient. Just try to do a little at a time but it's good to do all your re-planting in one day if you can because you'll have all the right gardening tools out and will only get dirty during the one day. Personally, I like to take a whole day off just to do landscape and gardening projects, or at least, a half day off for that.

Again, before you begin your time of tackling a gardening and landscaping project, assemble everything you will need, like a hoe, rake, shovel, saw, potting soil, gardening gloves, and clippers. When you are done, go all around the lot and retrieve all supplies so you don't forget anything. Quite often, something is left outside in the sun and rain, and can be left outside, for days.

If you want a real nice lot, you may need to work outside two or three days a month for a time, depending on what projects have stacked up. Gardening helps to keep your weight down, and it gives you a sense of accomplishment. Some people work more days, some work less days, but it's all good unless you become a slave to it, in which case, you may want to either move, or hire a gardener.

REMOVE THE UNWANTED, START SELECTING, AND GET STARTED

Aside from the Prickly Pear and the Cholla cactus, another planting that was on the lot when I moved in wasn't impractical, at first, but it became impractical—very—and it, too, had to be removed. <u>In planning out your landscaping, try to have vision</u>. This can apply to anything on a lot, if you are not a first owner. In my particular case, it was a palm tree that got to be too much for me (a desert fan palm of a particular type). I didn't mind trimming off the lower fronds for a while, but it got more and more difficult for me to trim them. By trimming, I mean sawing them off with a hand saw (or a power saw, if you have one). I used a hand saw. Every time I'd trim off the lower fronds, that had died and browned, it wasn't more than a month or two later that I'd have to trim off a row or two of dead fronds, again. The dead fronds were always unsightly because they browned and drooped down. If too many fronds droop on these palm trees, the tree acquires a grayish-brown beard, which looks pretty tacky. With every fronds cutting, my palm tree kept growing taller and taller and this was the problem.

This kind of palm tree provided little shade, too, which was another drawback. Some palm tree types provide more shade than others do but people don't usually have palm trees for the shade. They have them for the ambiance and décor. In tropical areas that are balmy, breezes cause fronds to pleasantly move about so these palm trees have a different effect on residents there than do the palms that grow around dry, hot areas that are not near water. For me, now, I only like the short palm trees, for practical reasons. Some of these, however, are so short that you can walk right into the fronds, once the palm tree is full grown. Some fan palms are more fern-like. In some foreign countries, the people use the fronds (or fan parts) as roof thatch, after the fronds have dried. These roofs last for years and years, too. You couldn't do that here, though. Fire department people would be on your case real fast. Some palm tree types, in some world areas, are protected by their government, and they cannot be dug up. Permits to remove them are not even available.

The palm tree I had cut down was a California fan palm (aka the Washingtonia filifera). These trees are all around California, Arizona, and Florida. They get to be thirty-five feet tall and get to have a three-foot diameter trunk. They're sometimes confused with the Mexican fan palm (Washingtonia robusta), that grows taller and has a broader base. Mexican fan palms are found in the same three states; both had originally come in from Mexico. This palm can get to be seventy-five to one hundred feet tall and get to have a fourteen to eighteen-inch diameter.

Both of these kinds of palm trees end out having beards if no one trims them. Sometimes, beards are called petticoats but they aren't at all pretty, like petticoats tend to be. I've heard them referred to as skirts, but that is not the best word, either. Therefore, that word isn't the one I would use. They look more like beards to me, since you can only see what is in your vision and can't see all the way around. Besides, beards you usually have to trim. Who trims petticoats and skirts? When a palm tree has just had its dead fronds cut off, its beard has been trimmed. I tend to consider palm types that need to be de-fronded 'hes' and the ones that don't 'shes', but that's, maybe, a little silly. In any event, the 'shes' tend to be shorter palms, and some she-palms can be very short. They are easy to keep trimmed but you may not need to or want to trim them because the fronds don't die. This is just my way of looking at palm trees—i.e. referring to some as being he-palms and others as being she-palms. The reality of it, though, is that they are really both 'its'.

Frankly, some beard-prone palm trees never get trimmed and this looks so tacky. As certain palms grow upward, the dead fronds droop, all the way down towards the ground. This really looks unkempt. Dead fronds keep on adding, as time goes by. These dead fronds spoil the look of an area, especially when passers-by see several of them as they go through an area. Dead fronds can obviously be a fire hazard, too. You only want green on a palm tree, other than its base, which tends to be light brown or tan and has scales that stick out from the base. Some people shave off the outer scales so the tree base looks thinner and smooth and can be easy to climb when the tree gets real tall (but no one ever climbs up them). Some ladders go only so high so in some countries, a frond trimmer might have to scale the upper part of the tree to get to the upper area. They use a special kind of rope to get up higher. Sometimes, a special kind of truck that has a ladder built on it has to be used for the really tall ones.

It gets more difficult to trim fronds, and usually gets to be more expensive to cut them off because the tree continually gets taller. You keep having to cut the dead ones off, on a regular basis, until the tree finally stops growing, which can take years and years. For this reason, some people seek out other types of palm tree—that don't get much higher than a one-story home. There are shorter types out there and you won't need a big ladder to trim them. The lowest palm tree fronds, you can saw off when standing on the ground. Again, some palm trees you don't even need to trim, once they reach their full height.

Because palm tree types have scales along their base, when fronds are cut off, more scales will be present. You will see the recent blunt-cut frond scales, as well. People will remove these outer scales so the base of the tree is smooth, but also because it reduces or eliminates insect problems because insects can live in these scale areas. (So can wasps, which especially like to be up higher on the tree.) Some think that certain palm trees look better descaled, but this is a matter of opinion. Many businesses prefer the descaling because if customers were to run into a non-descaled one, they could get scratches from the scales that are left from the cuttings. Some businesses may avoid cacti with sharp quills and needles, for this very reason.

The State of Florida has many different kinds of palm trees, more so than other states have, including the State of Hawaii. Hawaii is loaded with palm trees, though. Texas has palm trees, too, and a number of them originated in Mexico. You'll see the occasional palm tree in the other southern American states. Most coastal areas in warmer areas all around the world have palm trees. This is why there is such an amazing variety of them. They can be tall, short, wide, thin, large, small, and their fronds do not all look the same, either. Many palm trees are transported to other countries, to be sold there. Some are special ordered. Some come in to other countries when they are very tall, indeed. I don't know how they are transported but it must be a very expensive operation. Others come in as baby palms.

It is unwise to plant a palm tree if winters get too cold. In fact, severe winters are bad for many desert plantings. Many palm trees do fine if the soil is somewhat sandy and so do certain other plantings. Such trees hold in better than if soil is real loamy and soft. Some plantings don't fare well in sandier soil, though, so know your soil, and your plants. There are temperature zones that relate to temperature range, amount of moisture and rainfall, and growing potential in general. The Plant Hardiness Zone Map is good to refer to. In the more southern areas, as a general rule, the zones range from zone 8 to zone 11. (Zone 12 is hot and desert. A desert area can be Low, Intermediate, or High, which gets quite hot.) Certain, specific plantings do well in only certain zones. Most palm trees do well in the southern zones. As a general rule, palm trees are very hardy. They're very adaptable to warm-climate areas.

Some palm trees produce edible fruit, but with some palm tree types, the fruit isn't very palatable. Palm trees all have varying growth rates and maximum typical heights. If a palm tree stays short, because that will be their maximum height, they won't be sprouting any new fronds. There is such a thing as a Dwarf Palm. Some people like the Date Palm, because of the dates. They get tall, but not as tall as the one I had. The Mediterranean fan palm (Champaerops huilis) only gets to be around twenty feet tall. The Chinese fan palm (Livistona chinensis) will end out being much shorter. For palm trees, you just have to shop around. You can even send for seeds. The ones that are taller are always in demand. The taller ones that produce lots of colorful fruit are also in demand, whether the fruit is palatable, or isn't. Some people will actually seek out Coconut Palms or Date Palms, for obvious reasons, but other palms that produce fruit are sought after, as well. They're generally found in countries outside of the USA.

Local businesses, including restaurants, seek out the prettier, more eye-catching palm trees. Some of the palms are from exotic areas, like Fiji and Tahiti. Some come in from Hawaii. They become a form of advertising for companies and they serve as beckoning beacons, quite frankly. This beckoning is usually something subliminal. Some types of palms are more prone to attracting certain insects, though, and they can become diseased so this factors in to people's selections, or at least, it should. Businesses usually hire out maintenance, to take care of their landscape problems. The better insect control requires a specialist.

Amount of space available for any of the palm tree types is important. Some of the shorter palm trees can have very broad crowns and so all that space is taken up by those palms. Many palms are not so tall that you can barely walk under them. Grown size—both height and width—can determine whether they are selected, or aren't. One of my favorite shorter palm trees is the Sylvester Palm. The different kinds of palms also have different kinds of leaves (fronds are sometimes referred to as leaves). Leaves (fronds) can be thin and bendable; others can be stiff and unbendable. Some palms have fern-like leaves; others have stiff and fan-like leaves (fronds). The fans of palm trees can be different shapes, too.

Some palms have a broad trunk or base, but others are slimmer. Some have downright skinny bases. When you see a palm tree that's eighty to a hundred feet tall, as some can get to be, and it has a real skinny base, you very much notice it. Most palms have what is called a swollen area at the bottom of their trunk or base. The bottom of the base is thicker there, and it tapers in as it goes upward. This gives the tree more security because it gives the tree more roots that can go down and keep the palm in place, even when winds blow strong. It's amazing that in certain high-wind areas, the palm trees are still well situated and haven't blown over.

Occasionally, you'll see thin-based palms with curved trunks or bases. Blowing winds caused this to happen. Still, the roots stay strong, which indicates something about the root growth. Hurricanes and typhoons are known to occur where palm trees are. If winds are high, where you live, you may want to choose palm trees with broader bases and ones that don't grow too tall.

Taller palms look good when they're near a street, where they are more easily seen by more people. You see them line avenues in certain cities. For this reason, people like to plant them closer in to the front of their lot. Sometimes, people plant them near a patio or pool area, particularly the smaller and shorter palms. It tends to be the smaller and shorter palms that are planted in gardens, to be garden specimens. If tall palm trees are planted, there may be more room underneath to grow other types of plantings, because of the thin trunks.

When a palm tree is planted, it is important to occasionally moisten the roots, but don't saturate or drench them. If you already have a palm tree on your lot and do not want it, get rid of it before it grows any more. You could perhaps dig it up if it isn't too large, and then give it to someone else, but even the small palms can be heavy, depending on the type. Once a palm tree ceases to be a baby palm, it's pretty hard to transplant it. This is because palm trees hold so much water and are so heavy. Also, when you plant/re-plant a palm tree, do not plant it too deep or too shallow into the ground. Either situation can end out being problematic.

Again, transporting some palm trees from area to area (to a new area) can be expensive, in large part because of bulkiness and/or weight, but rarity factors in to cost as well. Getting permits can be expensive. Some types (like with other kinds of vegetation) may not be allowed in to certain places. It's surprising where palm trees can come from, though. Probably all continents have palms, except for Antarctica.

Never buy a palm that has any yellow leaves (or fronds). It could be that they were in deficient soil for a while, but it could also be LY aka Lethal Yellowing. Leaf hoppers (insects) can cause trees to become diseased. To avoid decay, a tree doctor can inject the LY tree, off and on, with tetracycline antibiotics, but this will only slow down the inevitable and it is not a cure. Also, all around the tree will need to be sprayed, to kill any hoppers.

Contrary to popular belief, palm trees generally grow pretty fast. In only three or four years, you can have a pretty tall palm tree if the palm gets ample water. Some people will pay over a thousand dollars or more to have a taller palm tree transported and planted on their lot, but it really doesn't take that long for them to get tall. You can buy a small palm tree in a pot for from twenty to fifty dollars, on average, and plant the palm tree yourself. In three or four years, it will have fairly good height. If you really want them to grow fast, water them. People pay money to have large Saguaros put on their lot, too, but Saguaros don't grow nearly as fast as the average palm tree does.

Certain palm trees that end out being quite tall are not only quite expensive to bring in and plant on lots and land, but they're expensive to have planted. Just think about all that would be involved. You have to tip them up, for one thing. How easy would that be? Still, some businesses are rich and can afford this. They believe they will draw in customers. Certain ones can be in demand. Some palms are what I call exotic palms. Royal Palms, for example, are in demand by the rich. Certain other ones are, too. Some palm trees are from the South Seas, so no wonder they cost so much to bring in. Some are from Africa. Some are from Arab countries. Date palms don't end out with dead fronds, but they don't get all that tall and they have a very large base. There are a number of these palms in the USA already—from the California coast to the Florida coast—and many of them have come from Middle-East areas.

If you have the time and money, dead-frond cutting and removal won't be a problem. It got to be a problem for me. Every time I needed to cut off dead fronds, there would be around a dozen dead ones if I got to it fast enough. I had bought a ladder just for this project and I used the ladder several times when I cut the fronds off, but after a while, it got to be too dangerous for me, especially with the wasp problem. All it took was for there to be one nest of wasps up there in the palm tree to deter me from cutting off the dead fronds. I had to wait until the next season set in (after the wasps disappeared). It became dangerous to get up on the ladder, too, to cut off the fronds. I figured this out real fast. I didn't want to fall off the ladder because

I was trying to shoo away the wasps or because I got stung. When I was finally able to cut off the fronds, I had to use a saw on each frond and I sawed in close to the base. The sawing itself can be a little tricky when you're on a ladder and are up high. The ladder has to be set against the rather thin palm tree. For a time, I was able to use a long-handled saw trimmer while standing on the ground, but pretty soon, it did not reach the fronds.

There were two other reasons why I was disenchanted with palm trees. One was because throughout the year they would cast off long branches (or panicles), which have feather-like looking ends on them (the inflorescence). These panicles are as long as the fronds, and they look a little like the fronds except for the ends of them. Somehow, these branches break off and fall to the ground, especially after it's been windy. (An occasional frond might break off, too, but so often, it's the panicles that do.) These panicles grow in amongst the fronds. You see both of them here and there, laying on the ground, especially after a storm. The other reason has to do with seeds and offshoot growths from the seeds. They throw off many seeds and you notice small single blades shooting up from the ground soon after the rains have ended. You pull these single blades up but you don't get the roots because the main part of the plant is under the blade joint so the plant (the palm tree seedling) keeps on growing.

The only way you can get rid of these numerous palm tree seedlings is to use an old table knife. You insert it into the ground next to and under a seedling at an angle, loosen the dirt, and then pull up the seedling. But, you have to put your thumb and index finger way down close into the ground, as deep as they will go and into the loosened dirt. Then, you grab the seedling at or below the blade joint so you can pull it up by the root. It gets easier after you've done a few. If you don't do it this way, you'll only pull up part of the plant. After a rain, the seedlings will come up by the roots if you pull them out by hand, but it's still better to loosen the dirt with an old table knife when it comes to removing these particular seedlings. Loosening the dirt is the key.

Most weeds come up better by loosening the dirt with an old table knife. In fact, with some, this method is imperative. Almost always, though, after a good rain, all weeds can be easily pulled up by the roots. You just have to pull them up from <u>way down</u> on the base and right next to the ground. Little by little, a gardener learns what is best to do and when it is best to do it. You should remove palm tree seedlings (shoots) fairly soon after you first notice them. There may only be a few; there may be a blanket of them.

Keep in mind that these palm tree seedlings are going to keep coming if you keep the palm tree. Some palm tree types seed more than others do, and the number of seedlings will correspond to the size of the palm tree. Some people pot these palm tree seedlings, and give them to others, or sell them. I personally never did that because too many people neglect cutting palm tree beards in a timely way, or cutting them at all. It's kind of like when too many dogs and cats get bred so other cats and dogs end out being euthanized. So many that are, shouldn't be being bred. If they're not bred, they won't exist. You can stop the breeding. You can cut the palm tree beards.

It dawned on me one day that I didn't really need that palm tree on my lot. Other plantings on my lot added to whatever ambiance I needed. I could see palm trees all over town if I wanted too and I didn't need one on my own lot. So, I called around and finally found some men who were from Fiji. They were used to working with palm trees. They didn't charge me much at all, surprisingly. They cut the palm tree down at the base and real low to the ground but they didn't de-root it and remove the stump. (I saved money that way.) So, I piled and arranged different-sized larger rocks on top of it and around it and made myself a mound of rocks. The rock pile looked great. I recommend rock piles for decoration whether they cover something up or don't. Little lizards and horned toads lived in my rock pile, so that was nice. Fortunately, no snakes or scorpions were ever seen. (I never once saw a snake or a scorpion on my lot the whole time I lived in the desert area. They may well have been in the country, but I never saw any of them in town.).

I was able to use my ladder for other things, thankfully. You really need two ladders if you take care of a home and yard. One type is A-shaped when you open it up, so it becomes secure on its own. The other one you have to set up against something before you can use it. It is a linear type, and it's adjustable and can therefore get you up to higher heights than the A-shaped type can. You need ladders, and it's a pain if you have to borrow someone else's.

A ladder can be used for getting up on a roof, getting up to clean the grooves of awnings (to clear them out of pine needles and dirt, mostly), or getting up close to a tree so you can cut off and trim certain of the branches. The point is that all was not lost, relative to the somewhat costly ladder, after I had the palm tree removed. It was still useful. When I bought it, I got it on sale and it was only forty-some dollars. The A-shaped one I bought used, for the same amount of money, almost. Presently, collapsible and adjustable aluminum ladders can cost around a hundred dollars (or more). A-shaped ones are a little less. (They're both certainly worth it though.) I kept the linear ladder flat on the ground and to one side of the mobile home, behind where my raised, wooden deck was, along the side and so no one could see it.. I put boards to the side of it, so it was doubly hidden. No one ever saw it but me. The other ladder—the A-shaped one—I kept in the shed. I had to tip it to get it in the shed door, but that was not a problem. It stayed closer to the front. I needed both types for landscaping projects around my lot because of all the many plantings that were there to tend to. Plus, I had to get up on my roof.

Ladders fit nicely along the side of a mobile home (or a house), but you have to set them a certain way so the mobile home skirting isn't harmed by the weight of the ladder. You might need to put something between the skirting and the ladder, like a taller board or panel. (You don't want the ladder to dent in or scratch the skirting.) You want to set any ladder where it can't be seen by passers-by. Setting them next to an outside wall is usually best and is often the only alternative. My long ladder happened to be under an awning so it didn't get rained on and stayed in the shade. Some collapsible ladders can fit inside some sheds, but this isn't always possible with some of the long ones. It depends on how the ladder collapses, what type it is, and the size of the shed. My shed was about 8½' long x 9½' wide x 7½' high (with a tapered roof). That's a pretty good-sized one. It also has a top shelf area that can be used, but it is only to the back.

I personally do not recommend tall palm trees, just the short or shorter ones because they are safer. If you plan to plant one or more palm trees, you may as well go out and buy a good ladder, if you don't already have one, and also buy a hand saw or power saw with long cording. Buy some wasp spray, too. It's always good to have that item in the spring and summer because you never know where wasps are going to build a nest. (If you don't want to disturb them, wait until the weather turns cold and you can just knock any nests down with a broom or stick, pick them up, and put them in the trash; there'll be no wasp activity then, after the weather turns cold.) Wasps need water to build a nest and evaporative coolers are often up on roofs. Wasps get the water from coolers or cooler overflow, and they build nests in palm trees if the palm trees are not far from an evaporative cooler (or from any other water source). You can't do anything to prevent this, really. Even so, I dealt with very few wasps, year after year. Wasps get water from swimming pools, too. So do hornets.

By the way, many people keep their palm trees and don't mind the upkeep. They won't cut them down. I just wasn't one of those people (not with the tall types I had). Palm trees are really quite beautiful and, assuming they are the type needing trimming, as long as they're regularly trimmed, they stay beautiful. Otherwise, they're unsightly because of beards. There are many unkempt palm trees around many a city or town. In fact, there are perhaps more unkempt ones than otherwise. Sometimes it sure seems that way. You see palm tree beards all over the place and in some less affluent neighborhoods, especially, but you'll even see unkempt ones in wealthier neighborhoods.

Again, some types of palm trees don't need de-fronding, and the other ones that do will one day grow to their max and then won't need to be de-fronded anymore. But, by that time, they're skyscraper palm trees (well, maybe not quite, but it sometimes seems that way). They will have required a lot of trimming from time to time, up until the time that they max out in growth. Some people are not bothered by palm tree beards and so they don't trim their palm trees, but some neighbors don't like looking at them and they look so much better when they're trimmed and only green is showing. It's a night-and-day difference. I so much prefer Cyprus trees, instead of palm trees. They, too, are tall and somewhat thin. They're stately looking and also have ambiance. They never need trimming and they do amazingly well in desert areas. They withstand 110-115° heat, and need little water (but you have to monitor that). Some people love palm trees, though, and feel the need to have one or two on their lot. They usually don't need any watering.

If you are interested in palms (and cyads), get some books on the subject before you zero in on what to plant. This book provides you with some key basics and a little more, but books that are only on the subject of palms would obviously cover more and you could learn about all the types. Check the Internet, too. Go into Landscaping business sites, as well as general information sites.

As noted earlier, here were two other trees on my lot initially, and I ended out keeping both of them around. Those two trees became dominant and since they were to stay, I was eager to get going with other projects. There hadn't been much on my lot, other than the unwanted cacti and palm tree, and other than the acceptable two trees that I kept (the Arborvitae and the South-Western White Pine), so I was somewhat starting from scratch. I realized, early on, that my landscape should have high-level plantings, as trees and taller hedges, mid-level plantings, as bushes and shrubs, and low-level plantings, as plants, flowers, small cacti and succulents, and lower-growing bushes and shrubs. (I wasn't into groundcover too much, but some people are.) Shrubs and bushes of any height can be full or sparse, when they are full-grown. They can be very leafy or sparsely leafy. They can have lots of pine needles, or not that many. It just all depends on the type. In other words, you can either see through them, or it is difficult or even impossible to see through them.

Succulents and cacti are popular plantings in the southern areas of America. (Even people who live in northern areas like to have them, but they keep them in their home and they are the smaller ones, as with the cactus they'll sometimes buy.) It can sometimes be very difficult to tell one succulent from another, so you have to look these plantings up. The process of grafting can be done on certain known varieties. Grafting is done on succulents and cacti. It's done so one type of succulent or cactus will live, or live better, because of the other plant or part, and it is also done to produce a certain effect or specific shape. Sometimes grafting produces plant art. The two plants have to be compatible, and there is skill involved and you have to know what you are doing.

Some people don't know the difference between a succulent and a cactus and there is a difference. A succulent is sometimes considered a cactus, as well, but a cactus, if it is a true cactus, isn't usually considered a succulent. Cacti are usually firm plants, having many quills (or spines). Some quills or spines go straight out, some curve around and are even like hooks, but there are many, all around the cactus (and I do mean many). Some cactus types are absolutely loaded with them, though. Some have a lot more than others have, per square inch. Succulents are safer to handle and to be around in that only a few of them have anything sharp on them. Some may have some sharp points on them, as some aloes and virtually all agaves have, but they don't have a number of quills or spines all around them, like cacti have. They do not have tubercles and areoles, that dot all around a cactus and quills and spines that emanate from them. (It is the Mammillaria group that has the tubercles (and areoles), but other cacti only have the areoles.)

Many succulents, as the aloes and agaves, flare out, like a flower does. These flare-outs resemble petals, but they are very thick and firm. They're also greenish. There may be small hook-like ends along the branches or blades that encircle certain succulents so you must handle these particular succulents with care, just like you would any cacti, though less so. Many succulents have no quills or spines whatsoever. They are smooth, in fact, and are also not as stiff and dense as cacti tend to generally be. If they have petals, or branches/blades, they are of crisp composition and can break or snap off relatively easily. Cacti tend to be rounded or columnar, and they are loaded with quills/spines; in general, succulents are not as dangerous to handle, compared with the cacti but always take a close look before you handle anything that falls into either category. Some succulents are tall and thin, and some are flowery. Some are quite exotic looking and come from far-away areas. Succulents also make nice indoor plants (that you can later put outside if you want to). Also, some succulent types work very well as hanging baskets. Their branches are loose and dangly. Both succulents and cacti tend to live a long time, but succulents are more temperamental.

Succulents have large fleshy pads or outcrops of some sort, which enable the plants to store water for long periods of time. If there is little rain, which is the case around desert areas, then the native plants must store what water they can. There are a number of succulents that come in from parts of Africa, the Mediterranean, South-East Asia, and some even come in from Middle-East areas. These succulents have come in to the United States over the years. Many succulents, of course, come in from Mexico. Some come in from Central America and South America. A few have come in from countries that are somewhat obscure. Even though a number of succulents you see in America are not specifically native, but they grow fine in many areas of the southern United States. Of course, this is the same case relative to the many kinds of cacti found around the southern United States areas. The two plant types are often lumped together.,

All the different kinds of succulents and cacti seem to have adapted to different regions and areas that tend to be warm. Succulents come in from here, there, and everywhere and there are also some hybrids now. So, too, with cacti. Cacti stores or saves water for long periods of time. For example, Saguaros have pleats or folds that cause them to expand when they hold water. Some will call this phenomenon ribbing or pleating. A Saguaro can store water for a year or two before it begins to fade or die, assuming it doesn't get some water. (Both succulents and cacti store water and some are able to do this more than others are.) When it rains in desert areas, the water often disappears fast, not only because of the dry heat and breezes, but also because the roots of desert vegetation and plants soak in the water so quickly. Gulp, gulp, gulp, they all go.

In the South, cacti can be in a high, mid, and low-height range. It all depends on the cactus. Succulents usually don't get too very large, or tall. A few do, but most of them don't. In a landscape and on a lot, you can mix cacti in with Evergreens and also with that which is deciduous. You can have an eclectic garden. Some people will only landscape with plantings native to their area, but others choose plantings that come in from other areas or will mix the two types in together.

When you landscape in the South, cacti and succulents do well, but the more prickly, thorny cacti are more popular in certain parts of the South-West (with certain people). Aloe and agave plants are considered succulents because they take in and store water for long periods of time. To emphasize, they aren't so thorny, compared with cacti. For this reason, they are very popular plants. The aloe-type plants, and there are several varieties, tend to be more sun sensitive than real prickly, thorny cacti is, at least as a general rule, but, there can be some exceptions (like agaves, for example—they can take lots of sun). Aloe is used in health preparations, and cosmetics. There are many other kinds of succulents besides aloe plants. Some agaves can be in sun all day long. Many succulents need more shade, however. In fact, there are some succulents that will thrive in full shade and they don't need any direct sun at all, only some indirect lighting from the sun. If you have areas around your lot that are full shade, consider planting certain succulents in those areas. Some succulents do fine with sun, but very few succulents do well if they're in too much direct sun and if the temperature has been exceeding ninety degrees Fahrenheit or thirty-two degrees Celsius. Their branches/blades (tips, especially) can become beige/tan in color.

Some succulents and cacti can be sun sensitive past a certain temperature—they can get sunburned—and you may need to transplant them (or cover them for a time). As a general rule and in summary, cacti can take a great deal of sun but succulents cannot take as much. Still, either type may need to be moved elsewhere on a lot (or covered) if it is getting too much son and the sun gets too intense. Some succulents can take more sun, depending on the particular plant, but many of them are more sun sensitive, past a certain point. When you buy any planting, you do not want that planting to die. Unless you were able to get some baby plantings from it, it will have been a money loss, plus, no one wants a plant to die.

Until late autumn and early winter, hand watering is occasionally needed in southern areas. Too much watering when it gets cold turns some cacti and succulents purple for a time, and this is not ideal. You'll notice the purple around the edges of the blades on certain succulents, and at the top, on certain cacti. The water, retained in the plant, can freeze inside the plant and cause damage if it has just been watered and it is cold (especially noticeable at night). The plant can come back, though, in the spring and summer. The purple will go away, under the right conditions, and all the green can come back. Therefore, wait until spring, and don't get rid of the plantings if they have turned purple. It is always worth it to try to keep a plant that has become purplish, because they may well come back to being green. Too much water can kill any plant, whether it is summer or winter. The speed of such a death will depend on the size of the plant, its type, and the amount of watering that was done. Also, it's just not good to water plants after the weather turns cold. As noted earlier, nights get cold, before the days do so when the nights are getting cold, don't water anything.

A book on the subject of cacti and succulents, with pictures and descriptions, can easily be found at most any library. Some succulents can take real intense heat even if they don't get much water from rain or the hose. Others absolutely cannot take intense heat without more water. Gardening can somewhat be trial-and-error, despite what any books might relay. Some things you plan and try just don't work out, or something can be thwarted. Carefully read what is noted about the plant when you purchase the plant. The information will help you to take better care of the plant.

Again, and to summarize, succulents are generally more sun sensitive than cacti. Succulents may do all right in the winter but not so well in the summer, unless they're always or partly in the shade. Some cacti and succulents can actually get sunburned. Other plantings can, too. Cacti and succulents can get parched, and die. You have to be careful where you plant certain cacti, and succulents. Some desert plantings may need to be protected from the sun, when it gets really hot. They may do fine up until around 90° Fahrenheit or 32° Celsius but after that, harm can come to the plant. Some will need shade covering. Plantings that get full sun and zero to little shade are the most vulnerable. You can put pieces of cloth over the top of some plantings if they seem to be getting sunburned. I usually put the cloth on the top area. The quills (or needles) hold the cloth on so the wind doesn't blow it away. When the temperature cools in autumn, I pull the cloth off or cut it off with scissors. Sometimes, I put an open-patterned plastic crate on top of certain areas, to give cacti some shade, or I put an open-patterned board in front of or over some cacti; it is securely braced in. When summer is over, I remove whatever is the protection. You can put plastic chairs in front of the groups of cacti, too. You do what you can to give them enough shade, during all subsequent hot seasons.

I separate cacti or divide cacti up this way—small balls (but they aren't really balls), larger balls, solo column, multi-columns, armed columns, clump groups, multi-parts, spherical, and hybrids. I don't take into consideration any ribbing or tubercles or areoles with this simple classifying or cacti dividing. I separate or divide succulents up this way—bladed, multi-leafy (but they aren't really leaves and some of them look more like pods or beans), flat florals (but they aren't really flowers, even though some will call any petals they have, rosettes), spatial florals, full flatter florals, danglers, clump groups, tree-like, thin, hybrids, and miscellaneous (if they don't fit in any of these others very well). This dividing up is really just an effort on my part to give each one a perspective so they can be better remembered and so there is less overall confusion about cacti and succulents. I call this dividing up Type Divisions. These Type Divisions help me to remember the different cacti and succulents a little better. Anyone can make up their own Type Divisions, for better recall. For someone who plants many cacti and/or succulents, it is good to visualize each plant in the place where you think you want them to go so they can better be placed.

Some cacti and succulents may be hard to find. One thing is for sure, there are <u>many</u> specimens of cacti as well as succulents—way more than most people realize. Some are commonly known while others are not. I sometimes look for the more unusual ones that tend to be eye-catchers, for some reason or other. Some of those can be a bit temperamental, though, and may require some extra care. Sometimes, I go for the ones that are a lighter green (they're more easily seen than the darker ones are) and I like the two-toned ones, sometimes known as variegated. (Variegated ones tend to be succulents.) There is a two-color agave that is green and yellow (so it is not really variegated). I have several of these now. I've grown to love them. The two-colored agave I have on my lot is the Agave americana—the Marginata variety. The Agave americana, otherwise, is what some people call the Blue Agave. It is not two-toned but is a bluish-green only. It tends to grow larger than the americana one does. Some call the Blue Agave a Century Plant, possibly because some of them end out living a long time. I've also heard them called Cathedral Plants, but the two are really slightly different. One is a little smaller than the other. Century Plants do not live to be a century but some of them will live a long time.

Another succulent I've grown to love is the Red Tip Yucca (aka Hesperaloe parviflora). It has long, very thin blades that shoot upward and outward. From its center come very long shoots that are loaded with red color—not just at the tips but all along the way of the shoots. The color and its size, that is medium, makes me think of another plant that does really well on the desert, even in full sun, year round. That plant is called the Mexican Bird of Paradise (Caesalpinia mexicana). It is full and has feathery tiny-leafed branches. It's a bit fern-like because it is light and airy. There are teensy thistles on the branches, though (unlike with ferns). You can trim the plant back and it always comes back. You can even trim it way down. It is loaded with reddish-orange blossoms, and I do mean loaded. Bees love it. There are many plusses, relative to this planting. It's one of my favorites. It is colorful and hardy. It requires little water.

Another plant that produces color—red in this case—is the Pyracantha. It is sometimes called Firethorn. It produces red berries but it is an extremely thorny Evergreen and the thorns are long. It is very hard to cut and shape if you must touch the branches. After trimming this plant, which becomes a tall bush (but it is technically a shrub), removing any thorny or quilly branches off the lot can be a little problematic. You must look before you touch if you are bare-handed. You must handle every branch with extreme care because of all the thorns/quills.

I personally try to find hardy cacti and succulents that do well in the sun and don't need much water. I want low-maintenance plantings. About cacti, though, it is well known that they don't need much water, but they need enough water to look their best and to grow well. Cacti absorb water by way of their roots, but also by way of their small dimorphic areoles that are all over and around many cactus specimens. Look carefully and you will see that they surround where the quills/spines come out from. Some cacti could use at least 'some' regular watering, independent of getting occasional rainwater, and the extra watering would be done in the warmer months (of spring and summer).

Clearly, cacti don't require as much watering as leafy plantings do, but it's good if they get a little more watering than they usually get from just the rains. Water plumps them up, greens them up, and enables them to grow better and faster. Eventually, they will grow to be their maximum size and won't need much extra watering.

Giving cacti a little extra water all along the way is something to think about doing, but it is probably not required. Pay attention to rain patterns and amounts, though, because they may not need any extra watering. Realize, however, that Global Warming is throwing rain patterns and temperatures out of whack. Keep in mind that cacti rarely die from lack of water, but they can die when they've been given too much water.

Agaves don't need to be watered and this is one reason why so many agaves are chosen to go somewhere on a lot. They look nice in corners or along edges. They make good border plantings when they are between lots. They also live a long time. They have sharp hooks all along each of their blades/branches, though, and a sharp point at the tip of each blade/branch (that you can cut off if you want to, and no one would notice it if you did).

After an elderly agave shoots up a high stalk, it will die. When the Agave tequilana shoots up the stalk and it blossoms, around its twelfth year, that is when they get the liquid out of the plant, but I have seen them cut (aka harvest) whole agave plants without stalks, down in Mexico (most notably around Jalisco, Mexico), for the purpose of making liquor . The liquor—Mescal—is also made from this plant. Tequila varies as to quality and cost, just like wine does. The mash used for distilling it is from the plant's core. Some people grow this kind of agave on their lot or property. It is not against the law, unless they use such plants for distilling, without the proper permits.

Century or Cathedral Plants, also agaves, are very popular in the South-West. These are a bluish color and they get confused with are sometimes called the Blue Agave Plant. They get to be rather large in size. It's thought that the Century Plant can live up to a hundred years (but I don't think they ever do—not even close). These plants are a lovely aqua or blue color. (Some will say they are green, but they are more bluish.) A two-color type of agave that has green and yellow blades or branches is many people's favorite of all the agave types. It stands out on a lot, because of the yellow, and also because of the light green. These get to be pretty big, too, but not as big as the Blue Agaves get. They do well in full sun, and hot sun. They're native to the United States. Most agaves found in the United States are native to Mexico.

It's sometimes hard to know where certain succulents actually got started—Mexico or the United States—because the two countries are so close together. Both countries might claim an origin, of a number of cacti and succulents, in other words, and this might even include some hybrids. Claims by countries relative to much that relates to specific plants, get disputed all the time. With the cacti from more distant places, origins are generally agreed upon amongst Americans. There may be disputes amongst countries neighboring those other countries, though. For example, the Cereus peruvianus cactus has an origin that is believed to be Brazilian, not Peruvian. The two countries dispute its origin. The Echeveria succulent origin is also disputed—amongst people in Mexico, Central America, and, South America. And so it sometimes goes. It is not easy to keep up with it all; I'm not sure if it matters because if you like a cactus, you like a cactus.

People call the blades or branches on agaves rosettes, in part because many other succulents have rosettes. In fact, some succulents can tend to resemble plump, green flowers. Rosettes can resemble flower petals. But, what agaves have do not look like rosettes, at all. They look like blades, which branch out from the plant's center. (A few small agave plants might have actual rosettes, but most all of them don't.) As noted before, you have to be real careful when handling both the agave and the aloe because their blades/branches and rosettes can break off rather easily. In this respect, they are delicate. Some succulents are quite colorful. They look as if they may have come from a Rain Forest. You very much notice red and orange on some of these succulents.

With certain agaves, the sides of the blades or branches, with their sharp, curved hooks edging up and down each blade/branch, will easily cut through skin. They're like teeth (as teeth along a sawblade) and some people even call them teeth. You have to be careful when handling these plants or when walking next to them. These curved teeth easily hook on whatever brushes up against them. Then, there can be a small slice into the skin, a rip of the clothing, or a pulling of yarn from a sweater. If there are children running around, or pets kept outside, you might want to avoid planting anything thorny, quilly, or that has sharp hooks. There are a number of smooth succulents that do not have anything sharp on them, and lots of Evergreen or deciduous-type plantings to choose from. On occasion, though, certain Evergreen needles can be a little sharp. Also, don't forget those Italian Cypress trees. You can brush up against them, no problem. They are 'soft' plantings, like the Oleanders and the Arborvitae.

As previously noted, at the tip of each blade or branch of the agave plant is a needle-sharp point. I cut these points off with a pair of old scissors that I only use for gardening. Otherwise, the tips can be dangerous. Any children in the area should be warned about them. Dogs, cats, or other unfortunate animals can run right into these sharp points so it is advisable to cut those tips off. This does not make the plant look funny. You hardly even notice it. No one will even know that the tips have been trimmed off, except for you. They cut off fairly easily. When new blades/branches begin to be added to the rest of the plant, cut those few tips off, too. You can't do anything about the sharp hooks at the sides of the blades, though.

In northern areas, gardeners have to be concerned with multi-freezes, and with snow, ice, and sometimes hail. Only certain kinds of plants/vegetation can withstand cold climates. The overall subject is a study all in itself. Many generic northern plants and vegetation do all right down in the southern areas, but generic southern plants and vegetation do not do all right up in the northern areas. Even desert climates can have cold areas to the north, where it snows in the winter. Much will depend on the elevation and the average temperatures from month to month as to whether or not a transplanted planting will thrive or live somewhere else..

I don't have plantings that I worry too much about when there's frost. (Ice is a different thing.) Many people have plants that will be harmed by frost, though, so they have to cover certain plantings at certain times. You'll want to have plant covers handy, in case you ever need them. I'm careful not to water any and all of my plantings right before a frost or freeze.

Be careful to not water a plant right before a frost or freeze. Some plants will even die, not because of the frost or freeze, but because of the watering that's combined with the frost and freeze. Some cacti might end out with crinkly skin. The skin of a cactus is simply what is covering the cactus, like the skin of a human being does. Some plants and cacti and succulents will develop both purple areas and wrinkly skin when watering and cold weather combines, but, again, they may lose that color and wrinkly look after it warms up outside, later on. If you water before a frost or freeze, cells absorb the water and then that water, in the cells of the planting, freezes. This, of course, shocks the plant. Plants can go into a type of shock for a number of different reasons.

It is at night, when temperatures dip, that the plant experiences some shock. After some or all of a living plant gets excessively cold, especially after having been watered, if the next day is sunny and warm, the plant may be able to stabilize a little, until the next night, when the temperature again dips. If there are a number of sunny, warm days, the plant may end out being all right. Just don't water the poor plant again, if you think it will be cold.

Some plantings do all right when it gets cold, this we all know, but when it is really cold, watering plants can ruin them. They don't all come back when it gets warmer, later on. Usually, rains stop or at least cease significantly, right before the weather starts to get chilly/cold, but, it may still occasionally rain through the winter, especially in southern areas. Some plants might turn purple even because of just the natural rain. Again, purplish plantings often come back to being green in the spring, after a time of rehabilitation and because of warm weather and sunshine. You have to give them time to recoup and don't assume they're permanently damaged because they may not be. Some leafy plantings, if too many leaves died because of too much water combined with cold, may grow the leaves back, given time, but if they don't, you'll have to trim off the bare area parts and then hope for the best. It may be a while before the leaves come back, so be patient. New branches with leaves can grow in, too. I've seen some sick and seemingly-damaged plantings come back to normal after a time, so don't give up too soon on what might appear hopeless. Don't throw away the plant.

A week or two before it turns noticeably cold, you'll want to go around and put a slow drip on several plantings, assuming they're a little dried out from lack of rain. Usually, there isn't much rain between the middle part of the summer and middle fall. You will want to decide if you want to do an overnight slow drip for certain plantings. You will want the water to get down to all the roots and be absorbed into all of the plant. Figure out how many plantings on the lot will need this last watering before winter comes around and get it done so the ground will be completely dry when the cold comes in. Do this before you begin to notice cold nights starting up. It will be cold nights that first enter. You can't go by day weather because day weather is warmer.

In most areas, it is not wise to water any plants during the wintertime. In the desert areas, there's sometimes a little winter rain, and so manual watering, unless plantings are in areas that can't receive the rainwater, not only won't be needed but it can be damaging.

Realize, though, that rain clouds form only in certain areas; some rain clouds are real small as it starts to get colder. One part of a town or city might get rain but another part will get no rain. Rain can be more scant during a rainfall than is thought, too; rain amounts can be confusing. Cacti and succulents (most all of them) should not be watered in desert areas after mid-October, and if you water them before then, after summer is clearly over, water them early in the morning so they'll have all day to absorb the water and the ground can dry out before nightfall. Don't give them much water, either. Be very careful about any watering during times of any colder weather in the southern states. Most plantings should get no hose water at all when it becomes colder. Some kinds of plantings may need occasionally watering, but be careful, if it is too cold.

The rule of green thumb is 'leave be through the colder months but be watchful'. Cacti and succulents almost always have enough moisture inside them to get through colder months. You don't need to bother with them. Many other kinds of plants will be fine, too, but keep a watch over them anyway. If you live in an area that has snow-and-ice winters, you can water nothing, but if winters are warm and temperate, regularly check all lot plantings. At the very least, skim and scan.

It's a good idea to put cacti in corners or along edges, and not in the middle of the lot that you are landscaping. These areas would include the front, back, and sometimes side areas, if there's room. If you create one or more rock-enclosed areas (gardening beds), in the center areas of a lot, flowers, bushes, or trees are better to use there than cacti are. This is because you don't want cacti that close to a walkway or walk-around area. It's also not good to have cacti along the path that a dog might take, in the event you have a dog or plan to eventually get a dog. Also, I've seen where cats have actually run into cacti. Such kitties likely had to be taken to the vets. It helps if cacti and succulents, especially really quilly ones, are put in corners and along outer edges, especially if a fence is to the back of them. Cats really belong inside, though; some dogs have to be outside, or they are indoor/outdoor dogs. I know people who will keep their big dogs inside, though. They let them go outside only to relieve themselves; plus, they walk them every day. Cacti can be perilous to pets. Not so much the succulents, though.

I put a variety of cacti on my lot but they were all either medium-sized, small, or very small, except for my Saguaro, that loomed tall and stately over the rest of the cacti. It was another planting that was there when I moved in. It got to be about fifteen feet tall. Last I saw it, it had grown two long arms, and another one had just started. The new arm looked like a little ball but it would have grown out and would not have continued looking like a ball for very long. I eventually had to remove the Saguaro, for a number of reasons. For one thing, termites kept chewing up the base. When some of the bottom area of Saguaros dries out and becomes wood-like, the termites go after that part, strange as it might seem. For another thing, I began to be concerned that it could fall over on top of a neighbor's parked car, or on top of an awning. It is rare that this kind of thing happens, but it can happen. This can happen with any tree on a lot.

I have had very few agaves on my lot (always in out-of-the way spots). They get to be rather large. Again, there are different kinds of agaves. They get to be about four feet tall, with blades or branches that shoot out from the base and have all those teeth all along the edges of the blades or branches. Most animals don't get close to these plants because the plants are so large and full. These plants get to be quite wide, or broad. Agaves are nice-looking plantings. (Aloes look similar to agaves but they're small plants.) Again, they make tequila out of some agaves, but those agaves are getting harder to find. Agaves (on average) can live for around eight to twelve years. Then, some of them shoot up a tall stalk that blossoms at the top. Seeds from these blossoms get scattered with the wind. This is how agaves can multiply in an area. There are also offshoot baby agaves or replica plants that grow out from the sides of some agaves. These small offshoots will also have roots and the offshoots can be removed and planted elsewhere. As a result, the plant is a mother plant.

To unloose these babies, you have to well wet the dirt around the mother plant first, and then gently work out the small offshoots because the roots can break off fairly easily. There is an attachment or connector part that extends from the mother plant. It can be cut but cut it real close in to the mother plant. It will, then, suffice as a root. It is planted as part of the small planting. These small plantings are baby agaves and it's an accomplishment to nurse them to full stature. It's so easy to do. Perhaps it's the mother part of me that enjoys doing this? Men can enjoy doing this too, though.

Other cacti also have prototype plants growing to their sides. Like the agave, there are quite a few cacti that have what looks like separate prototype plants growing to their sides, but some of them are not really separate plants, per se. They're actually joined to the parent plant. They're a part of the cactus, in other words, so you have to just leave these be. Some types of cacti, however, will have offshoot cacti that have tiny roots and can be removed from the mother cactus. You just gently remove them, using tongs and after saturating the spot with water. Usually, roots are quite small on baby plantings. You have to always be careful with their roots. Sometimes these baby adjuncts are called arms, but they can be next to or even somewhat under the ground so they're more like feet. You can get confused and think that some particular offshoots have roots when they don't, or, vice versa. Roots are only on certain cacti offshoots. Be careful and look before you leap, if you can. You may not want to detach anything if it's an actual part of the cactus and the parts do not have roots of their own. Figure everything out and know what to do before you do it. Also, though, with some cacti, if an offshoot has no roots, roots might grow if the tiny planting is set on top of potting soil and watered at intervals. It's worth a try.

On my lot, I had regular Barrel cacti (very green) and also Golden Barrel cacti (yellow green), and I had other cacti in several areas, but most of the others were smaller. None of these were next to a walk area. Sometimes Barrel cacti are called Ball cacti. The regular Barrels got to be rather good-sized plants, and the Golden Barrels got to be a pretty good size, too, but they don't get as large as the regular Barrels do. I was surprised the Golden Barrels ended out getting as large as they did, but it took years before they did. The two main types of Barrel cacti (or Ball cacti) are Echinocactus and Ferocactus; these are both classed as being larger cacti, but so many of the smaller cacti types are barrel-shaped and especially ball-shaped.

Quite a few cacti types tend to be columnar. One that comes to mind is the Eulychnia saint-piena type. Some of the Cereus types are columnar and ribbed and are often night blooming, for example, the Oreocereus, Espostoa lanata (Peruvian Old Man), azureus (Wooly cactus), hendriksonianus donsilanatus, Echinopsis subdenudata (Easter Lily cactus), Philosocereus azureus, Philosocereus pachycladus, and Stenocereus pruinosus. Sometimes the columnar ones start off with a single column but later, other columns sprout. The columnar cacti all vary in height, whether they are Cereus types or other types.

One columnar cactus that gets really tall, and sprouts more and more columns and acquires arms later on, is the Organ Pipe Cactus. It does well when it's very hot. You can shape it if you want to, by clipping off one or more columns or one or more arms. It is of the Stenocereus thurberi that can get to be huge—a range from sixteen to twenty-five feet tall and twelve feet wide, but the smaller species, the littoralis, only gets to be around ten feet tall. The flower on this one is large, and white. It's a gorgeous plant and can get to be quite jam-packed because of all the columns. Some people call these cactus types branch cactus because it looks like they have many branches.

Again, quite a few columnar cacti end out having more than one column. Sometimes, they just go on and on. I planted a variety of different cacti all around my lot (but only along the sides and in corners) and it was fun to see how they each flourished. They all flowered at different times, but each almost always seemed to flower after a rain. I don't know why, but some cacti flower at night, when it is cooler (and that actually might be why). Cacti flower more often than you'd think if they get watered enough. (It's always nice to take a picture of a cactus when it flowers or blooms.) Some cacti flower well and easily; every so often one won't flower all that well. All cactus flowers deserve center stage and to be well noted because they are lovely. Some are different and unusual. It's fun to take pictures of them. They don't usually last that long and that is why pictures are good to take.

The small cactus plantings were all inside beds that were edged with good-sized natural rocks or scalloped bricks. Actually, all my cacti were outlined (protected), in some way, by whatever materials I had on hand or could find around town. I use rocks and stones of different sizes to edge enclosures for the cacti or general vegetation and different types of plantings. I tried to match the general size of rocks for each, separate enclosure or bed area. I had small, medium, and large rocks that I used for the different beds. I also had a few of the more jumbo-sized rocks. I put them in various, different spots.

Frankly, there are so many of the smaller Mammillaria cactus plants that you can't list them all. These tend to be ball-shaped and are purchased a lot. Some are cylindrical or columnar, and a few are really odd-ball shaped, like they're from the Twilight Zone. A few of the rounded, ball cacti are the Mammillaria compressa (White Wool), the M. rhodantha (Easy Flowering), M. zeilmanniana (Pink Crown), M. spinosissimi (Red-Headed Irishman), M. candida (Snowball), M. camptotricha (Bird's Nest), M. germnispina (Satellite), M. hahniana (Old Lady), M. nejapensis (Silver Arrows), the M. pringlei

(Pincushion), the M. pilcayensis (Bristle Brush), the M. bombycina (Silken Pincushion), and the M. parkinsonni (Owl's Eyes). Most of the simpler common names seem fitting and help you remember the cactus better.

There are many other Mammillarias (200 some species), but they are but one kind of cactus and there are many others. The list goes on and on so before you buy any of them, check around and learn about them, especially on the Internet. Mammillaria is the most popular genus because they grow well and are small. I have several different ones and most of them are mixed in and amongst other types in my yard. Mammillaria grow as isolates or in groups or clumps. You can order cacti from various Internet sites. Many of them show pictures.

You can order all kinds of plantings from Internet sites, when it comes right down to it. Packing cacti with lots and lots of quills would be a challenge. Other species or types of cacti are diverse. It gets confusing, frankly, when you go to decide on and want to buy plants because there's a Kingdom, an Order, a Family, a Sub-family, a Tribe, a Genus, and a Species. All within these categories have hard-to-remember names. It's worse than what you'd find in the medical field, with all their terms. Most people are lucky just to know the Genus and the Species. Again, knowing the simpler common name helps a lot, when buying cactus.

With my numerous smaller cactus plantings that go inside the rock-enclosed beds, I sometimes used an old toothbrush to get tiny rocks or debris out of the cactus sides. Sometimes, when I watered them, small rocks got stuck between quills when the water level rose. Dirt pieces got stuck in the quills, too. Also, on occasion, debris got stuck in between or on the quills because wind blew it in. Pine needles got stuck in between the quills, too. A toothbrush got into the quills without hurting them, and debris was safely brushed out. On occasion, too, I used a nut pick to pry something that was stuck, out of a cactus. I'd usually tend to do this when I was cleaning out the beds.

One point to be made about cactus is that once you plant a few different ones, you get other ones for free. Again, because certain types of cactus sprout new cacti off to their sides, you might want to look into getting those. You wait until the sprouts are a little larger, thoroughly wet the area down, and then carefully and gently pull the new sprouts away from the mother cactus, using tongs or some kind of separator, so it is all very easy to do. If you can reach way down to the root and avoid touching the cactus, you can sometimes pick the larger babies up by the roots and then hold them upside down by those roots until you get them in to their new spot (or over to a planter). The roots won't likely break. It's good to loosen the soil first, with a gardening tool or old table knife, so the roots will come out easier. But, with the real little ones, they're pretty small roots and can break easily. First, loosen the dirt around them and under them. When these plant sprouts have their own roots, you must pull each one out very slowly. Two gardening tools in combination (one in the left hand and one in the right) can also be used to pull out small cacti, once the roots are well loosened from the dirt. You just put the young cacti between the two tools and take it over to where it needs to go. You can place small cacti on a spade blade, too. You can use old potholders for this task as well, to avoid the quills. You get pretty skilled at doing this removal after you've done a couple (and so, too, with re-planting and so, too, with removing weeds).

Other types of cacti throw seeds so you find little prototype cactus plantings on the lot that way, too, and they're sometimes found in unexpected places. Often, the seeds lay dormant through the dry season, and then you see the actual seedlings sprout after it finally rains. Seeds can be flung far distances by winds, but many times, there's only light breezes so seeds may not go very far before they settle in somewhere. Generally, new seedlings aren't too far from the mother plant. You can put these sprouts and plantings in pots or in one of the beds on the lot. Other non-cacti plantings on a lot will throw seeds too, so there could be some tree and bush plantings around, as well. Over the years, if you're patient, you can benefit from these kinds of plantings (of various types). It doesn't take these baby plants all that long to get larger.

Again, you always have to envision the maximum size that a planting is going to end out being when you select a spot to plant anything. All plants must have room to grow to be their maximum size. And if they grow feet, sprouts, or extensions to the side, as some cacti do, you have to allow room for that, as well, but you can contain this growth by putting up a rock enclosure so the whole planting cannot grow beyond the rocks because the rocks will serve as barriers.

You can put these new baby plants in pots, and just keep them as potted plants. When you get enough of them, you may want to design a bed for the grouping. You can re-pot the plantings if they get too big for their pots, but re-potting can be hard work. Dumping in potting soil, lifting heavy and filled-up pots, fussing with this and that, and the re-planting itself—it's sometimes just easier to plant plants into the ground than it is to re-pot them. But, you do whatever is before you to do at the time and you do whatever seems best to do when you are developing the best yard and landscape you possibly can, and, when you are trying to be utilitarian.

Relative to transplanting, when you re-plant or pot, if you take a plant out of the ground, sometimes there will be a lot of soil still on the roots when you dig the plant up or pull it out and it is best if you try to get as much of that soil (that is still on the roots) back into the hole area where the plant came out of. You can gently shake off the dirt, gently hit the roots with a garden tool, or hose the dirt off and back into the hole area. Some people use a hand spade to knock the soil off of a plant, but you can just use your hand, if you want to. You want to get into the habit of saving all the topsoil you can each time you remove any plant from the ground, because of the topsoil nutrients.

You never put potting soil in to these ground areas. Only ground soil and dirt should be used to refill the hole. Thicker, heavier compost could be added in with the dirt, but not potting soil. If you put potting soil into the hole, the potting soil will always float when that area gets watered, and it will go all over the place. It is very light in weight. It is fine in pots, but not on top of the ground. Plus, if you put another plant into the same spot, you'll need as much actual real dirt in there as possible (but not potting soil). Dirt is the right consistency for such planting, compared with potting soil, which people sometimes use to fill in such holes (because they removed too much actual dirt or soil and was not able to put all the dirt back in. The lightweight granules of potting soil will become problematic). The same principle applies to when you remove a plant from a pot. Try to separate all the potting soil from the roots. Some people re-use potting soil if it has not been in the pot too very long. You can mix previously-used potting soil with new potting soil to save some money, but don't ever mix ground dirt with potting soil. It is not so easy to work with, makes for a heavier pot, and reduces water drainage so a plant can get waterlogged.

Never use regular ground dirt or soil in a pot for a plant of <u>any</u> type. Water collects on top but does not soak in—well or at all—and the plant will die. The dirt or soil gets way too compacted. Ground dirt or soil works fine in the ground, but not compacted in a pot. If water ever does get down to the plant roots, it takes too long for it to evaporate, so plants get waterlogged and watersogged, and die. They will completely wilt and this death will not take very long.

In summary, there are a number of projects you can begin with when you first start to landscape and garden a lot. Selecting major plantings is a first step. (Remember, there will be baby plantings, along the way.) Deciding which plantings to keep, which are already on there, is another first step if the lot already has some landscaping and plantings. Also, preparing areas on the lot will have to be a priority if new projects are going to be started. Decide what all needs to be done first, and then get started. When the first group of tasks is done, then you can get going with the second group of tasks. Some people like to divide up their projects by groups.

PLAN FOR VARIETY, WITH PLANTINGS AND ROCKS

One plant that I love is the Spider Plant. It has thin blades that shoot or flare out from the center and a cap look is created as you look down on the plant. It is not a succulent or cactus, but a regular plant. The thin blades of the Spider Plant are two shades of green or variegated. It's popular everywhere—north and south. It is easy to grow indoors. It can be a hanging plant or a ground plant. It is found, now, in many areas around the world. The baby sprouts stem outward, at the end of a thin, yellowish stem or shaft, which extends from the plant. When the tiny sprouts get heavy enough, they weigh down to the ground, whereupon the roots grow and go into the ground and presto, you get some new plantings from the parent plant. It's like they're splayed out from the center. You can clip the new stem or shaft and uproot the offshoot planting after wetting the area down (so you can get the roots). It's very easy to do. If the offshoots are somewhat established (into the ground), there will be one or more linear bulbous roots attached to the new plant so dig down fairly deep to get all those bulbous roots out, if you decide to grow more Spider Plants, and start up new ones around the lot. Some people like to have Spider Plants inside, even, but they actually do well outside, even in the southern areas. It is rather surprising. I learned this by accident. I tried it out and it worked.

Spider Plants grow outside, even in the desert-type areas, but you have to water them. They're actually pretty hardy. If they're in the shade, you don't have to water them as much. If they get some sun, you have to watch over them, especially in the summer. They must, at least, have partial shade, perhaps especially in the afternoons when it gets the hottest. They live through frost in the winter, at least in the desert, they do. (But desert areas get very little frost.) Most people think that Spider Plants can only be indoor plants, or porch or deck plants, but they do good outdoors and in the ground as long as you water them when they need watering. They take more sun than you would think, for being a thin-blade plant.

When the weather is <u>really</u> warm, or hot even, water any Spider Plants <u>well</u>, let that water soak in, then do a second watering application, let that water soak in, and possibly do even one more watering application (perhaps just a short one). This is the multiple-watering procedure. You may need to do this with other plantings, too, whether you are in northern or southern USA areas, or anywhere else. You can lose certain plantings fast when the weather is hot, if you do not water them consistently and well. Water will enter the roots of the plant and then travel up and into the plant. The plant absorbs the water. The plant will perk up considerably, if it had been drooping. When it's been hot, plantings may need a slow-drip application or multiple watering applications, to really get that plant filled up with water. It will take some time for the plant to drink enough in to get the water in to all parts of the plant. I've seen where these plants were almost dead and with the multiple water application, they came back to life, 100%.

Even though it is good to do two or three watering applications for many plantings in arid climates, so often, only one application is done and may not be enough, or be barely enough. The water in the ground can dry up rather fast. When the weather has turned hot, when you make your rounds watering your plantings, decide how many applications are needed. One week, only one application may be needed. Another week, two or three applications may be necessary. If you do two or three applications, you may not need to water the plantings quite so frequently. Some plantings may not need any watering.

I like to walk around my landscaping and garden periodically so I can enjoy the sights and the fruit of my labor. As I do, I take note of the condition of the plantings, and I assess whether or not any of them need watering. I look for other things, too. I take note of what needs to be done, in general. Even if you are quite busy, make time to do this. It only takes a few minutes. Many plants and trees die because they do not get water when they need it.

Spider Plants (or similar plants) don't need much watering in autumn and winter and do not water them if cold is present or expected. They will get through cold weather but maybe not real cold weather. If the day is sunny (during autumn), give them a 'little' water early in the morning so they can take in water when it is real warm and sunny during that day. If they take in cold and chilly water, the blades may completely wither and wilt and will end out needing to be cut off. The plant may 'come back' after a time, after certain care is given. You can trim blades off Spider Plants on occasion, and more blades will come back later. They grow from the center and so will grow over all the other blades, and any cut-off blade areas. Generally though, you don't want to cut back Spider Plants. You want them to be full and spread out.

You can get extra Spider Plants only one way, and I do it all the time. As with my extra agaves, I sell my extra Spider Plants or give them away. Again, when a Spider Plant becomes a certain size, it begins to establish real thin yellow shoots that end out being longer than the blades are. At the end of these shoots is a baby Spider

Plant, but it sometimes isn't able to implant itself into the ground without some help. You have to help these baby plants along so you carefully bend down the thin yellow shoot and put a small rock on top of it, next to where the baby Spider Plant is. That way, the baby plant can get its roots into the ground because it is now right on top of the ground. For a while, it gets its nourishment and water from the shoot so do not cut the thin yellow shoot until the roots of the baby plant are well into the ground and established. You may want to leave any growing-in-the-ground shoots alone until you are ready to pot or transplant the new Spider Plants. As several, thin yellow shoots with potential baby plants grow out of just one mature Spider Plant, you can get several baby Spider Plants every time the shoots have tiny plants at their ends. You just have to put small rocks down on all the shoots and then wait for a while for the roots to go down in the ground.

It's good to have a variety of plantings, but some repetition within that variety works very well and cuts down some costs. It's a good feeling to benefit from free plantings. If you wait long enough, you'll get a number of free plantings. (I've already made note of the cactus freebies, but there can be other types, as well, including trees and bushes.) Random plantings come around every year, so look for them every year. Sometimes, seeds blow in from neighbor's lots, too, and the plants that sprout up can be added to your group, if you want them. Weeds grow too, and you have to be careful to not pull up and throw away nice potential plantings when you pull up the weeds. Plant sprouts (seedlings) almost never come up in a spot where you want them to stay so eventually, you have to find a place for them on your lot or give them to someone else. Either they need to go into a pot or over to a special spot, to enhance the landscaping. It's good to have small pots with potting soil in them ready to use, every year.

Keep in mind that plants can also be sold. I've sold some, but most people seem to want larger plants and not the baby plants.

They sell better if they're in a decent pot, too—be it plastic, clay, or 'other'. Those cheap, black plastic pots they come in when they are store-bought have little appeal. You can use those as interim pots.

In any landscaping, the point to be made is that a variety of different sizes of plantings create a more interesting landscaping and it doesn't matter whether you mix diverse plantings together, or whether you don't. Whereas I have actual cactus gardens, where a number of different cacti are put together, I also have solo cacti in areas around other kinds of plantings. This principle can be applied to all kinds of plantings, anywhere. You can create, and do what you want, when you select potential plantings. You can mix or match, and it's always fun to go on a hunt for just the right planting. I have many garden beds around my lot. They are away from walkway areas. They are along inner edges or outside edges.

People like cacti and succulents because watering will be much less, and sometimes, will be nil. Cacti and succulents should be watered, however, on occasion. In the summer, when it is extremely hot, I give them a good soaking every so often. I douse them once real good, let that water soak in, and then I douse them again so the roots can drink up even more moisture. That way, moisture gets into all of the cacti. You don't have to do this very often, though, and if the plantings look all right, you really don't need to give them water. As it gets cooler, I water all my plantings less often or I don't water them at all. Presently, there are a number of plantings on my lot that I don't need to water at all, unless they look wilty or like they need it. (I try to keep to as low a maintenance lot as I can.) The few I do water (in that I have a low maintenance yard), will perhaps get one douse, at most, after it has become cooler. I no longer grow Spider Plants but I miss them. They required more watering than my other plants did. I gave them to a neighbor and put in aloes.

Most of my plantings could live without any watering at all, because of rainfall, but the extra, occasional watering when it gets hot plumps them up and makes them look healthier but they all generally only need a little extra water, for that to happen. They also flower nicer, when they've been watered. Rains are always very helpful. If I know that rain is expected, I don't have to water (unless the rain passes by, which it often does). Gardeners must pay attention to weather forecasts and occurrences. You can play the watering by ear. Just be watchful. A glance here, a glance there usually does the trick. If you have to, and have lots of plantings, take some notes as you go around inspecting.

Actually, even in some desert areas, the Saguaro, regular Barrel, Golden Barrel, the Italian Cypress tree, certain Evergreen bushes, certain Evergreen trees, certain Arborvitae trees, the different Oleanders, and some cacti and succulents don't ordinarily need any watering at all because rainwater is enough for them. This is why they're so often chosen by desert residents. Global Warming has set in and rains have been affected but they still come around. If you live in a desert climate, especially keep watch over the condition of plantings, now. Plantings I just noted can live in most American desert areas and probably in a lot of warm climates.

Plantings (or plants) are an investment, and they are living organisms that are in your charge. When you go out to water some of the plantings, remember to scan the <u>whole</u> lot to see if any of the others will need watering soon. See if there's any kind of problem, anywhere, and be quick to take action if you need to. Especially, check on the condition of all plantings. Also, check for insects. (Check for spiders, too; they aren't classified the same as insects but most gardeners just limp them all in together and put them in as insects). Like scorpions, mites, and ticks, spiders are arachnids—i.e. arthropods, which have jointed bodies and limbs that are segmented. It may seem like a lot to have to do all this, but all you need is a good-thinking brain, good eyes, and two good hands. The walk-around is always enjoyable to do, too.

Keep actual records about the amount of rain you have been getting or are getting in your town or city. If rain has been scant, you'll know what needs to be done. If you have Oleanders—and quite a few people do because these plantings are very popular—yellow leaves usually mean 'not enough water'. (It can also mean that the planting isn't getting enough Nitrogen or that it is dying of old age.) Way more yellow leaves than usual point to drought conditions, though, assuming the plant is fairly young and not dying from old age. In other words, rain has been scant in your area, or, you have not been able to water when watering was needed.

If you see too many yellow leaves on any bush (including Oleanders), again, give the plant a good watering so the water saturates way below, because the roots go down deep, usually. This will prevent even more yellow leaves from forming, drying, and falling off. Yellow leaves can possibly point to a Nitrogen deficiency in the soil, too. Yellow leaves can also mean there is a fungus, or that there is a lack of Iron (which is a condition known as Chlorosis). But, more often, yellow leaves means that the planting isn't getting enough water.

The yellow leaves of an Oleander, as an example, will turn to a tan color, once they dry out. With deciduous trees, they are supposed to get yellow leaves, in autumn. They're supposed to turn tan, and brown, after they have fallen off the trees. Green leaves will then come around in the spring. You can't miss yellow leaves on Oleanders, since all the other leaves will be green. Yellow leaves are easily seen after they fall to the ground, too. That's why you want the leaves off your lot. I have many Oleanders on my lot. They make great space fillers and windbreakers. Whenever I make note of Oleanders in this book, I'm roundaboutly including other bushes with many of the points I am making. There are many similar kinds of plantings out there, besides Oleanders, and maintaining them has some parallels.

If there is not enough absorbed water, regarding any Oleander leaves, certain of the leaves tend to absorb what water there is first, and so those leaves get to stay and won't die, but other leaves will die and they drop off, once they are dead. They didn't get the water. Sometimes, one or two leaves on each branch (or more leaves than that) will die, whether branches are higher or lower. The leaves that don't soak in the water are the ones that die. They turn yellow, fall off, and then brown and dry up while they are on the ground. The wind breaks or snaps them off when they're yellow, and most dead leaves stay fairly close to the Oleander bush once they fall. Eventually, new branches (sometimes called shoots) grow up from the ground area, and they eventually get tall enough to fill in the Oleander. New leaves may not grow in where the old leaves dropped (at least not for a while) so you never want your Oleanders to be without enough water for very long. When they lose too many leaves, any plant looks skimpy in spots, and for some time.

If Oleanders are given too much water when it gets real cold outside, the upper leaves may turn brown because the water that goes into the leaves freeze, and destroys the leaves. The Oleanders may or may not be able to be saved. Oleanders need little water in autumn and winter, in warm climates. (Oleanders are very popular in warm-climate areas.) It sometimes rains in autumn and winter in desert areas and this is usually all that desert plantings need (including Oleanders), during those seasons.

My Oleanders don't usually need much (if any) extra water during the warmer days. They will blossom better and more regularly with extra watering, however. If they get droopy, and if I notice any yellow leaves, I put the hose tip next to the Oleander's base and they get a slow drip for some time. If they don't get enough watering (rain included), more yellow leaves than usual will be seen in amongst their green leaves, and when the yellow leaves eventually drop below and turn brown, they leave a mess. I go around and remove browned leaves from my lot about two or three times a year. (I probably planted too many Oleanders, but I so love the planting, even when they drop leaves.) There are many other kinds of shrubs and bushes, though—many, many. Not all that many of them don't drop leaves, unless you get into the Evergreen ones and decide to plant them. Oleanders are good for shade, privacy, and wind-breaking. They can even make up a whole wall/. When they're planted in fairly close together, they as 'as' a fence.

In southern areas and especially desert areas, because of the sun, and heat, when it comes to watering from early spring on (until winter), you will especially have to focus in on the condition of all plantings on your lot. Dry-out can occur in the winter as well as in the summer. In warmer seasons, as soon as you see there is some dry-out, put those plantings on a slow drip. Again, dry-out is easy to spot because some of the leaves or any green areas will be yellow or brown. In some cases, there will be a fading of the greenery. A first sign of water lack is drooping leaves. Any walkabout you do should be done at least once a month, but it would be better if you did this two times a month. You can look out of windows in your home on occasion too, to check on condition, but it is best to do an actual walkabout. You want to see everything up close and also, some plantings cannot be seen or seen very well from any of the windows around the home.

Sometimes there aren't enough spring showers or there aren't many lengthy rains so that water gets way down deep; therefore, do not depend on spring showers. In warmer areas, many people lost plantings or they've had plantings that lost too much of their greenery in April and May because no one focused in on the condition of the plantings along the way of those two months. 'April showers bring May flowers', as the saying goes, is generally true because flower roots usually don't go down all that far into the ground. April showers may not be enough for trees, bushes, and the larger plants but they are enough for the flowers. Be very watchful during April and May and look at all plantings more frequently than you might expect to, and during the three principal summer months—June, July, and August—be even more watchful. In fact, be very watchful until winter actually sets in (when you can do very little or no watering at all). More dry-out has been occurring because of Global Warming. Also, some rains can be scant. You have to pay attention to number of inches of rainfall.

Some plantings will replenish their lost greenery, given enough watering, while other plantings will not. For example, again, once an Oleander loses too many leaves, those particular leaves won't come back—not for some time, and maybe not ever. New leafy stalks will shoot up from the ground after adequate watering, though, and especially after adequate consistent watering has been done. Eventually, those stalks or offshoots will become tall enough to fill the plant in. If the non-leafy stalks still have life, you may not want to cut them down or remove them if they are alive, since new stalks will eventually fill them in. This same principal applies to other plantings. Pruning and trimming will give space so that new branches or growth can occur in and around the open spaces but there may be times when you don't want to prune and trim.

The taller and larger the Oleander (some of them can be very full and rotund), the more leaves you will get. The less water the plant gets, the more leaves you'll end out having to scoop up. For me, scooping the leaves up and then picking the remaining ones up, one by one, works for me because I have the river rock landscaping rocks so if they're raked, there is too much breakage of the dropped leaves. You cannot pick broken leaves up, as there are too many little pieces. They settle in between the rocks and can't be raked up. Certainly if they break, the leaves can't be raked up and you have to pick up broken pieces with your fingers, which becomes much more work (too much work). Once you get the knack of picking up whole leaves, however, it can go fast and become easy. You can use a small whisk-type short broom to gently sweep leaves into a dustpan, too, but you cannot get them all that way. Hand picking is the best way.

To minimize the number of leaves and blossoms that fall and that you must remove, you can cut Oleanders way back—even the really tall ones. You can cut the really tall ones back to be quite short, in fact, so they are only two or three feet high. The bush (in this case, the Oleander) will look stubby at first, but it will fill out and new shoots will come along and the plant will no longer look stubby. It will take quite a while for it to grow back to full size. You can cut back many bushes or tall plantings, actually. You can even shape them. I personally don't mind that stubby look for a time, but some people don't like it.

I finally got to where I cut most of my Oleanders back just so there would be fewer leaves and blossoms to have to pick up. I did this after I started feeling my age. You can cut the tall ones down to be only around four or five feet from the ground if you want, and then shape them a little so the plants won't look so stubby. At this point, you won't be getting many blossoms on the plant, nor on the ground. Therefore, you won't end out having to pick up very many blossoms. After a time, not only do new shoots come up, but new side branches on the shoots that are already there, start to grow. The bush will fill out and smooth out. It will just be shorter and have fewer or even no blossoms. You will get more blossoms the next spring, however. Eventually, if you stop cutting a bush back, all the blossoms will return.

You can trim Oleanders or other bushes way down and they'll eventually come back up to full height and won't look like they've ever been cut back. They'll get their height back and fill out. It doesn't take all that long for some bushes to come back. Some people trim or cut their bushes back every April, right before any blossoms come out but most people like blossoms and do not cut back bush branches if they tend to blossom. It is optional to do this. When it comes to landscaping and gardening, there are many options.

If you trim off the branches and offshoots that are going to bloom and cut an Oleander way down, the Oleander will look more like a good-sized plant. You can buy shorter Oleanders, and they grow to be two or three feet high and will be blooming very nicely. You can even trim those down in April so they will not bloom so much and you won't have to pick up so many blossoms after some of them drop. The plant will then be considerably shorter but you don't want to cut it back to be too short. Oleander blooms can be white, light pink, peach or salmon, or red (which is really a red/pink—almost a fuchsia). Some people just want the Oleanders as greenery, though, and don't care about the blooms, so they cut them or trim them back, every April. When they drop or throw leaves and blossoms after it gets quite hot, there is much less clean-up to do if they have been trimmed.

You don't want to cut Oleanders back more than once or twice a year. If you keep cutting them back down, you obviously, won't ever have any blooms. Cutting them back is, of course, not the same as just trimming or tweaking them. If you like the blossoms, you'll want to think twice about trimming off any branches or shoots from Oleanders (or other bushes that blossom) because you'll lose blossom potential. Blossoms suddenly show up at the end of Oleander shoots and if you cut off the top of the shoots, you won't get any blossoms there. With Oleanders, some people want as many blossoms as possible, and for them, it isn't good to trim anything off of their Oleanders. Some may want absolutely no blossoms, for already-noted reasons. The blossoms can be really lovely, though; they can be prolific and even awesome. Always—to each his or her own.

You'll have to go around once or twice a year and do some slight trimming and shaping of Oleanders, and of any bushes and trees. If you want lots of height and fullness, then do little trimming and don't cut the plant down. Many bushes don't have blossoms, though, and only some leaves drop from them. Some bushes (even high ones) don't drop any leaves, or they don't drop very many of them. (Those are really the best ones to get.) Anything 'Evergreen' should drop very few leaves or nettles. Whatever is deciduous is another matter. Leaves will fall in the fall (autumn). (Is that why fall is called the fall? That makes sense to me.)

If there is a lack of water, it's almost as if the plant 'knows' that some leaves must take in the water for it to be able to survive, and that other leaves cannot take in any water, since there's only so much water. (Therefore, some leaves have to die and drop off.) To keep the plant looking its best, it requires water going in to as many of its leaves as possible. Again, though, generally Oleanders don't need regular watering or a great deal of water. Still, you have to keep watch. You're likely to get some yellow and dead leaves, even if you do water Oleanders. Also, who can monitor everything perfectly, and do so every year? You are going to end out with at least some dead leaves, from time to time. You also want to keep your water costs down, so if you have to rake or pick up some extra dropped leaves, you won't feel so bad.

It is especially a good idea to go around a lot if there has been no rain for a while, and check each and every planting. It is relatively easy to lose a plant or even a tree if the tree doesn't get enough water on a consistent basis. You can miss noticing the deterioration of a planting, and it can essentially be on its way to dying even if you routinely walk around. Some plantings may not be able to be seen—well or at all—from a window in the home and at any time, so you can even miss seeing any drooping, drying, leaf yellowing or browning, and leaf loss. After a certain point—of not getting enough water—a planting is likely not able to be saved. You can't reverse its death, in other words. If you ever notice plant deterioration because of lack of water absorption, you'll need to put the plant on a slow water drip, possibly overnight and perhaps even longer than that. You want all branches, twig areas, and leaves to have time to soak in the water. (At least you tried to save the plant.) During all warm and hot months, observation especially becomes a part of routine maintenance.

When a plant is receiving too little water, you may not be able to realize it right away. Even plants you haven't had to water over the years can suddenly die from lack of water. Obviously, drainage is a factor. If the land incline goes away from the plant, the plant may not be getting enough water. If the rains do not follow a specific pattern of regularity, plants can be vulnerable. Most people haven't the time to keep track of rain patterns and rain amounts. When leaves are needing some water, they'll droop and perhaps crinkle up a bit. The next stage is that the green on some of the leaves will fade in color because of the drying out. As this is happening, they will be easily pulled off. If you pull at them, they'll come off really easily because they were almost ready to drop anyway. If you shake the branch, off the leaves will come.

A good rule of green thumb is that if any plantings look even a little dry and droopy, and especially if leaves start to turn yellow or brown, the planting will need to get water to all its parts. This rule should be in the forefront of any landscape caretaker's thoughts. And, realize that if one planting is lacking water, it may well be that others are, too. It may be a few hours after watering before you see a planting perk up. Droopy leaves will spring back to a healthy-looking form. Sometimes, I forget to water my outdoor Spider Plants. They got real dried out and the ribbon-like blades looked very thin and they even looked to have a real pale cast. They almost looked dead. If I watered them really well, I'd come out the next day (these plants don't take that long to rejuvenate) and they would look like brand new plants. All the green came back, the plants were suddenly much fuller, and they had a more rounded shape. This plant resurrection never ceases to amaze me with Spider Plants and even certain other plants. Unfortunately, not all plantings bounce back that well, and, even Spider Plants will die after a while if there's been too little watering and you don't catch that in time. I had the Spider Plants for around five years, then decided to put in some aloes.

When it comes to removing fallen, dead leaves for that season (or whatever else, like dead blossoms or Evergreen nettles), keep in mind that you can sometimes use a broom and sweep them up, even from the ground; you can use a dustpan, if there aren't that many. A flat piece of cardboard or flattened wood would also work for collecting the leaves and then dumping them into a box. I tend to use a three-sided flat box (3" high) that is larger than a dustpan. You may want to wait until it becomes generally clear that there will be few to no more fallen leaves for that season (or whatever else, like dead blossoms or Evergreen nettles), but if the dead leaves, etc. have become a fire hazard and are piled up, you will have to do the removal then, and then likely a second time, later on. Dead leaves, etc. tend to collect in certain areas especially, so be careful about that. A smoker could walk by, and drop a cigarette.

On the subject of rain, right after a rain (that same day or the next) can be the best time to go out and do your gardening. After a rain, the air is fresh, the ground is wet, and the leaves and debris on the ground are moist and without dust. You can easily rake or pick up leaves and debris then, and you can easily pull out weeds. The ground is easy to dig in and it's also a good time to remove unwanted plantings, and to plant new ones. Right after a rain is the ideal time to work on gardening projects.

Many of the insects are underground right after a rain so you won't be in contact with very many of them, which includes stinging ants. When it rains, all ants go underground, for example. They remain safe down there and will wait until most of the puddles are gone. The return of the sunshine is a green light to them. These are all good reasons why it is good to go out gardening immediately after it rains. When you garden or work out in the yard, ants can be a problem. Some areas and lots have many ants, and many types of ants. They eat leafy vegetation (and whatever they can find). If you pull up weeds, ants may be at weed areas and even on the weeds. Ants don't usually bother me too much. Every once in a while, I get a few stings but that has never bothered me. Anyways, I've since started to wear socks if I think ants will be out when I need to garden.

Insects aren't around much in autumn and winter (in the north and even the south). Some ants are, in some southern areas, but flies, stinging insects, gnats, termites, fleas, and mosquitoes don't come around until spring and summer. With Global Warming, they tend to stay around a little longer now, in autumn. Possibly, some of them come back around earlier than they used to, in the spring. As noted earlier, all landscape workers and gardeners must be careful about Africanized Killer Bees now. Someone brought a bunch of them to South America a long time ago and now they are in the United States and are entrenched. Hundreds and hundreds of stings, etc., is an awful way to die—for a human or an animal. (Now we have the new Giant Hornets, too, to be concerned about.) Certain kinds of ants should be avoided, too. Fire ants, for example, if they are in your area. Also, if you can get some landscaping and gardening work done before the mosquitoes come back, all the better. Early spring is a good time to get most of your projects done, if you can. Then, everything will be prepared for the summer. Spring is really the best time and it slips by all too easily. Planning, and organizing time needs some forethought. Do not ever let yourself procrastinate. Do as much as you can before the insects settle in. This is another rule of green thumb.

Insects can be a problem anywhere and they can be a problem to varying degrees. All kinds of insects can plague plants and trees of any type. The scale insects, whiteflies, and mites are but three types. I have never had a problem with beetles, but in some areas, beetles need to be tackled. I consider beetles to be bugs but they are also certainly insects. I only consider some insects to be bugs. Beetles range in size. Bark Beetles can be a problem. (They feed and breed inside of bark.) There can be an infestation and they can kill trees. They like both the thin and thick-barked trees. They go for the Evergreens and the non-Evergreens. They've destroyed whole forests. They get underneath the bark so they are hard to see but there are tiny holes that can be seen if you pull back the bark. If you get them, you will have to call in a specialist. It is hard to kill them because they're under the bark. They can be on one of your trees, but not all of your trees, so you have to look at all your trees.

There are many different types of Bark Beetles and they range in size. If you get them, it can be hard to get rid of them. What is known as Sevin will get rid of some types. It is a dust or powder but it can be in a spray. In the Mid-West, quite a few Ash trees were lost to Bark Beetles. Cedar trees can get Bark Beetles, too. Cedar trees are supposed to be able to live a long time. There are some in Lebanon that are said to be 1,500 years old, but that could be a bit of a stretch. Still, Bark Beetles will cut short the life of trees. Some tree types are not so prone to getting them. You can have several different kinds of trees in an area and only one or two might be infested with the Bark Beetle. A bark beetle will bore into a tree and have their young in the tree. National Park areas have infestations. Forest areas have become dryer because trees die from their infestation and wood rot gets burned fast when there is a fire. If there's been excessive warming where there are Pine trees, more pine needles will have fallen and those will also be fire fodder. It's important to be careful about blaming Global Warming on every little and big thing, though—some things, yes, but some things, no.

Certain beetles are helpful, on the one hand, because they loosen the soil so water holds better in it. They do this when they are grubs in the ground. After they leave that stage (and about the time the rains hit, they turn into beetles. However, they will, then, start to eat vegetation and sometimes fruit, wherever the fruit is found, which would include on trees.

One beetle found in the South-West is the Fig Beetle but it doesn't only like figs—it likes most any fruit. It's one of the more beautiful insects because of its iridescent greenish color (that is on top of black, so the Beetle is really dark). There are a number of beetles all over the South and South-West because of the warmer climate but there are rare ones mixed in with the more common ones. There's some larger beetles but not many—like what you find in certain foreign countries. Beetles can range in size—from small to mid-sized to large and to huge. They aren't ever tiny, though. They're generally easily seen.

Most beetles generally don't get much larger than a fingernail. They move slowly, and they aren't dangerous to people but they could be to a garden or field so you have to know what kind they are so you can, somehow, get rid of them if they are doing any real damage. There are ways to exterminate them and there are ways to simply get them to leave an area. You have to decide what it is you want to do.

Some insects may be hard to see or detect. Different insects cause different kinds of problems. Certain ones will cause damage but not all will. Insects can affect roots, bark, branches and twigs, leaves, blossoms—in other words, all total, they can affect pretty much anything and everything. You'll have to identify the insect type as best you can and talk with a specialist about how to get rid of them. Certain relevant books will also help. In some cases, you can only keep them under control. Many people will hire out for insect control, which may include bombing, spraying, sprinkling (powder or granules), and/or using underground pellets. Insect control is a specialized business. Some places are relatively free of insects that harm their plantings, or harm them significantly. Cold weather will, of course, kill them, but certain types will return when it gets warm.

One insect that is very easy to detect is the locust and the reason why it is, is because they tend to increase so fast. They can take over whole fields and pastures and multiply and become hordes or swarms. They can take over large areas of a country, and they have been doing this in Africa. It is a type of grasshopper, of the Locustidae family. Whole areas must be well and repeatedly sprayed (with Chlordane or Toxophene, and all the crops are destroyed and then the eggs have to be plowed and dug up. They invade the garden and landscape lots of people. You want to get rid of them fast, before they multiply.

One insect you'll run into in southern areas is the cucaracha, otherwise known as the cockroach, but you won't find them around gardens. They don't like outdoor temperatures. They like being deep down in sewers and sewer lines. They like being hidden. They get into your home by way of sink and sometimes bathtub openings, usually (so keep them plugged). They are not a garden insect, nor are crickets, really—grasshoppers are a different matter. Crickets like to get into homes. They usually don't multiply too fast. They do not like being outside in the open, unlike grasshoppers (and locusts). Grasshoppers are leaf chompers. You don't want too many grasshoppers (or locusts) around, which leads me into another point (again). Try not to kill insects unless you know you have to. It's not the end of the world if there's been some occasional leaf chomping. It's when there's been a little too much of it that you'll need to get out the insect spray. Again, some you'll only want to leave or go away; others you'll probably want dead.

Ants can become a problem. They get in the house. I toss a couple of grapes outside my door (but a distance away from it) every so often so they won't enter my home. Find out where they enter, and toss out the grapes (or whatever else). That is where they will stay.

They also cluster on melon. They seem to really like fruit. You don't need much fruit, to deter them. Or, you can get out the insect spray or hire a pest-remover company to spray them for you. Ants sometimes bite you when you're working in the yard, and they can ruin the look of certain flowers. One particular plant can be their breakfast, lunch, and dinner, if they especially like the flowers on the plant.

If you grow fruit, you might get some fruit flies. These are tiny insects that look like gnats but they get to be a little bigger than gnats, though not much bigger so they get confused with gnats. You have to get a special spray, just for these tenacious insects. If you bring any fruit inside, you have to wash the fruit immediately in case eggs are on the fruit. You do not want any eggs to hatch in your home. If they do, you have to go on the attack right away as there will be many fruit flies. I've only had one home invasion, and they were hard to get rid of.

You have to put cut fruit in the dish, let the fruit flies come in to the dish, and give one good spray every time you see some gather. They'll keep gathering even after spray has been sprayed. If they eat the cut-up fruit (they especially like tomatoes), they'll die. The spray will kill them, too, but more will keep coming around the fruit. You just keep spraying in the home (one short shot of it, per time), being careful where any excess spray lands. Clean those areas later (or sooner would be better).

You may have to buy fruit-fly spray at a commercial insect spray company outlet. I personally tried the traps and for me, the particular ones I put in my home did not work and I had to use the spray, which was a little over a dollar an ounce. Whenever you need to kill insects, you want to try to find something that will kill eggs or stop any reproduction and fertilization of eggs. Not all insecticides will do that. Fruit flies in your home are a nuisance but they don't sting or bite. They pester you. They are nuisance pests. Also, fruit flies like cider vinegar and wine and beer. Put a little dish soap in with one of the three. The insects will stick to the soap upon entering where the smell is that is captivating them.

Some areas get more insect pests than others do. Different types of insect pests are found in different areas so you'll have to do some research. Insecticides are purchased based on what kinds of insects they will kill. People have to be very careful when handling or using insecticides. They can get into skin pores or be breathed in. For a long time, insecticides weren't noted as being harmful to humans, or to all the wildlife animals found in nature. Insecticides were lavishly sprayed down on areas, indiscriminately, and wildlife was grievously affected. Many animals died a horrid death. Reproduction of animals was adversely affected. DDT was used all over the place, for years. In 1962, a book came out about insecticides and about DDT. It was titled *Silent Spring* and was written by Rachel Carson. She was a leader in proclaiming the dangers of DDT and other insecticides on wildlife. Her book made a huge impact at the time and it still does.

Wherever insecticides are sold, before you buy anything, read all the labels. Consider tracking down an actual commercial insecticide if you can get it (ones that are used by an actual insect spray company or pest removal company). Some of those types can be stronger and more potent than what is sold in stores (and so, too, with weed spray). You may be able to buy larger volumes at such stores, which are usually specialty stores. They may not sell to the public so, first ask if they do when you call them up.

When it comes to ridding plantings of insects, do you want to kill the insects or do you just want them to leave? Remedies you buy or make up yourself can do one or the other. There are many natural remedies you can use and there are books out that specialize in these, or there are chapters in books about such remedies. The natural products that can go into these insect sprays are garlic, red pepper, and salt. Everything has to be mashed and squeezed out and mixed with water for spraying). There are others, too, like certain spices. Liquid products that can be used are milk and vinegar. Also, dish detergent has been used and mixed in with water. Not much is mixed in, however, as with baking soda, which can also be used. You make up actual recipes with these products. Then, you put them in a well-functioning spray bottle or spray apparatus and mix and then spray.

If you want certain insects to be dead, just be sure you identify what insect it is that you want to kill. Don't just seek to kill all the insects because some insects are good. They don't do damage to the plants. Certain insects will kill the unwanted insects. They are carnivorous, and either eat no plants or very little vegetation. It can become a bit of an Entomological Science determining what you want to kill. Before buying any commercial insect poison, see what it kills first. Does it kill the kind of insect you want gone, in other words? Again, you don't want to kill the good insects. Most areas, there are <u>only</u> around two to four percent of the insects in a garden or a landscaping that are truly pests. The rest of them really do no damage or very little damage and most are either helpful or basically neutral and do no damage. So whether you go with a commercial remedy or a natural remedy, determine what specific insects you want to be rid of.

What can be another problem is fungus, so realize that the problem you are noticing could be fungus, not insects. What can occur at times, too, is mildew (though it is rare in desert climates), but mildew isn't a very common problem anywhere—not in general. Sunburn, and the effects of frost and snow on plantings, may cause you to think there is a root problem or some kind of internal problem, but you'd be wrong. You could also be wrong about insects. Perhaps the planting is being frequented by certain insects, but those insects may not be affecting the condition. As a layperson, you can determine most of these conditions on your own, but when in doubt, consult a specialist and ask a number of questions.

On occasion, you may have to contend with bees around the yard. Wasps, hornets, and yellow jackets are less often encountered. (The yellow jackets and hornets are specific types of wasps and they all sting.) Bees fly and buzz around floral blooms and you want them to because they pollinate, which may or may not affect your lot per se but that's beside the point. They pollinate in many places where it matters. So do butterflies, which, of course, you'll want to see from time to time around your lot. They're so lovely.

Wasps, yellow jackets, and hornets make nests (with chambers in them). These stinging, flying insects do not build hives, nor do they make honey. They can spread pollen around, though. If wasps, yellow jackets, or hornets have built a nest on your lot (it will be brownish or grayish in color, and will be rounded), they will sting you if you come around close to their nest. If you try to knock their nest down, they will really go after you and sting you. Several will come after you. I wait until it gets cold to knock any such nests down. They are not around then. Bees usually build hives in rural areas and the country, but they've been known to build hives in eaves of houses and similar places. Often, if they're in eaves or nooks or crannies, they cannot be seen, and this can get to be dangerous, particularly if they are Killer Bees. I had Carpenter Bees build a hive under my mobile home one year (so I couldn't see the hive). I kept bumping into them, the hive got to be so big. They do not attack you but they can come in close and startle you and you will want to get away from them. It may only be one or two bees that come in close. We should have a lot more of these Carpenter Bees around than Killer Bees. I paid a professional to remove the hive. I really didn't want the bees killed, but I suppose he may have done that. I should have asked. They're a very cute and relatively harmless bee. Perhaps certain bees don't need to be killed to remove them. It would be good to look into this when you contact a bee control company. I would want any Killer Bees or Giant Hornets killed but not Carpenter or Honey Bees.

Carpenter Bees are large, black, rounded, and they have a louder buzz than the smaller more yellowish-orange bees have. They look scary but tend to leave you alone. If I was wearing anything floral, one or two would come around, which I did not find amusing. They'd buzz around me like I was a bunch of flowers and I'd have to go inside. Carpenter Bees are louder than regular bees but they are not the large, yellowish Bumblebees. Those are big and rounded, too, and they also buzz fairly loud. They're also social, as most bees are because they live together at a hive.

You might also see a few Mason Bees flying around your landscaped area. You might even want to get some via the Internet if you have a larger area. They wouldn't be good to get if your lot is small. It is not good to keep bees on a small lot because neighbors are usually too close and so you would get complaints. Mason Bees are rather small bees and they are non-aggressive. They are docile, for the most part. People buy them and tend to them but there is more to beekeeping than meets the eye and over the course of the year, specific tasks must be completed.

Africanized Bees are more apt to build hives around where at least some people are, compared with regular Honey Bees. Killer Bees will sometimes build their hive in eaves of homes, or in any hollowed out area on a home or shed. They do not prefer the rain, and they like to be safe and secluded and so they'll try to build a hive higher up (but not in every case because they can be hidden somewhere lower down, too—like in a hollowed-out log). Their hive can also hang from a tree branch. Regular Honey Bees will often build their nests or hives in ground hollows that will stay dry.

These bee types—Killer Bees and regular Honey Bees—are not distinguishable to most people, even some experts. The regular Honey Bees have fewer and wider bands of black along their thorax and abdomen areas; sometimes there's only two bands, whereas the Killer Bees will have four (thinner) bands. Regular Honey Bees just look fatter and more filled out. The regular Honey Bee will have a black head but the Killer Bee will have a golden-colored head. When Killer Bees are around, you must always be looking both high and low. They kill humans and pets because a whole hive will aggressively go after whatever they perceive to be a threat, and they'll attack fast. Any walking person, or pet, would be vulnerable to these more southern menaces, and killers. The minute you see a couple of bees flying near you, go the other way from where you suspect a nest of them could be.

As noted earlier, insect-rid companies should be government paid to go out on a hunt and kill the killer bees so all the other types of bees will come back in and dominate. There are ways to track hives so the insect-rid companies would have to be detectives. This should have been done as of yesterday. They do not belong in America, and never did. It is too bad the problem was not nipped in the bud.

It is good to have non-hostile bees around, every growing season. We have to have them so plants will be pollinated. If ever you don't see any bees around (and you usually did in the past), report it to the local Agriculture Department because a lack of bees is a very bad sign for any locality. Too many Honey Bees have been strangely dying off and disappearing and a number of people believe it has to do with pesticides. Industrial pesticides have been widely used on crops all over the world, really. There are just so many toxic chemicals around and bees find their way to areas that have been sprayed. There's been a world-wide dying out of very important, valuable bees, and it's been proven that pesticides are culprit. They've found pesticides in bee tissues. From plants and vegetation, the pesticides get rubbed off on the bees and get into their nervous system.

One half to two-thirds of dead bees has caused beekeepers to lose their business (or businesses). This has increasingly been a world-wide problem. Some countries are now banning certain chemical insecticides or pesticides—almost too late, I might add. One day, will there be no honey? Everyone hopes all bees will 'bounce back'. We aren't so crazy about the Killer Bees, but the Honey Bees have never been aggressive. Have Killer Bees been killing Honey Bees? They are looking into this. For sure, they drive away Honey Bees because they are so aggressive.

There are products around that are not so toxic that can be used for some and certain insects. You can get these on the Internet and find them locally. Again, you can even make them up yourself. Certain garden nurseries will have these products, and large marts will, too. There are companies that will come out and spray your yard; ask any company rep if they have less toxic sprays, even natural ones, which will do the job. Call around if you need to. Visit more than one retail mart or garden center. When it comes to the Killer Bees, do not try to spray Killer Bees yourself. Let the experts come out and do it. You may want experts to come out and spray all aerial stinging insects. You need special protective clothing before going out to spray. You have to wear a well-covering face guard or mask, and, be careful if there is wind and people are nearby.

The problem is, how do you get rid of some pests without harming others? What happens when there are unwanted infestations and disease-causing insects? Countries must all proceed with great care. Certain chemical insecticides may have a number of brand names so it can get confusing. In Taiwan, ten million bees disappeared in only a couple of weeks because of insecticides. Regular Honey Bees could be wiped out very easily. (Killer Bees are also honey bees but how many people want to breed them for honey—not many but believe it or not, some do and some are.) You'd think there would have been more tests done and done earlier on and much better government observations going on in many countries around the world. Even when there were reports of losing a few bees should have alerted them, but up to as much as an eighth or a fourth of them! Where were the inspectors? Even when bees come across low doses of pesticides, they are still affected and cannot function properly. They become disoriented and disabled. They cannot pollinate plants when they're in that condition. They cannot work around the hive. They have trouble moving about and flying. It is a cruelty that's been put upon them, really.

A few gardeners will also keep some bees, for the honey. (Even though a few people have kept Africanized ones, there are other problems with these bees, besides their being so aggressive.) You have to know what you are doing if you keep any bees, at all. What are you going to do if your neighbor suddenly decides to set up one or more bee colonies? Well, it would depend on if it's out in the country in a real rural area or if it is in a more close-quarters area, where more people are around. For me, I would like to know if any of my neighbors were keeping bees.

If bees are known to be in your area, keep a good watch for the Africanized Killer Bees, as well as a sudden lack of Honey Bees around your area. Again, the Killer Bees will drive off the less aggressive bees. Keep a <u>constant</u> watch for them, too, especially if you are out in a less-populated area. As a reminder, don't be slack. Be ready to call in the bee exterminator.

The Africanized bees are considerably more fierce and aggressive. Again, they may bump you first, as a warning to get away from where their hive is (that may not be able to be seen); if you don't get away and take the hint rather fast, get ready for a full-scale attack (but how can anyone get ready for that?). Again, get away quickly from where you <u>know</u> their hive can, if <u>ever</u> you are bumped by one or more bees. As noted before, animals of all types do not know what is happening, if they're bumped so they do not quickly leave.

To emphasize and make very clear because life/death is involved, bees send out some guarding bees if someone (or an animal) is within about twenty-five yards of their hive and when you see any bees flying around and they aren't on flowers, even if you aren't bumped, get away from where you think their hive could be. It could even be a ground-area hive. Leave fast. Run even. Get away no matter what the bee type, in fact, because it can mean you are too close to a hive. A few Carpenter bees did that to me, one time, and I left but they followed me because of my floral dress (three or four of them did) until I got far enough away from them. They didn't sting me, which is the way it should be. We've never needed the Killer Bees and we don't need them now. It's just like—do we need the pythons in the Florida Everglades? No, we don't, and we don't need the Killer Bees, either. The USA was doing just fine, before they came in. They are invaders.

These Giant Hornets could become worse invaders, too, if we don't get rid of them, fast. They kill whole hives of Honey Bees. They chew their heads off, and then just leave them. They will do this to whole hives. Some are calling them Killer Hornets. They can be around two inches long, which means their stinger is quite large. It is two to three times longer and thicker than the Honey Bee stinger. You do not want these aggressive invaders around your landscape and garden. Their spreading must be stopped, in a focused and deliberate way by local and state governments. Perhaps the Federal Government should intervene.

All beehives have to be and stay dry. Bees can be in lumber piles, tires, unused vehicles, and unused containers lying around. The Africanized ones can especially be in tipped-over containers or anything similar. They can nest or build hives in chimneys so be careful about burning wood in a fireplace. They'll get into plumbing, sometimes, but will obviously leave if there's too much activity in the plumbing. But, bees need a water source, too. The best beehive remover is a beekeeper who might even want to keep and preserve the hive and take it elsewhere.

Even though Killer Bees are somewhat smaller than regular Honey Bees, they are unusually fearless for an insect. If you don't get away, fast, a whole horde of them (thousands, even) will assemble to attack an animal or a person. (Some believe Africanized Killer Bees are killing the Honey Bees, which is another reason why people want them all exterminated.) In many areas, it is probably not just the Killer Bees that are killing the regular Honey Bees, which have been dying all over the world. (Killer Bees aren't even in Europe where so many Honey Bees are dying.) Again, it is the toxic insecticides that are killing the Honey Bees and this has been proven.)

When you first see Killer Bees, call in a specialist to get rid of them, even that very day. You don't want them around. You don't want them multiplying. They have the potential to bee killers. Lives are in danger when they are around. You cannot leave them be when they are too close to where people live. All farm animals have to be kept safe, too. You do not want the bees to be on your property. In some areas, be constantly on the lookout for them. Go out and find them, in other words (in protective clothing). Don't let yourself get caught unaware. It is not illegal to kill Killer Bees.

Africanized Bees tend to be in larger groups than regular Honey Bees are, and a person or animal that threatens the hive will end out with so many bee stings that it can be jaw dropping. With the Africanized Bees, there will be hundreds of stings but with regular Honey Bees, there'll only be around ten or twenty, depending on how fast the animals or the person being stung can get away. Because the nests or hives of the Killer Bees are often much smaller than those of regular Honey Bees, it becomes harder to see them and this factors in with the overall problem of Killer Bees. Still, all bees have more of a tendency to be in more rural, sparsely populated areas so most city dwellers and homeowners are not so apt to run across a beehive. Look around for them anyway, whenever you are gardening. Rural people garden, too—sometimes quite a lot.

Those big, black Carpenter Bees do not mind being around people, but you cannot miss seeing them, or hearing them. If too many of them are around, there could be a hive nearby. Carpenter Bees are quite rotund. You almost wonder how they are able to fly. They're almost cute (because they're rounded). Giant Hornets look a little rounded, too, except their bodies have more than one section. Don't get near the Carpenter Bee's hive, though. They won't look so cute when they start stinging you. They aren't usually attackers, though, but they'll defend their hive if you get close to it. They like to find safe, hard to get to places for their nest, or hive. They'll go under homes so you have to find out where they are entering. All beehives have a number of small chambers in them, so they're sometimes called nests. Chambers are where new bees come out of. Eggs are laid inside them. Wasp nests also have chambers. All wasp nests are gray in color and they hang from vines, branches, or whatever the wasps can attach the nest to that seems safe for them. The nests aren't too large.

All bees do not want to be killed, and they don't like their honey taken. It is a food supply for them and they especially need it during cold winter months when they can't get nectar from blossoms. If ever honey is removed from a hive, it shouldn't all be taken because the bees will need it. So often, it all gets taken. It's no wonder the bees get angry and sting people when their honey is at stake. It's like someone coming in and clearing out your refrigerator and taking all your money so you can't buy food.

America did fine with just the Honey Bee before the Africanized Bees were snuck in to South America, bred with the European Honey Bee, became aggressive, and then made their way up to the United States. We don't need the Africanized Killer Bees. We need to take care of the Honey Bees. We need to try to protect the Honey Bees so should we go to war against the Africanized ones? From March to July, swarms of bees will leave one site to go to another. They follow the queen bee. Some feel that before they leave one site (and if they are the Africanized bees) they should be eradicated before they can get started up somewhere else. Most people feel that no Africanized bees should ever be bred by anyone, anywhere. We need more Honey Bees and not Africanized ones. Bees are useful in gardens, landscaped areas, and in the natural world, but the Killer Bees are not wanted. Before the Killer Bees came, there were only Honey Bees and everything was fine. We had enough honey and plants got pollinated. Then came the Killer Bees and all the pesticides.

A beehive is a home for bees. It is where they live and take their meals. When a beehive is taken or destroyed because someone wants the honey, any straggler bees may well die. You can't always know where Killer Bees and the hive will be but again, they are exceedingly aggressive in their defense of their hive. Even though they are smaller than Honey Bees, that means nothing if someone gets attacked because so many bees will attack. It takes about 1000 stings to kill a grown person (on average). It can take less if there is a heart condition. Once a bee loses its stinger, it dies (but more will be born to replace those ones). Africanized Killer Bees are in all southern USA states but especially Southern California, Southern New Mexico, Southern Nevada, all of Texas, and all of Arizona. When a hive is exterminated, the queen bee must be killed.

We need more Honey Bee types because they are in decline for more than one reason. The Killer Bees are killing them (as are the Giant Wasps); toxic agricultural chemicals are, too. There are reasons that relate to Global Warming affects, too. All the dryness in places, the storms, in some areas, and the fires that seasonally flare up do not help. We need more beehives and beekeepers. Global Warming affects all animals, right down to the insects and spiders. I cover this subject in my book *Global Warming Causes, Solutions, and Theories*.

Beehives are being put up on rooftops by beekeepers, now, but the roofs are on multi-storied buildings in towns and cities so the bees can never bother people walking below. They have to be set behind an affixed obstruction so the wind cannot bother the bees. Several 'boxes' with pull-out honeycomb trays can be up on a roof. Doors are locked to such roofs. If you own an office building, and like bees and honey, and if you get city clearance, then consider keeping bees, there. Many will keep bees on their land, though. There is a lot to know if you ever keep bees.

A gardener should stay away from any and all bees. Be very careful of them. Be extremely careful of trimming trees and weed-whacking. Call an exterminator first, if need be. And be careful about leveling or digging dirt when landscaping, since they are sometimes in the ground. Consider wearing bee-protection clothes and a head guard or cover if you are in a John Deere or Caterpillar work vehicle. Also, if you have farm animals, don't let them be near any hives. Go out routinely, find them, and get rid of them. They'll attack any moving creature even if they are as far away as 100 feet, which is twenty to thirty feet longer than most mobile homes are. If you are closer in to them than that, start running. Farm animals can be fenced in so they are possibly more protected. Dogs and cats sometimes go under a fence (not good). Probably some birds have been killed by Killer Bees, too, if stingers can go through some of their feathers.

If mosquitoes are out, wear sweatpants, socks, and a long-sleeved shirt or blouse. However, if your arms are always moving, mosquitoes tend to avoid the lower arms, even if that part of the arms is exposed. It's because the lower arms tend to move around more that they don't land on arms. Mosquitoes tend to avoid the face area, as well, if you are in motion. Why they tend to avoid the face area could be because of movement around the face area. Mosquito repellent might be a good idea, at times. I now wear socks (along with the sweatpants) so I'm less apt to get any mosquito bites on my ankles or feet. I don't get ant bites, either, because of the socks. (Fortunately, mosquitoes aren't around during the colder months. They are summer insects, like so many other insects are.) This is one reason why some gardeners try to get as much done as they can in the early spring.

I have yet to encounter a rattlesnake, so I don't worry about that, but in some areas in the southern American states, there can be rattlesnakes (or other snakes) in and around a yard, especially in real rural areas and the country, where snakes can come across lots of small critters to eat, and for their young. A rattle can sound a little like a hissing sound (but it is not like a cat sound, it's like escaping steam that is constricted and going through a small area, thereby making the hissing sound). You do not want to continue gardening when you hear any rattling (or hissing). Get away from the area and the snake as fast as you can. Find out, in advance, exactly where you need to go for emergency medical care before you do your gardening, in the event of a snake bite. Try not to garden if any snakes are out. In a number of areas, there are no snakes. They are only in a few areas. Always know, in advance, where the poisonous snakes live. Constrictor snakes only live in certain areas. Some people carry a knife with them, if they know some constrictor snakes could be nearby.

Learn to differentiate different snakes, since only some of them are poisonous. As a general rule, snakes like the privacy of rural and country areas and don't like cities, towns, and noise. They could still be around any area, though. They tend to breed in areas where there are no people. Their babies are born from mid to late summer. If your residence is more rural and there could be rattlesnakes around, wear high boots if you garden and be very careful where you put your arms and hands. Look around before you do something. Rattlesnakes hibernate in the winter but come out in early spring to mate. Most anti-venom costs can be quite expensive. Always try to guard your pets from rattlesnakes.

You have to be very careful of alligators in some of the south and South-Eastern USA areas, too. (You have the rattlers in the west and the gators in the south and South-East.) The State of Florida is loaded with gators—some say there are a million of them down in Florida (and there's some in Mississippi, Alabama, and Louisiana, too). They're also in western Texas, eastern Georgia, both Carolinas, and to some extent there are some in Arkansas and Oklahoma. Anywhere where there is water (and fish), in these southern areas, is where they can be. If you are near water where gators can be, you must be wary and vigilant. You must also watch your children if there's even a slight chance there could be alligators around (and watch your pets, as well). All it takes is one alligator to take a life and they can do it so quickly. It would help to learn how to fight off a gator. Punching them in their eyes might help. They might let go. People have started to eat alligator meat, but alligators are still increasing. Certain reptiles generally have a lot of babies (like snakes).

People who live where snakes and gators tend to be or could be will want a nice yard, regardless of these dangerous animals. A particular type of fence would help with the snakes. It could possibly help with the snakes if it is a wood-plank fence and there are no openings in it anywhere. Always check for burrowed holes, though. You will want to fill them all in and even collapse them, if you see holes.

In Florida, another danger now is pythons. People started dumping their pet pythons out in the wild, rather than having them euthanized. Since the mid-1990s, they have been breeding and pets and even people have been attacked or even killed by them. A large enough python can eat a child, and most any pet. Anyone who gardens, especially in Florida, has to be very careful of these snakes. Again, be very careful about burrowed holes. Pythons do not like to be in the open. They hide inside places, and between and in tight places. Some anacondas have been dumped, too.

For sure, do your best to snake-proof your yard, relative to any and all snakes--always. Don't leave your shed door open. Be wary of any spot where a snake could be (including the burrowed holes). You might need to remove something that is on your lot, or move some things around. Snakes try to avoid too much direct sun. They like the shade. They could be under something on your lot. They are not real fast movers but they are stealth and can move fast enough.

The gators kill pythons, but pythons can kill gators, too. Still, more gators eat the pythons and for this reason, the pythons haven't been able to spread north, but a python could be dumped anywhere, and not just in Florida. Even if a python is dumped in a forest or heavily-treed area, it can slide over to where people are. People who dump pythons know this, too, and they are criminals. If a python kills a person (or a pet), whoever dumped the python is responsible for the death. <u>Any</u> python-related death should go on any person who has <u>ever</u> dumped a python; certainly such deaths should go on those people, morally. Some shelters will take pythons. Also, check with local Animal Control if a python has been spotted.

Sometimes, it's good to do certain gardening projects during late autumn and the winter because when it gets cool enough, most insect pests disappear. This includes ants, termites, fleas, flies, bees/wasps/hornets, and many other types. In warmer areas, about the time you start to need to wear a sweater or jacket outside, the insects are gone until springtime. When it starts to get pretty cold at night (but the days may still be warm), the insects may die off or hibernate, because of the cold nights. Insects can be a nuisance, when you are gardening.

During warmer months, after a rain is a good time to garden because insects aren't usually around. I've even done yard work when the rain outside has been really light but the temperature was fairly warm. If I need to pull weeds, I very rarely miss the opportunity to pull them out after a rain so I can get the roots, but other tasks can be done then, as well. I am now conditioned to go pull weeds right after a rain; it's the first think I think about when it rains. It's a good time to clean out beds, too.

Frankly, most people only want to work outside in the spring, and in the early morning hours of the summer, but there are advantages to working outside during late autumn and winter, too (unless there is snow on the ground). You can do quite a few gardening and landscaping tasks so you will be ahead of the game when spring comes around. Some things you cannot do, though.

Most people who landscape want to get the front of their lot landscaped first because it is ever in plain view of the neighbors, of people who drive by, and of visitors who come over to the home. Arranging rock gardens in front is often done and usually some kind of symmetry is preferred in the front area, from side to side. (This will depend on the design of the home, though.) Or, you can go with partial symmetry as long as there is some kind of balance. Balance is something to consider when designing and organizing a landscape. Harmony is too, but only to a point. There can sometimes be a harmony in diversity, in other words. So much will depend on what is planned for the overall landscaping.

Most mobile home front areas are rectangular in shape. As you work towards the sides of the mobile home, you don't have to be concerned about symmetry anymore. For one thing, one side of the lot is generally wider than the other side is. Rock garden partitions are popular, and easy to do. You can put in all kinds of plantings to be a part of a rock garden. Use medium to large-sized rocks to edge rock gardens, and use them as separators if you want a particular rock garden to have one or more sections. Rocks that are from three to five inches long/wide look good and enclose plantings very nicely, but, you can use even larger-sized rocks if you want to. You can use bricks as edging, too.

There are many things you can do with small, medium, and large-sized natural rocks, when creating bed areas for plantings. I used these rocks for edging, all over my lot. I had to carefully place each rock in so that the edging looked its best and stayed intact. I'd maneuver each rock. Sometimes, I tried two or three rocks before I found the best rock to place in with the rock next to it. Once this got done, it was done for good. The rocks absolutely had to fit in well with the next rock. Sometimes, I had to readjust rocks in spots before the edging looked just right and the rocks fit in real well. I tried to keep to general same-sized rocks whenever I put edging around an area. There has to be general compatibility and uniformity even though every rock is different. Some people just put rocks down willy-nilly, but I prefer more precision so I take more time to establish my rock gardens. I'm meticulous about how I place the rocks. I will sometimes even move them around until they look better. Once established though, the rock edgers or other kinds of edgers (like bricks or scalloped-designed edgers), will stay as they are. I never look back.

When the rock work looks good, the rock-edged beds become permanent. You can also edge garden areas with railroad ties or with planks of wood. Redwood 4" x 4"s work very well. There are also rounded redwood logs that roll. Water doesn't rot out redwood and insects (mainly termites) don't eat redwood. All kinds of bricks work good for edging. Some people edge their gardens with short metal-wire fencing. I prefer natural, good-sized rocks. I use ones that are different shapes because it can't be otherwise with the rocks from nature. All edger rocks should be in the ground, at least a bit, so some dirt has to be removed first before each rock is put down. Rocks stay in place better, if they're recessed in the ground just a little.

I generally bought plantings after I made up a rock-edged bed (if I didn't have any free plantings available, that is). I'd look for a plant, or several plants that I knew would look right in the newly created bed. You can do this the other way around, though—create the beds around the plantings that you plan to put in or that you've even already put in. Wherever I could establish a rock-edged bed, I did, but I did these one at a time and over a period of time. I also put the same kind of natural rocks around some of my solo plantings, for example, around my Italian Cypress trees. It's nice to put rock edging around all trees but it certainly isn't compulsory; some people prefer leaving tree areas alone.

With the rock-edged beds, you can always make them larger, smaller, or divide them up. Rock-edged beds add to the charm of landscaping and give the landscaping a finished look. As noted before, seeds are blown around and therefore, wanted plants to be used elsewhere on the lot can sprout, and so when these sprouts are to be planted elsewhere, a rock-edged bed may need to be expanded to accommodate these sprouts. Someone may give you some new plants, too, or you may see some new ones at a garden shop that you can't resist buying. All cacti should be in a rock-shaped partition. The rocks serve as protection for people who walk by the cacti. Rock-edged areas may also need to be expanded if a particular planting grows. It all depends on the planting and the space. Plants flare out and tree trunks expand, for example. So do enclosed cactus partitions. It's always good to have extra rocks around so you can expand any edging areas.

Concerning buying new growths for my own lot, I tend to buy small plants, to save some money. Sometimes, it's wise to buy a larger, established plant or tree but they will cost you more money. For some people, however, money is no object. Larger plants are heavier to handle. Potted plants and trees at garden shops or plant nurseries are sold in different-sized planters, so obviously they are going to vary in weight and size. Whether a planting is large or small, it will still need nurturing. Sometimes, you can only find a certain, specific plant or tree that you want in a certain, specific-sized pot so what are you going to do? Buy the plant or tree, obviously, and pay what the plant or tree is priced at; however, at some nurseries, sometimes you can ask if they will reduce the price. On occasion, they will.

Edger rocks and rocks in general make a yard look filled in and complete. They're nice because they all look different. They're different as to size, shape, and color, although there aren't too many colors—just the white, beige, brown, golden, reddish (rust colored), gray, and sometimes you see a black or greenish one. Still, they all look different and add a natural look to a yard. Some of my rocks have turquoise streaks in them, and these ones are easy to notice. When all the rocks are put in together and nicely and evenly placed, they look great.

Pavers, of course, are man-made but they can look natural because they are usually the colors found in nature. I have pavers here and there. You can get pavers that are different sizes and shapes and they can help to fill in your yard. You can actually put a group of pavers side by side and use them to form a floor, for a patio, a barbecue area, a shed, or anything else that needs a stone-type floor. One type of flooring can be done better using flat 12" x 12" pavers, not the 16" x 8" ones, but sometimes, it makes no difference and sometimes, it all depends on how you want to lay out a floor.

Pavers can be put down to make a linear footpath, too. Such a path can go from the front of the lot to a door area, or from a door area to a shed or patio area. Of course, round concrete pavers (that are flat) can be put down to provide a linear footpath, as well. Sometimes, these kinds of pavers are square or hexagonal and these, too, can be used. They have to be distanced just right so that the average person can step on them with general ease, as they are walking along. Packed-in cobblestones, or what might be similar, are sometimes used for a footpath, but they're not always so easy to find and they can take more time to lay down if you do find them because cobblestones tend to be small. Any step-stone should be flat, or ankles can turn, so carefully select any stones that will be used for stepping. They shouldn't be too high up from the ground, either. You have to dig up some of the dirt and smooth an area out so they'll be imbedded in the ground and be a little lower in the ground. When putting down pavers or stepping stones, you should dig an area out that is about a half inch to an inch in depth and make sure the surface is flat before you put the paver or stone in place. That way, the paver is securely in and down in the ground so it's not so easy to trip on it. Cobblestones or pavers will be in more securely and be less apt to be tripped over if they are set lower down in the ground.

Some people are very careful when they lay a concrete path or walkway. The right grade of concrete has to be selected, as does the right mix. As soon as concrete is mixed, it has to be laid down quickly because it immediately starts to dry. Therefore, the pegs and board framing for whatever it is that is being concreted must be installed in advance. Walkways can be in several places on a lot. You don't really need them, but they add a great deal to a lot and they can make an area look much better.

Be careful where you plant if you are planning to put down a footpath of some kind. Know how wide any plantings are going to get because plantings can encroach on a footpath. If you can trim back any encroaching planting, then that is something you must take into consideration before deciding what to plant in a spot or where you will put down a footpath. Only some people will actually lay down concrete, to create several walkways or paths. Do a study of the mixing and spreading process first because there is much to know about mixing concrete and laying down concrete. Keep in mind, too, that concrete can be stained a nice color afterwards, and staining is very simple to do. Pavers can also be stained, but they can be found already having a color, as terra cotta, green, brown, gold, and gray, which is likely uncolored since they are concrete blocks and concrete blocks are naturally gray.

Generally, you use pavers to step on. I have paver paths, and then I have pavers packed in side-by-side in a few isolated spots and they serve as outdoor flooring. If I need to step somewhere, there are pavers down for that. Pavers are like stepping stones. I have put in a few flat natural stones around the lot, too, and these are natural stepping stones. Natural stones, if they're flat, are not so easy to come by; they're hard to find. Man-made pavers or stepping stones work better because they are always very flat and equal in size.

Everything takes time and effort, and you don't do everything in a day. You can't cut corners (or you shouldn't). You really don't want to do things slipshod (though some do). You want to do everything right. On occasion, I've had to re-do something, so it would be right and would look right. When everything is done right and looks good, it is an achievement. You feel good about your labor and about the result. It's not much fun when you know you have to re-do something or improve on something you did but sometimes, this is the way the cookie crumbles.

Many house lots and mobile home lots have small rocks or pebbles on them. They pretty much cover the whole lot. They make the lot look better and they help keep the weeds down to a minimum; however, you will still get some weeds. The seeds land between the rocks and germinate and the weeds sprout up. The thicker you put on the layer rocks, the less apt you are to get weeds. Often, a resident who rents the lot space at a mobile home park must pay for these small rocks or pebbles, on their own. The park management maybe used to pay for them, but they may not anymore. Ask if they do, though, because they just might. Before you sign anything with park management, try to squeeze that in, and anything else that might be possible. If you own the land, you most certainly will have to buy the rocks and whenever you lay down landscape cover rocks, it is better to have too many of them than too few. Over the years they can dig down in the dirt and not be seen any more so you may need to lay down more.

You can choose from different kinds of layer rocks. There are different sizes—for example, the half inch or the inch ones—and there are different colors, as reddish (rust colored), peach, mauve, pink, golden, white, or gray. You can buy the tiny gravel size, but usually people use this kind of layer rock for a carport or a garage area, and also for a road. People like it for driving on. You use somewhat larger rocks on an actual lot. I chose the River Rock to put on the lot because it is a mix of natural colors, and I chose the inch-sized stones or pebbles. I also chose the River Rock mainly because it had more of the smoother edges and it was composed of genuine rock. I passed over the white layer rock because looking down on it was too bright and hard on my eyes. I certainly passed over the tiny gravel-sized layer rocks. They go all over the place—on sidewalks, roads, carports and driveways, and into planting beds. They're just too light weight and can be a nuisance if they aren't somehow braced or bracketed in or set down in specific separate areas. Just avoid them in the first place (except to drive on) is what I would suggest. Some like the tiny ones for driveways so they don't have to lay expensive concrete down.

On many different kinds of smaller lots, especially in warm-climate areas, people have been using and are going to the landscape rocks to cover the lot, so they can avoid using grass. Though one name for the larger of the smaller rocks is River Rocks, there could be different names. River Rocks have a smoother edge than chipped landscape rocks do so they cost a little more than chipped landscape rocks cost. Chipped rocks are harder on your feet when you walk on them (even with shoes on). Rocks about a half to one inch long or round are best for covering the ground. Again, those really small and tiny rocks can be a nuisance. They shift around a lot and go places where they shouldn't (especially after a rain) and they can also get in your shoes, especially when you are wearing sandals. They're just too tiny and too light in weight; still, a lot of people get this kind of layer rock, and probably, a lot of people are all right with having them all over their lot, as well as in their driveway. Some of the River Rock will naturally be broken when you first get it so there will be some rough edges but there will be considerably fewer sharp edges than if you'd used the chipped rocks. Walking on top of the one or the other makes a big difference and you will notice that difference. Some chipped rocks are dyed and of a uniform color, too, whereas River Rock will be of varying earth-tone colors.

You don't see grass on lots all that often in many areas in the South-west, particularly areas that get very hot and tend to be dry. You see more grass when homes are close to a coast or on a coast, because of the humidity. In the dryer areas, if a lot does have grass, it does better when there is a watering system installed and when a timer is used. Nowadays, rolls of grass can be bought and the grass on the rolls has been pre-grown and is usually thick grass and it has a consistent-growth of grass blades. The rolls are easy to install; you simply roll them out. If you use grass seed instead, the grass tends to grow in slowly and unevenly, and often the seeds get blown over to the neighbor's and they will come to be hoppin' mad when the blades start sprouting.

The windblown seeds may grow into grass on a neighbor's area, and do so not just once, but periodically. You may see new grass growing over at your neighbor's every time you look over there. Your neighbor will be secretly or openly fuming. Rolls of grass, when they are used, are not so apt to throw seeds because there are essentially no seeds. The grass blades are already mature. The grass may throw a few seeds, later on, but not for a while.

Grass requires regular watering, and quite a lot of it per watering time. When water gets rationed, grass watering can become very problematic. Still, people like grass. Grass can cool an area down a little, especially after it is watered (whether there is a watering system or isn't). Grass can also keep the dust down. Once grass is all laid down and installed, it can be great. It will die in the winter, and come back in the spring and summer, after some watering. Many are opting for the landscape rocks, though.

One advantage of using landscape rocks on a lot is because no lawn mowing is needed. Those who have grass must regularly cut it, even if there is only a small amount of it. Mowing grass can be quite an effort, even when using a gas-powered lawnmower. What to do with the grass clippings can be quite a job or a bit of a job, depending on the grass clipping apparatus (or holder). Not all electric mowers have such a bag attached so grass clippings have to be raked up. Gasoline must always be around for these mowers, too. Electric or battery-powered mowers are extremely expensive. They are sometimes used on really big lawns.

There are quite a few battery-driven mowers around now, that you can buy. You just re-charge the battery. There is no need to keep gasoline around. There are also small, low-to-the-ground units that are remote-control and computer-generated ones. One such unit will automatically go all around the yard and cut it because it is programmed to; it knows when the grass is high, so the cutter is on, or when it is low, so the cutter is off. It even has its own little garage-type unit it rolls into when it is done. This grass-cutting unit is costly and how many know how to repair it? Probably not many.

With the landscape rocks, you don't have to buy a lawnmower of any kind or be concerned with lawnmower repairs. It's good, though, to find out what choices are present with the landscape rocks because there are different ones around, especially if you live in a larger city. Many people prefer using landscape rocks to having grass because they conserve water. And again, with lawn mowing, they'll be using up gasoline. Many people have to hire out to lay out the landscape rock. Usually, though, the landscape rock company doesn't lay the rock out for the customer; they just dump a large pile of the rocks on their lot. People with homes in northern areas and along coastal areas are even getting landscape rocks put on their lots—in the front, back, or in both front and back. Once grass is established on a lot, it is not easy to get rid of because even it is dug up, it can come back up, in patches.

It is best to wait to see if dug-up grass is going to come back up before any layer rocks get spread on the lot. You'll want to dig up any grass areas that come back up, and you may want to use a strong grass killer. If you remove grass, you may need to put down a topsoil afterwards, before you put down the layer rock, depending on what you want to do with the ground area.. Most people won't bother to do that, though. Topsoil would replace the soil that was taken out when the grass was dug up, however.

In some parts of the country, people don't have to use the layer rocks because they can have grass, but grass does not grow real well in desert areas. For one thing, so much water is needed to keep grass alive, and cost of water is going up, especially in the warmer and hotter areas. Water can even be a little scarce in places. Sometimes, it is rationed in some areas, at certain times of the year. They are still working on desalination of ocean and sea water so there can be more available water, but use of this water will be expensive. The process of desalination is expensive. Mainly, governments are concerned with irrigation on a large scale. So much water goes to irrigate agricultural areas.

One subject not yet all that highlighted in America is the water that ebbs and flows in America. (Ebbs and flows essentially means goes and comes.) When it ebbs, there is a water shortage. In half of the American States, there tends to be occasional shortages. There are times when a town or city must impose water rationing on its citizens. This can happen anywhere but it happens more readily in the warmer southern states, particularly where it is dry. It certainly happens in the desert climate areas. With Global Warming upon us, water rationing is likely to increase but we'll see. Some areas cannot use well water anymore, or get into the underground water table, which is now lower in, at least, many areas, but certainly not in all areas. I write about this topic in my *Global Warming Causes, Solutions, and Theories* book. The desalination of water is being perfected. Rain is probably not going to stop any time soon. Reservoirs will probably stay filled. They'll go up and down, so it will depend on the season when the level is being measured. There is also snow and ice-melt run-off from hills and mountains. Only some South and South-West areas get snow and ice. These areas are more northern and they are in different temperature zones and require a different approach to gardening and landscaping.

One problem occurs if people forget to water certain plants. An irrigation system, once installed, is good to use if it has a timer. There are drip-method systems and overhead watering systems, the latter of which uses more water, but it can be on a timer, too, so everything gets watered enough and forgetfulness won't matter. Always, no matter what, try to water earlier in the morning if you know the day will be hot, or later in the day as it starts to cool. There will be so much less evaporation that way and less water will need to be used but always, water has to be enough to get down to the roots. Plantings and vegetation must have enough water so that as they drink in the water, the water will get into most all of or all of the planting.

During more drought times, more watering will be needed; timers can be very helpful. If you live in a drought-prone area or desert area, or even in a warmer area with a more Mediterranean climate, like you find in California, Florida, and USA areas that border the Gulf of Mexico States (except that parts of those areas are a little too hot to be considered 'Mediterranean', per se), you will have to more carefully watch your plants, and probably water them more frequently. To save money on water, don't plant anything that requires a considerable amount of watering. Plant either what is generic or is very conducive to the area because those plants will have a better chance at continued survival.

To even be safer and to better guarantee that your plants will survive (and to end out using less water), get plants that come in to garden centers that are from areas that get (and need) even less water via rainfall than your area tends to get. There are some good plants that come in from Africa, trees included. Look for certain South American plantings, too. These would all be adaptive plants and some might be similar to certain of your native plants.

Adaptive plantings that require less water, overall, yet will still grow well and are also attractive plants, are plants to look into, when you are planning out a landscaping. Take your time when searching for your plantings so you'll get the best possible ones. You are likely to have them for a long time. Also, when you must replace a plant, bush, or tree, look into the adaptive plantings. In some areas, you absolutely must use less water. It is prudent, ethical, and efficient to do so. This is when the adaptive plants can be most practical, as long as they truly are ones that will require little water.

In the South-West areas, particularly, people are concerned with water-usage amount. It's so hot and dry in the South-West anyway. Much of the South-West relies on the Colorado River; it is projected that this large, flowing river will continue to reduce in its water volume amount. How fast or how much will depend on greenhouse gases, fossil fuels, and emissions; by 2050, for example, how many of these emissions will have been reduced? Unfortunately, so many live in big cities now and so emissions collect in these areas all the more but they're not so easy to reduce, in the bigger cities. Everything is so unwieldy and there are clashes. We need top people in Water Management, and even Forestry. We need more Clean Energy but because it is warm and dry in many southern areas, there's an abundance of wind (for wind energy) and sun (for solar energy), but, what about the rain issues, and all the water and river issues (aside from just the Colorado River)?

Some are saying that Global Warming is causing less rainfall (but this is disputed), which means that there will be lower levels of water, all over, and so everyone, all over, has to be concerned about that. We don't really know if there's been less rainfall and it almost seems like there's been more rainfall, at least in some areas. World storms have not seemed to stop. Unfortunately, we don't have a centralized weather-reporting headquarters anywhere and all aspects of weather reporting has been non-standardized and piecemeal (so, yes, we need such a national center and also an international center and headquarters). How are we ever going to know what past reports have been ball-park? None of the recording equipment has been standardized. Reports—certain of them—have been biased. There is no sole and central database for Global Warming.

Since temperatures 'seem' to be up, there will be more evaporation of what water there is. All the wildfires contributed to some of this temperature increase. That heat gets added in to many towns and cities and sometimes these wildfires have lasted for weeks and even months. Some say that some aquifers are sinking, too, as water is being pulled out of them for usage. Some also say that a number of water levels in many places seem to be going down. It is sometimes hard to trust what you hear and read these days. Even statistics can be off the mark. Nothing is, yet, excessively desperate—not concerning Global Warming but, then, there's been the coronavirus and it had made many people desperate. Perhaps too many calamities are being blamed on increased temperatures? Some can be, but not all of them can be. All factors have to be studied and recorded in a consistent manner by a trusted and objective source and this is not the way things have been or have been going.

Other reasons than what are believed can be the cause of Global Warming, and, situations can be temporary and create an illusion. Still, to one or one and a half degrees, max, Global Warming 'seems' to be here, and it is problematic. In my good-sized book titled *Global*

Warming Causes, Solutions, and Theories, I present some new ideas and theories, as to the causes of the increased temperatures, aside from the greenhouse gasses, fossil fuels, pollution, and emissions that are considered to be the sole cause. Greenhouse gasses, fossil fuels, pollution, and emissions are likely the main reason for Global Warming, granted, but there could be a number of other causes, or at least, contributing factors, which could be considered and that could also relate to what has been going on. I cover twenty theories in the noted book. One or two of those reasons (causes) could be dominant, too. Some are likely valid. Some are likely not provable, some are likely provable.

Since water could be decreasing in amount, now, measures may have to be taken to reduce water usage. (There is still a need to more diligently look into this, however.) Public access to water could, one day, be significantly rationed. More energy-efficient water taps, laundry machines, hot-water heaters, and toilets are now being sold. Grass at homes and business sites is being removed. (Some are even using artificial grass.) Sometimes grass is purposely allowed to dry and die by not watering it, and then it is dug out, once it's dead. People are going to pavers and landscape rocks and pebbles. People are much more conscientious about leaks anywhere, too— be they inside or outside. Presently, swimming pools are made to be much more efficient. Smaller swimming pools are being built. Some people only need to change the water in the pool once a year now, too. Also, any drip systems used to water plants or trees do not use any spray, only dripping. Spray evaporates so fast, even in the air, when it is hot outside. Obviously, no drip or spray system is needed if there is no lawn. Some cities are even making drinking water out of sewer water, and who knows how many more cities will go that route (and don't forget desalination). Some people are purchasing water meters so they can test for leaks anywhere in their outdoor watering system or indoor plumbing. They track leaks faster with these meters and take care of leaks faster, as a result. Overall, water reduction is not going on as much as some believe but it is on the rise. Yards and gardens can still be maintained, however. Water has somewhat been increasing in price, though. Still, it does not yet appear that we are really short of rainfall.

More water is lost from leaks than people realize. It can add up to hundreds, even thousands of gallons. One's water bill can go up a little or a lot and accumulate month after month, year after year. In cities and towns that don't have much water availability (and even if they do), it can all add up to be a significant loss because many homes can have leaks. So often, the residents don't even know there's a leak. Water bills, per gallon, can then go up so that watering a landscape can seem like it is even more costly when it could be related to something else, i.e. to a leak somewhere. Many times, leaks are underneath a home and can't be seen. If you look under a house or a mobile home, it is very dark.

It is good to plan out a minimum-water usage type of landscaping and certain plantings are quite good to use in such cases. (Cacti and succulents are especially good.) The way the ground is contoured around the plantings, when flowers, trees, shrubs, and all else are planted, has to be concave and not convex in any way, at all, so water can collect in where the planting is and more water will, then, be provided to the planting when it rains or when the lot is watered by an installed water system or by hand. Water collecting in divoted and concaved or recessed areas around plantings saves water and money and gives more of a guarantee that a planting will live. It mainly has to do with rain water, but also with hosing water.

If the area around the planting is not concaved or recessed, there will be more hose run-off. So, too, if there is a watering system in place. You want to go around and make any bed areas around a yard or area to be at least a little concaved and recessed, even before you do your planting. On the subject of watering systems, a number of them can end out wasting water. It depends on the type and it is all relative. Unless you have grass, it is really best to go around and water everything by hand and hose. It is not so hit-and-miss when you water by hand and hose. You also know what to come back to, what to water twice, and what you can delay watering until another time. Play-it-by-ear hand watering will save on water usage.

Even if you only remove a little dirt and dig out or recess the area around a planting or several plantings, that will make a huge difference relative to the amount of water a planting gets, over the years. So often, plantings die prematurely. In the case of a tree, though, a dug-out ring all the way around the tree (even if it is slightly dug out) can end out saving it, especially if it starts to look all dried out. If you ever see a dying tree and it does not have a recessed area all the way around it, dig one out right away and water it well and then put the tree on a slow drip for some time. Water the tree like this at least once a week for a while. If the whole area around the tree is initially dug out, even slightly, to cause a concaving, the tree will thrive much better over the years. This dug-out encirclement is actually a type of safety feature—for the tree. Most trees do not have this dug-out encirclement and so for years and years, a lot of water has been wasted. Many times, even when it rained, water was not able to get down to the roots of certain trees.

Again, somewhere along the line, I dug out some dirt in any and all beds because I wanted to make sure the ground around the plant or plantings was recessed and a little lower than ground level. It's best to do these recessions/indents early on and from the get-go. These recessed indents I prepared are down to around an inch to an inch and a half. Therefore, as it is now, water collects there whenever I water or whenever it rains. In other words, the plantings can thrive more than they would have had I not made the effort to do this. Doing this is important, especially in your warmer climates. It doesn't take much time to do these extra tasks.

For sure you don't want your plantings to be higher up from the general ground level because then there will be water runoff away from the plantings and the plantings will be adversely affected. This problem occurs more often than you'd think. For example, plants on hillsides will look much less healthy than plants below a hill will look. The hillside plants may be alive but they may look sickly and they usually have a shorter lifespan than the ones that are below a hill have. All plants have to have enough water to stay alive and how much water that's needed varies from plant to plant and area to area. Sometimes, for some vegetation, rainwater is enough to sustain what grows (unless it is on a steep incline or on a hillside).

When you check trees periodically to see if they've been getting enough water, you sometimes have to look upward. Check their bark area for insects, while you're at it. There are insects that can quickly kill trees. When there are bark strips on the tree trunk, insects can be hard to spot because they can be underneath the bark. You can strip off a small piece of bark and check for insects. Some insects on some trees you simply cannot see. There may be browning of what was green if there are insects—like on an Italian Cypress tree. Some of the green will be brown in spots, but you can't see the insects. It's hard to see the tree stem or trunk because of the foliage. The insects can be real small, too. You might need a tree specialist who sprays for insects, to come out. There are a few types, however, that insect spray or poison doesn't work on.

You have to inspect trees, bushes, and plants all over for insects, too. Some insects can be hard to spot if they're under leafs or under bark. Some are even underground but come up to infest plantings from time to time. Some are tiny, too, and hard to see. Wear eyewear that helps you see close up when you check for insects. For example, aphids can be hard to see on bushes, plants, and flowers, yet they can be quite problematic and you really don't want them around. Some insects can cause large spaces to be showing up on leaves and do so fairly quickly so you must have spray ready to go as soon as you first see clear and obvious damage to leaves and/or bark.

In the City of Phoenix, Arizona, there is quite a lot of grass growing around the City, but in the City of Tucson, Arizona, a two or three hours' drive to the south of Phoenix, grass is not very common. Both cities are desert cities. Some businesses in Tucson, Arizona have grass, but most of the homes don't. Las Vegas, Nevada has quite a lot of grass too, overall, for being a city in the desert. Even though many homes in Phoenix have grass, many people have been digging up the grass and putting down layer rocks because doing this ends out saving them quite a lot of money over a period of time. They don't have to water any grass, just their plants (that they can go around and water by hand and hose). People in Las Vegas, Nevada, are going to the layer rock covering too, and so are people who live in other hot areas. Layer rocks are just so practical. More people in the more northern areas are also going to layer rocks. If people would produce more colored layer rocks, they would make a fortune. I would buy the green.

Layer rock is no maintenance compared with the grass, which needs cutting and edging on occasion, along with watering. Mobile homes that are found in the north of the United States, and also in Florida because of the rains and the humidity, often have grass lawns, but a grass lawn is always optional and it's one of those things a mobile home owner can change around at any time, no matter where they live. Small rocks, if purchased in a fairly large supply, are not all that expensive. Ordinarily, a rock company will deliver a large load of it and they'll dump it, usually in front, but they won't wheelbarrow it to places on the lot, or spread it with a rake. You have to do that or see that it gets done by hired help. Delivery cost for load of landscape layer rocks isn't usually all that high in price.

It is a little difficult to completely rid an area of grass before ordering layer rock, but it can be done. You usually have to dig grass up and get it all up by the roots. You loosen <u>all</u> the top area with a shovel, down to under the grass roots. You create dirt clumps, lots of them. Then you remove all the grass pieces by hand—one by one—shaking off as much dirt as you can and getting all the grass up by the roots. It's best to do this when the ground is wet. The grass and the roots get dug up, lifted up, and sorted out from the soil. You leave as much of the soil there as you can. If the lot is small, this won't take all that long if you are a fast worker. Two working on this would be best. When done (and you may only want to remove grass from one area at a time), wait several months to see if more grows back before putting the landscape rocks down. Get rid of grass that seems to want to grow back, first. Be patient. Don't just throw the rocks down prematurely. Certainly, do not put them down over the grass from the get-go. The grass will keep growing and your lot will look unkempt and tacky. It will be a perpetual mess.

You can chemically spray the grass but it probably won't die down to the roots and much of the grass will still grow back. Some types of grass do not respond to chemical weed spray, so you may as well dig it all up by the roots from the getgo. If it is a large area, no matter what you decide, you are in for some labor and time, to get rid of it all. Perhaps a commercial spray that is quite strong might kill it but then, you'll want to get rid of the dead grass. Putting on a really think layer of landscape rocks could be enough, after such spraying, to keep the grass from re-growing and coming through the landscape rocks, but it is best to get rid of all the dead grass and the roots before you put down the rocks. There are so many rocks, that you can't do much afterwards if the grass shows through or comes through, which it probably will because it is imbedded in the ground. So again, just get rid of all the grass.

Layer rocks can also be used inside the rock-edged spaces or gardens. You can fill in the rock-edged beds with small layer rocks or pebbles after you have selected and planted whatever it is that you want to have in the beds. I like to wait until the plantings are somewhat established first, just to make sure they are going to make it. I prefer leaving the area circling the plant clear of the small rocks for a while so the plant will have room there, to spread out. You don't need to put small layer rocks in beds, though. It's optional. Some people like to use wood chips. At first, I used wood chips in certain bed areas, but now I tend to leave bed areas free and clear and empty, but for the plantings. I don't even use the layer rocks anymore but to each his or her own. I like the larger layer rocks—for these sections, if they are colored.

Laying colored rock down in beds looks pretty but there is one type called lava rock that has so much Iron in it that the Iron gets into the soil after some rainfalls and this hurts the plantings because the roots soak in all that Iron. Therefore, you have to be careful about lava or similar types of rocks. These rocks are dark reddish and even a wine color, and they are very rough. They tend to be light in weight. They make you think of lava from volcanoes. The plantings will sometimes take on a dark reddish tinge in their leaves or in their exterior because of these rocks, and some plantings may not grow well, at all, because of the lave rock iron. Other colored rock has worked for me, though, but colored rock is hard to find. As far as I know, most colored rock is safe but be careful where you put the lava rock.

Wood chips look good in beds. They don't cost much, either. You can use either layer rocks or wood chips in the different beds around your lot. You can use both, but in different beds. You can use larger rocks than pebbles, too, to fill in rock-edged beds (rocks approximately two inches by two inches or even more, for example). Some beds you may want to leave be, though, if a number of leaves, blossoms, needles, pods, etc. drop from whatever is planted there or nearby, and that will therefore, get into those beds. It is hard to remove leaves, blossoms, pine needles, pods, etc. from beds with somewhat larger layer rocks because they tend to settle in between the rocks. If there is only dirt, you can easily scoop out whatever is in the beds. That is why I like them free of anything now, except for the plantings.

Most people buy that which is practical, for their lot. What is practical is likely to be successful, work better, and last longer. Practicality is a good word for people who landscape and garden to keep in mind at all times. When you deviate from practicality too much, you get into the explorative and experimental arenas, which sometimes works but not always. You can also get into the sub-standard arena, if you deviate, too much, from practicality.

LOT CHORES AND PROJECTS

<u>It is important to at least consider planning a landscaping that is going to be low maintenance, in advance.</u> That's what I did. I did some extensive landscaping, and the lot ended out getting filled up, but, it was low maintenance afterwards, for the most part. I watered, particularly in the summer. I trimmed. I cleaned out beds. I pulled up weeds. And I raked up pine needles. I did all these things at different times of the year so it was never a burden and it was actually enjoyable for me to keep up the yard. Gardening exercise was always welcomed and it was cheaper than going to the gym.

Whether a lot or yard is low maintenance or not, there will be occasional weeds. If you have a blockage-type fence that does not have open areas (as wire-mesh fences have), you'll get very few weeds. Wood-plank fences are good, if the planks are side by side. In southern USA areas, weeds tend to grow at any time of year unless the winters are cold enough to have snow and ice. You'll especially see weeds after a rain or two. Rain, and then sunshine, causes them to grow amazingly fast. I noted this before but it is important enough to note again--I always go out after a rain and pull up weeds by their roots because when the ground is wet, weed roots come up and they don't break off. I sometimes use an old kitchen knife for a real tough weed so I can loosen the dirt the weed is situated in first. Then, the weed is guaranteed to not break when you pull it up. Usually, though, if it is after a rain, they will all come up without using the knife blade; even the big weeds will come up if it was a ground-soaking rain. The old table knife is useful when the ground is dry and if you absolutely have to pull any weeds up when the ground is dry.

If the ground is dry, that old kitchen knife will always work. You stick it in the ground as low as you can and at an angle, and cut the main root by moving the knife and presto, you pull the weed right up. It will come up easily. Very rarely will it grow back, too. Weeds grow back when you pull them up and they snap off above the ground but if the old table knife cuts the root under the ground, the rest of the root will die (almost every time).

To add, when you use a knife to de-weed, you stick the knife down in the dirt at an angle and move the knife back and forth a little. You will then cut the stem with the knife, but you may not even need to cut the weed if you simply loosen the dirt around the weed with the knife. The loosened dirt should enable the weed to be pulled out, in total, rather easily. Up will come the weed, but your thumb and index finger have to be down as low on the weed stem as possible when you pull it up. Sometimes, you have to move small landscape rocks out of the way first, before you can get the best possible grip on a weed stem. If a weed is real big with a long, thick root, you may have to use the knife. If the weed is at all thorny, pulling it up way down on the base and next to the ground is generally safe because there are usually no thorns or bristles that low and around the base.

Again, cutting the root under the ground will usually eliminate the weed because if the rest of the root is down that far, it is likely to die because the sun can't get to it. It's when weeds are weed-whacked or pulled from just above the top of the ground (and snap off) that they are likely to grow back, which, of course, defeats the whole purpose. When they grow back, the roots end out being quite large so the next time around, they're even harder to get rid of. They're more fragile at the top than at the bottom, for one thing.

Amount of weeds, each year, will vary. Some years, you get a maximum number of weeds. Other years, you get a minimum number. Most years, you get the in-between number or amount. Much has to do with previous rain amounts, but also with amount of previous wind because it is the wind that blows around the weed seeds. You have to get and keep control of weeds, even if you get a proliferation of them and they seem to be overwhelming. (This has happened to me a few times.) If you have an excessive number of weeds, there is a procedure to follow.

After a rain (again, always take advantage of wet soil after a rain because it's the best time to garden in general, which includes the pulling out of weeds), go out and at least pull out the big and mid-sized weeds if that is all there is time for you to do. With the big/mid-sized weeds, usually the stems don't break off (when the soil has been saturated). Then, either wait until the smaller weeds get mid-sized, or, spray all those little ones while they are little and low to the ground. You use less weed spray when weeds are small, obviously. At least get the bigger weeds first because they will be first to throw weed seeds and you want to prevent that. A stitch in time saves nine.

Weeds always come up fast and easy when the ground is wet, down to so many inches. If any roots go way, way down, you may have to tug a little. Use an old throw pillow or piece of carpet as a pad for your knees. Like you would get rid of any dead, browned leaves, toss the weeds in a low-rimmed box; then, when it gets filled up, put those in a larger box and then dump that box into your garbage bin once it gets filled up. Again, you must put you thumb and index finger at the very lowest part of the weed stem, grip the weed base, and pull up each weed like that. You have to concentrate on doing this and go at a good pace. If you try to pull up two or more weeds at a time, almost always, stems will break off above the ground. Pulling just one at a time goes very fast if you just keep at it. It's the only way, really, if you want to get them all up by the roots. It can be done. If you even, accidentally, grab several weeds at a time, most of the weeds won't come up by the roots and they may all break off above the roots. Therefore, they will just grow back. It has to be a one at a time endeavor.

To repeat and clarify, if you do not get the roots of the weeds, the weeds will grow back and as the weeds grow back, the roots will become even larger, making it more difficult to remove them the next time around, especially since the roots will be larger compared to the new weed stem and top. It sometimes takes the same amount of time, or even less time to go around and pull weeds up by the roots, compared with going around and spraying all the weeds. Furthermore, weed-whacking is essentially just a Band-Aid but is even worse than a Band-Aid, unless you go in afterwards and spray what you see is still on the lot—i.e. the stalks and stems and any leaves still on the stems. All those weeds will grow back and may even grow back if there is spraying.

If you have the time and stamina, try to pull up the smaller weeds when you pull out the larger ones. They come up easily if you pull them up the right way after getting a good hold of them at their base. Even with the small weeds, you will have to pinch them at their base close in to the ground area and before you pull them up. If too many stems of the smaller weeds are breaking off when you try to pull the small weeds up by their roots, then just go around and spray them, instead. Certain kinds of small weeds, in certain kinds of soil, will come up so easily by the roots, right after a rain. The smaller ones will get bigger and sometimes fairly soon, if rains have been plentiful. A lot of people will just get the mid-sized and the larger ones and will leave the small ones until they get bigger, especially if they're short of time. Then they'll pull those weeds up later but do so before they are big enough to start throwing seeds. You always hope to get as many weeds up as possible before they are able to throw seeds.

Small weeds are different from baby weeds. Baby weeds are much smaller. With the really baby weeds, some will come up by the roots if you pull them up, but with many of them, when you pull them up, even after a rain, the weed stems break off and the roots stay in the ground. This is because they are so tiny and fragile. Baby weeds almost always continue growing after they've been broken off from the stem and are without their top growth. More top growth will occur if you wait until baby weeds are adolescent, and then you just pull them up, after a rain. When they are larger, you will usually get the whole weed because the stem is thicker and stronger and won't break off.

On occasion, you may have to wet down an area yourself, if it has weeds and if there has been no rain. Then you can pull up the weeds. An oscillator can be used for this purpose, after it has been attached to your hose. Because water has to soak into the ground at least four inches, you have to water the area for a while. Generally, oscillators are used to water lawns but here, they would have another use... pulling up weeds.

On rare occasion, certain types of weeds will not come up by the roots, even after it has rained. If you pull them, the weeds break. Even if you do a pinch hold on the weed, at its lowest base, it will break. Sometimes these weeds can be very leafy—more so than usual. You may have to use a spade and dig these ones up. Or, you can spray them but if they are quite leafy, the plant, itself, might not die. Go around and cut off everything but one leaf and part of the stem so that will be all you need to spray. Then, the plant will likely die. Use scissors, probably, because they work fine. Instead of squirting weed spray (with the spray bottle) five or six times with the spray bottle, you only have to squirt the weed spray out once or twice because the weed has been cut down.

Do this only when specific weeds won't pull up by the roots because, again, there are some weeds (but not too many) that won't pull up by the roots even after a rain. If you try to pull them up, they break and may, therefore, still grow. When the leafy weed is prepared and cut so there's only one leaf and the stem, spray that area once and save on your weed spray. If a weed is real leafy, spraying all the leaves may not kill the plant anyway because you need to get at the stem. The stem, as well as some of the lower leaves, will be hidden by the other leaves and therefore protected from the weed spray. Doing this extra work really doesn't take all that long.

Amazingly, spraying an area with weed spray takes less time than many people realize. Going around and clipping the top of even quite a few weeds doesn't take that long. Again, if certain weeds on the lot break when you go to pull them up, cut off the tops, leaving the stem and at least one leaf still showing and then spray those weeds (for better killing success). Many bigger weeds will pull up by the roots, though, but you must almost always pinch-hold way down on the low part of the stem and just above the ground and gently pull the weed up. Again, you must only do one at a time and not try to grab several.

Weeds on a lot also have to be inspected; and, to spray or pull—that is the question. Because I pull weeds out after a rain, the roots always come out easily. If you have landscape rocks on the lot, you pretty much have no choice but to use an old pillow for your knees so you can get low to the ground when you pull the weeds. If you decide to use weed spray, it is better to go out and spray when the weeds tend to be juvenile and smaller. They'll die faster and there will be smaller dry, dead weeds on the lot after they die, which is less of an eyesore on the lot than the larger ones are after they die, if they die because some of the larger weeds won't die. Also, the wind will blow the dead ones away much easier, once they break off. If you spray weeds when they are very tiny, all the better. After they've been dead for a while, you'll have to go out and remove whatever 'brown' is still on your lot, i.e. the dead weeds. Heat from the sun will speed up the death of weeds, after there's been spraying. Any rainfall right after spraying, and their dying will be slowed down or can even stop. You may have to re-spray.

Weed spray tends to kill most weeds, especially the ones that are small to medium-sized. There is a way to spray weeds without using chemicals, however. Many people prefer using natural ingredients. You mix one gallon of white vinegar in with a cup of salt and a tablespoon of dish detergent. Even just the 5% household vinegar will work in this mix. Find a good sprayer bottle and voilà, you will be able to kill weeds naturally. Even without the salt, the weeds won't grow back; with the salt, the soil will not be receptive to future weed seeds. You do not want to spray this mix so it gets on your grass, if you have grass, but if you only have landscape rocks, it's a good weed-rid mix and the weeds will die in three or four days. The salt serves as a preventative.

If you spray the whole lot with this mix, assuming the lot is covered with the smaller landscape rocks that have open areas to receiving weed seeds, the added salt in the soil will, assumedly, keep weed seeds from germinating. If you have a large weed-sprayer, this task can more quickly be done, compared with if you use a gallon-sized spray container that has a manual squeezer method for spraying. In this day and age, many people wish to avoid using chemicals and poisons, both in and outside their home. Use this natural weed spray (with the salt) perhaps every time you spray. Test its workability and longevity along the way. Spray the whole lot with it, as you need to.

As a part of general maintenance, not only will you have to go around periodically and check for overgrowth, insects, water lack, and general overall appearance, but at times, a very close look will be required. Anything needing doing should be jotted down so when you have to do the required tasks, everything will get done in a timely way and nothing will be forgotten. Since plantings can die, some things will have priority. Sometimes, even the roots of plantings might need to be checked because specific bacteria on roots can cause their death. Outdoor home care is similar to indoor home care because always, there is something needing doing.

One of my trees (the big South-Western White Pine) continually tossed off thousands of pine needles (so pine needle removal is another task that may need to go on a to-do list). That pile-up happened on one side of my home. On the other side, I got my neighbor's pine needles. I only had to rake all the pine needles up when there was a buildup. You can just roll these needles up as if they're a blanket, too. Both of the trees (mine and my neighbor's) were tall, full-shade trees so we all just put up with the pine needles because we liked the shade in the summer. Pine needles rake up pretty easily, off a lot, even when there are landscape rocks. I just used my fingers when it came to picking them out of beds. Sometimes, even in the beds, you can just roll them all up together and remove them that way. It's so easy. They roll up because the needles lay on top of other needles, like tossed pick-up sticks.

Evergreen trees are all over the USA and it is strange that they can grow in desert areas, but they can and they do. I happened to have a Pine tree. Pine needles go all over the place and get in the beds and between and over the rocks so you have no choice but to ease them out of the beds with your fingers and hands. You can sometimes pick up clumps of pine needles or, again, roll them up if they are stacked up thick enough. Anyone can roll layers of needles up, at least in spots, which makes it so much easier, but sometimes you can only pick or scoop them up, and this tends to go slower. You have to look at the various areas on your lot, and decide what will work the best. You can do this along the way while you are working. Some people never get pine needles. If you can get other kinds of shade trees, you may not want Evergreen needles to be concerned about. Some Evergreens shed few to no needles, keep in mind. It just all depends on the type of tree, and also on how hot it gets.

Once or twice a year, pine needles have to be cleared out from beds, but you should rake them up to get them off the main part of the lot more often than that, and get them off the layer rocks. That's if you have a tree that throws these needles. (Consider avoiding these kinds of trees if you can.) Again, certain kinds of trees are great for shade, but they require certain maintenance if they toss needles (or toss leaves or pods). Raking pine needles is why I prefer to have the larger, heavier layer rocks (the 1" ones), since they don't rake up so easily when you are raking up the pine needles. Smaller layer rocks rake up and mix in with the pine needles and that can become quite a loss, over time. You end out throwing away quite a few rocks, along with the needles. You have to think about these things, in advance.

One day, we had a freak storm. Winds were one hundred mph. The storm came in going west to east, which was not the usual pattern for storms that I'd previously been the brunt of. The trees that shed all the needles swayed and swayed. My Pine tree stayed intact, but my neighbor's Pine tree snapped off at the top and that large heavy part, instead of going over on to my awning and roof, bounced off their roof and awning, damaging both. I was a lucky camper in that respect, but I did lose my lattice work, over on the other side from that particular neighbor's place. It broke up and needed replacing. The result, for me, of a now-missing tree on my neighbor's lot (they had to have it cut down) was that the myriads of pine needles I got on that side, year-round, went down to zero. Both of our big Pine trees had been planted in a center area on our lots, not towards or at an edge. Whereas some trees look good along edges or as separates in corners (like the Arborvitae and the Italian Cypress), these big full trees that you can walk under, after some trimming, should go in a center area on a lot, wherever that center area might be. Once such a planting gets to be really tall, it could become vulnerable to wind snapping. It happens rarely, but it did happen to my neighbor so could happen to anyone. Mine provided so much shade, and was a long-life Evergreen.

Pine trees can be problematic if you get the real high winds. They can snap anywhere, causing damage to whatever is around. Branches easily snap, usually at a joint. Pine is not a real strong wood, compared with certain others. Other tall trees tend to snap off during high winds, too, so pines are not the only trees that are vulnerable. There are many trees that are tall and full. They will either have leaves or Evergreen needles to rake up. With some trees, the needles aren't too many. Dropping needles will depend on how hot and dry the area where they are located will get. Fairly high humidity will keep the needles on the trees, more readily.

The tall trees, especially if they are full, make the best shade trees. Evergreens are good because they do not lose all that many needles (for the actual size of the tree). Deciduous trees lose their leaves in autumn and winter (but they don't lose as many when, year-round, the weather is warm to hot (so they will give year-round shade). It's real cold weather that especially causes deciduous trees to lose leaves around autumn time/winter time.

The short but full trees, like the Arborvitae, are useful to have as windbreakers—big time. These trees can grow anywhere in the USA. They can be planted in isolation or as a hedge. It's good to put such full trees in front of a deck or as a protection for a swim area. These are durable trees and they come in different sizes but you'll want to get one that gets to be tall. They're pointed at the top and full all the way around and they can be used as a security and privacy screen, too. This tree is known as the Green Giant, or the Thuja. They get to be from eight to ten feet tall. They need no trimming or pruning, either. You can shape it, though, if you want to. You might need to spray them on occasion for spider mites. Some trees are vulnerable to certain insects but some trees don't seem to ever be bothered by any. It's good to be in the know about your local insects.

Very popular in the South-west is the Mesquite Tree. These get tall and large and are somewhat full and they can end out with a very thick trunk. They have thorny branches (that are often used for a barbecuing flavor), and, every year, they drop oodles of yellow-beige pods that are shaped like pea pods. These trees tend to go on the larger lots. I have seen them on mobile home lots but they tend to reach over to a neighbor's lot and the thorny branches and dropped pods can cause neighbors some irritation.

Another very popular tree in the South-west is the Palo Verde tree. You see it all over the place, quite frankly. Quite a few business lots have these trees on them. It is the State tree of Arizona. It is more of an ambiance tree because it isn't necessarily used for shading (except for pets) and it isn't necessarily used as a windbreaker. Like the Mesquite tree, it has more open branching. These trees can live for over a hundred years. It's a gorgeous yellow from the top of the trunk on up to the branching-out area, and the yellow is essentially small flowers. The tree has red seeds on it that you can eat. You can cook and bake, using the seeds.

If you don't have grass on the lot, and you have the landscape layer rocks instead, you'll have to get your flat pillow out, get on your knees on that pillow, and pick up pine needles, leaves, fallen blossoms, pods, debris, etc. by hand. You can do this quickly if you remember to put a small, flat, open box down next to where these eyesores are. Go around from place to place, and plop the pillow down. Any leaves would include Oleander leaves, if you have any (which I likely always will have, unless I were to go into a nursing home). I love all Oleanders. When your smaller box gets full, you dump everything into a larger box, or a bag, as per usual. This ground clean-up goes really fast and it only has to be done once, sometimes twice a year. Oleander leaves are but one of the concerns, assuming you have Oleanders because you may well have other bushes or similar plantings that drop leaves, needles, or blossoms.

Miscellaneous other things to pick up can be varied—like candy wrappers, bottle caps, cigarette butts, small Styrofoam pieces, and even thin paper strands from Easter baskets. There could be a few dead insects around the lot, too. I've had to pick up a few dried-out beetles from time to time. Quite often, debris is tossed on your lot or the wind blows it in. I don't drop anything on my lot, myself. This debris is essentially trash. Birds sometimes drop this and that when they are building a nest. You never know what's going to appear on your lot but one thing is for sure—you have to go around and pick it all up. I generally do this routinely and as I see it, but I sometimes pick debris up when I pick up leaves or pine needles.

Even if you have grass and rake up Oleanders (or leaves from any planting), some of the leaves will still break. You will still have to get down on your knees, using a pillow under your knees, and scoop up or pick up at least some of the leaves and put them in a lower-edged box and then dump the contents into a larger box when the lower-edged one gets filled up.

The leaves get removed faster when you are able to use a low box (like one that soda cans set in, at grocery stores). Any dried leaves can break because they are dry and brittle. The lower-edged boxes work well for other gardening and landscaping projects, too. Hand movement can be very fast, because it is low and set right next to you. I often use one or two of these boxes when I garden. They're included in my gardening supplies. Also, I pick up larger discarded cardboard boxes from time to time at various stores or wherever I see them. They are used to put leaves, dropped blossoms, branches, and pulled weeds in while I am gardening. Those large plastic bags work for this disposal, too, but sometimes I like the boxes. You can also put garden clippings, leaves, etc. in your garbage bin. They may, or may not need to be in closed-up bags. It will all just go to the dump. Any cactus should be in taped-down boxes, though. Anything with anything sharp should be.

I somewhat habitually used to grab empty boxes at supermarkets, or wherever I would see them. I'd set them in inconspicuous spots and I'd use them later on for putting in weeds, leaves, unwanted cuttings and trimmings, needles, dead cactus or dead anything, and miscellaneous other. Some mobile home parks have their own weekly curbside pickup of home-maintenance garbage, which includes for garden and landscaping clippings and cuttings. This is separate from City garbage pick-up. It's so much easier to put garden and landscaping garbage into boxes and not bags. Bags will sometimes work but boxes are better. If you don't have weekly curbside pickup where you live (other than for your household garbage), then you have to put lawn and garden 'garbage' into bags and put those bags in with your household garbage. Sometimes, boxes can go in these bins. You can put them in boxes but you have to tape down the boxes and obviously, the boxes can't be too big for the garbage bin. You can always take lawn and garden clippings/debris to a local dump, too. Again, I use cardboard boxes every now and again. You can pick them up, many places. They're always good to have on hand. You can flatten them until you need to use them. You can tape over these boxes whenever you need to. You will want to if you're disposing cactus or anything sharp.

You can pick up all leaves and debris around the lot at the same time that you go around and get leaves and debris under and around plantings so it will all go faster. It goes fast, too, because you get on your knees and use one or two small, flat boxes. If you keep having to bend over from the waist, in an effort to get rid of leaves and debris, it will be more difficult. On your knees, you're not constantly having to bend over. (I can't do this too much anyway, because of medical problems.) You can go from side to side, and reach out to areas further away; you will have to move along to a new area as soon as leaves within your reach get picked up. Doing that is no problem. You just slide the box over to the next spot and plunk the pillow down and set your knees on the pillow and then resume. And so it goes until you're finally done. Picking up dead leaves goes really fast, if you do it the right way. It can be methodical and done the same way every time, or, you can vary the general pattern. Whatever works is what you do.

There is apt to always be dead, dried leaves on your lot that you'll have to pick up. On occasion, leaves on Oleanders (or other plantings that have leaves) may just go brown without first being yellow. If this happens to an excess, it usually means that the planting soaked in water when it was extremely cold, or, that snow fell on the planting and froze the leaves and froze any water that was being retained in the leaves. If snow falls on and stays on the plantings, if you can, go out and <u>gently</u> brush or knock the snow off. Use a whisk broom or even a regular broom. Snow can brown cacti and succulents as well as leafy plantings. Snow rarely falls on the warmer desert areas, but it can happen and you want to get the snow off the plantings <u>right away</u> so the snow doesn't collect on them and stay for a time. Go out after a snowfall and remove all you can. If a pile of snow stays on top of a planting all night after a snow, it will be worse because of temperature dips after the sun goes down. Don't wait for the sun to come out and melt the snow on the plantings after it snows because by then it may be too late and the snowed-on areas will turn brown and no longer be green (because of the freezing). A snowfall can be harmful to many desert plants, but, usually, trees and bushes will be all right with snowfall. Evergreens are especially safe, since they naturally grow in snow country anyway.

I write about Oleanders so much because they're a very popular planting in all the southern states, and in other states, as well (though less so than in the warmer areas). Some consider Oleanders to be a shrub, and the ones that grow shorter look like a shrub. Some consider them to be a tree, and some of the taller ones do kind of look like trees, especially if they've been trimmed and shaped a certain way. Personally, I see them all as just plain bushes. Oleanders are pretty hardy. So is the Japanese Boxwood plant. That is one that also gets quite tall, if you let it (or them, because they can be lined up to create a hedge). These grow well in hot climates. They have no blossoms. They drop leaves, but not very many of them. You can even shape this planting to eventually be tree-like, if it is planted to be solo.

Actually, Oleanders are all over the world; they're extremely popular. They're an Evergreen shrub (perennial) that originally came from the Mediterranean areas. All Oleanders are from the genus Nerium. Some say they came from South-East Asia first, and Mediterranean areas, second. They are more prolific in certain countries, and are found on all continents but Antarctica. They may be the most popularly-purchased planting in the United States. You see them all over the southern half. There are different types of Oleanders in the world and they all get imported and exported. Many are now reproduced for selling in the USA, and in certain other countries.

Oleanders can be toxic to pets and sometimes to humans, if they eat enough of the fresh leaves or blossoms. Much is on the Internet about this. Pets don't generally eat it fresh off the bush (or shrub) so they're generally safe, in that respect. If you think your pet might ever eat Oleander leaves or blossoms and your pet goes outside, do not put in Oleanders or if you do, carefully watch your pet. Humans don't eat the leaves, obviously. Touching any part of the planting has never been a problem for me, which includes my having touched the green leaves. This does not mean that someone else won't be skin sensitive to Oleander leaves, however. The leaves or blossoms I handle the most are dead and on the ground, so there is nothing toxic about that. I have never seen any Oleander sap, but it's been reported that touching the sap can cause skin irritation. I perhaps have too many Oleanders, and again, they all drop some leaves (even if they get plenty of water), but I believe they are my favorite planting; plus, I have a variety of types of Oleanders—the short, mid-high, and tall, and they all have different-colored blossoms.

You don't ever want to trim oleanders because eventually the blades or shoots will become the same, general height. Sometimes the blades or shoots look a little uneven but they're somewhat supposed to. You can trim and shape a little but not too much. Trim away anything dead, as per usual with any plant. Do not trim off too many living blades or shoots or the plant can go into shock and slowly die. Many plantings are vulnerable to being over-trimmed. Don't get trim happy. Do only what seems truly necessary, unless you know a particular planting is hardy enough to take considerable trimming. In some cases, knowledge and skill is needed when it comes to trimming.

Tree leaves are another matter. Trees generally drop too many leaves to pick up, one by one. If you have landscape rocks, tree leaves can be a real challenge to remove without breakage. Some dead, dried tree leaves are pretty thin and so they break up into small pieces really easily when they're stepped on. Some people use a blower and blow leaves over to an area not having the landscape rocks, and then they bag or box up the leaves and sometimes the nettles, but again, with nettles, they can actually be rolled up, or large clumps of nettles can be lifted up because they all pack in together.

By putting a flat pillow down, my knees are protected and cushioned as I pick up leaves, nettles, and debris, and as I clean out beds around the lot. A flat pillow or some kind of cushion is as important to a gardener as a rake and shovel is. (You can even use an old throw rug or carpet mat.) I use the flat pillow for many projects around the yard—planting and re-planting included. In fact, I find that I use a pillow constantly. I definitely use it when I pull weeds, whenever a number of weeds have collected on the lot and they have become conspicuous. I usually get enough of them, year to year, to justify using a pillow as I go around the lot. If there are ever just a few weeds, why bother even getting on your knees on a pillow?

You may want to consider clearing off some or all the small landscape rocks around the Oleanders on your lot (or similar plantings). That way, you can scoop up the dead leaves with your hands every time the leaves collect. Put larger, edger rocks around the Oleanders so they have that enclosed look. It's the landscape rocks that make it hard to rake up Oleander leaves, or rake up anything, for that matter. I haven't, yet, cleared layer rocks from under all my Oleanders, but I have, with a few of them.

If you merely step on dry leaves, they break. Therefore, rather than using a rake, try using a broom and a dust/debris catcher or scooper and sweep up whatever leaves on the lot you can, and do so very gently. If you do this, considerably fewer leaves will break up into pieces. Try not to ever step on the leaves. You can also sweep them into a temporarily turned-to-the-side cardboard box. You'll lose fewer of the landscape rocks because if you rake them, many of them will get mixed in with whatever it is that you are raking and so rather than going through the rocks that mix in when you rake and putting the rocks back on the ground (somewhat tedious work to have to do), you can use a broom and flat dust pan, gently sweep up the leaves, and avoid picking up so many layer rocks. I noted earlier that if you wish to get on your knees, on a pillow, to remove leaves, try using a short whisk-type broom, and a dustpan to get the leaves. So, there's the long broom you can use, if you're standing, and the short broom, if you're on your knees.

You can use a broom for other things, too, when you do your gardening and landscaping; a broom is really multi-purpose. You can use it to clear out spider webs, separate branches, knock down wasp nests, sweep dust or dirt off of the home siding, knock down vacated bird's nests, and brace something in while you are working.

You may think twice about knocking down any bird's nest, though—it may not be vacated, and, the birds will return in the spring and so why not just leave the nest for them to return to? The birds will repair and fix it up and use it again. The same birds may well be expecting it to still be there, or their offspring might be.

Since one reason for using landscape rocks is to prevent weed seeds from getting through to the soil, you don't want to remove too many layer rocks off your lot (when they mix in with needles, leaves, and debris). It's somewhat a Catch 22. If you end out getting too many layer rocks mixed in with leaves and debris and therefore lose them, you'll eventually have to buy more rocks. This is one reason why I pick dropped leaves up by hand (when they're underneath certain plants and bushes). Frankly, I have seen where some hired-out gardeners will rake all leaves, and then usually scoop them up into bags. Homeowners don't realize how many of the layer rocks get mixed in and are thereby removed but I know, because I've seen them do it. Some hired gardeners cut corners rather often, just to get the job done, but the job is not done in the best way possible, if you get the drift. They can be good at doing some things, but not others.

When you're out there, getting leaves, nettles, pods, and debris off the lot, you might consider trimming and shaping bushes at the same time. It's good to trim and shape bushes, in general, and on occasion, to get right into the plant and cut everything out that is dead. Sometimes twig growth will die; less often, a whole branch shoot or larger part will die (i.e. that which is larger than a twig). When you cut any bushes back (so all main parts are about the same height and so the bushes are shaped and shorter than they would ordinarily be), new shoots will grow. For some time, the shoots will be thin but as they grow, they will thicken and strengthen and become strong branches. You'll eventually see blooms on these new branches that, all together, will fill out the plant (assuming the bush does, in fact, get blooms). You'll have to occasionally water the bush during warm to hot times when there is little rain. All the new branch shoots will eventually fill in the old cut-back branches.

Also, about bushes, over time some dead leaves will fall in-between all the branch shoots or divisions that are close in to the ground and you have to try to remove those leaves on occasion so the bush will look better and rain water can get in between all the divisions. I use a barbecue skewer to lift up these leaves so I can pick them out from between the stalks (that are growing in close together). Otherwise, it's a little hard to pick all of the leaves out of the tight-together stalks at the base of the plant with your fingers because some of the leaves are stuck or packed in between the stalks and some of the plant's stalks can be in the way, since there are several of them packed in together.

The reasons you may want to cut bushes back or down (or any planting, for that matter) are several. You may want more space and for the area to look more open. You may not want to have so many leaves or blossoms dropping. You may want to have more light coming into your home (if the plant has been blocking a window). You may want a more cleared area so security of your home (and visibility) will be better. You may want to get rid of an insect infestation. And, you may want a fuller plant because sometimes when you cut a plant back or down, the plant will grow back much fuller than it had been. This is not the case with some plantings, though, only certain plantings. If you have any Oleanders, they should never be cut down to where the lower stalks are less than two to three feet high, and most likely this applies to certain other bushes, as well.

Yard work gives you exercise and it burns calories. It can keep you more fit over the years. Some people absolutely love getting outside and doing yard work and outdoor projects. Some sun is good for you, too. You soak in Vitamin D. Yard work and outdoor projects can be mentally challenging; they demand decision-making and planning and organizing. Gardening and yardwork is good for the soul.

I make note of Oleanders so much because they are the perfect bush or planting for southern areas. You see them a lot around roads and highways. They're decorative, practical, full, and sun-hardy, among other things. My Oleanders are to the outer edges of the lot (but two of them are side-by-side, next to the shed and they are out a ways from it but they give the shed some shade. I also have one large bed of them, which is situated next to the mobile home, on one side and to the front. These tall ones give my kitchen area some shade. They are on the side where the sun hits. They are planted right next to the home. Even these are not in the center anywhere, though. They are along the side of the home. I planted five or six Oleanders there inside of a large rock-edged bed (there is a double row of Oleanders) and they're nice because they grow tall and they get filled with blossoms for several months. There is a path made of hexagonal pavers to the side of them that leads to the deck stairs.

For years, I didn't cut these Oleanders back since they're in front and the blossoms were nice for the neighbors to see and enjoy. It's when the Oleanders are in bloom that they're noticed, wherever they are. They stay in bloom for a fairly long time. I eventually cut some of them down, like certain tall ones, because it meant less work (with picking up or scooping up the leaves and the blossoms). I then let them grow back to full size, but I could cut them back at any time and well may.

Oleanders are low maintenance once they mature, except for having to clean out the bed areas a couple of times a year. When I hand pick or remove the dead leaves, I do the same with any dead, dried blossoms, wherever I happen to find them. The blossoms aren't as important to remove as the leaves are, since they're less conspicuous after they completely dry up. I suspect that insects eat some of them, too, after they drop. You still don't want them on the lot, though. It's better to pick the blossoms up with your fingers, one by one, once they are dry—if they are on landscape rocks. Sometimes you can pick up several blossoms at a time, but if you try to pick up several dried leaves at a time, somehow, they get broken. You can easily scoop up or rake all the blossoms, if there are no landscape or small rocks underneath them. With Oleanders, consider waiting until <u>all</u> the yellow leaves have dropped before you pick up the leaves. In the meantime, the Oleander could use a watering, most likely, and the yellow leaves can be indicators. If there's a few yellow ones still on the plant, go ahead and pick them off the plant. You might want to wait until all the blossoms have fallen, too (depending on time constraints and the number of blossoms). If you wait too long to remove anything dried on a lot, those places in the yard can become a fire hazard.

Oleanders can be tall, as trees, medium, as bushes, or short (even dwarf), as shrubs, or plants. Technically, they're all really either shrubs or bushes. You can't get away from all of them dropping at least some yellow leaves once or twice a year. A blower could work, if you could blow the leaves on to a flat, non-rocky surface so they can be swept up or raked up and then put into a box or bag, but frankly, blowers can be useless if all you're doing is blowing stuff elsewhere and it isn't getting picked up and completely removed from an area. I've seen maintenance men do that, and the blown stuff goes over to a completely different lot. How nice is that?! If you sometimes wonder where all the extra leaves and debris on your lot comes from and your neighbor has a blower . . . . You might want to spy on what they're doing if you suspect anything like that could be being done. The maintenance workers are not always very thoughtful. If you could only get it on camera. Some maintenance workers are great, though, and consistently conscientious and go the extra mile.

When you go about removing dropped leaves, you can get rid of dead wood at the same time. In fact, you may want to go all around the lot and get rid of all the dead wood, wherever it is. Parts of living plantings die, in other words. Dead branches, stalks, and twigs are easily seen if you are looking for them. They tend to be seen more around the bottom of plantings, but not always. They can be anywhere. If no leaves are growing on a branch, stalk, or twig and any of these look dried out and brittle, then get rid of the dead wood so new growth can fill in that area. Do this on any planting with branches, including trees. Dead parts can be removed from cacti, succulents, or low-lying plants at the same time. On occasion, you might even lose a whole cactus, succulent, or low-lying plant, which you will have to dig up.

Use both the long-handled clippers and the long-handled pruner when removing anything dead. On an Oleander, for example, a whole stalk or branch can be dead, or just a part of it can be. You may not need to get rid of what is dead on Oleanders all that often, but every so often, you should do this pruning or trimming. This is the case for other types of plantings too. At least every so often, get rid of all dead wood or dead anything. Doing this at least every year would be good, but even every two years might work if you are especially busy. Sometimes, there is more dead wood than you expect to find, especially if a planting is an older one.

Every so often, not only is it good to go in and trim off any dead branches, shoots, or twigs, but you may as well shape any bushes by trimming off some side branches or offshoots, at the same time. Some will trim off some bottom branches or offshoots, too, so they can get in underneath and remove leaves and weeds growing in under those areas. Try not to trim off too many branches, though. That can certainly happen. Most of what is still alive should be left. Some people get trim-happy and cut too much off. They tend to do this with rose bushes, too.

With Oleanders, branch-like stalks grow upward from the bottom of the plant, and each one grows out at a different angle from the others. Some shoots are shorter than others are only because some shoots start up later than others do. Eventually, Oleander shoots get to be about the same height or length as the others do. Again, once a year, preferably right before the rains, clip off all dead stalks and branches. Sometimes, there are dead branches off from stalks that are really still alive so you have to look closely for life. You have to get rid of what is dead, though. Cut off whatever is dead, but leave whatever is alive if you can. You may want to shape the Oleander with 'a little' trimming at the same time.

It's good to go around and get rid of anything dead around the whole lot or yard at the same time before the rains come. After you have clipped off what was dead, there will be bare or open areas in the planting, but after the rains, these areas tend to get more filled in, and all the shoots, branches, and leaves tend to even out fairly well. After the planting fills out fairly well, that is the best time to consider shaping the planting so it takes on the look you want it to. A little clip here, a little clip there, and the planting can look better and more symmetrical, although, some plantings have a constant, natural symmetry and may need no adjusting.

Oleanders are full and leafy, and attractive. They fill in spaces beautifully. Not having to water Oleanders very much (for the most part) is compensation for having to pick up the dead leaves. It's a trade-off. They're worth having, and they don't die on you. They live a long time. They do fine in direct sun and will survive even in 115° Fahrenheit (and 46° Celsius) weather as long as there aren't too many days of that. They endure cold, too. I've seen where they can tolerate slightly below-zero temperatures, at least for a time. All plantings have their tolerance point, though. This is why you don't see plants in some areas of the Sahara Desert or in the high Arctic or Antarctica. Once Oleanders get established, they do all right on their own if there is sufficient rainfall, and in most places, there is. Again, they really don't need that much water to live and to even thrive (but, you have to carefully observe them when it is warm or hot outside, and do so month after month.

Oleanders make great hedges and can be a type of fencing or barrier. Certain other bushes do, too. Some lots need hedges more than other lots do. Some people plant several Oleanders in fairly close proximity so they'll give a walled privacy and also reduce the amount of wind and dust coming in to an area. They're great plantings because they are so leafy. Many people put a number of taller ones in as a divider or border between two lots. The tall and even the medium-height ones can be used as dividers or borders, at any side of a lot. They'll make up a natural hedge. I have all three heights of Oleanders on my lot but I especially seem to have more of the white-blossomed ones—the Sister Agnes type. It is the tallest of all of them. Some people trim and shape these to be tree-looking, but I never did. The white ones can get to be from ten to fifteen feet tall.

Oleanders are a popular planting and they probably always will be. You see them all over the place, even around highways and freeways. Their profusion of blossoms is eye-catching, but even when they don't have any blossoms on them, they still look good because they're so leafy and full.

The bright red/pink, pink, regular pink or salmon, and peach-colored blossoms brighten up any area. I haven't seen any yellow Oleander blossoms but I know there are some. It is the Nerium Luteum Plenum and the blossom is yellow in its center and white at the top so it is not all yellow. The white blossoms are quite noticeable, too. Some Oleanders can end out being covered with clusters of white blossoms. The blossoms are eye-catching, and fragrant. They make you think of those cluster fireworks. To be precise about the more general names of the Oleanders, there is the Dwarf Red Oleander, the Little Red Oleander, the Petite Salmon Oleander, the Rainbow Tiny Peach Oleander, and the White Sister Agnes ones. The genus and species is Nerium Oleander, and it is from the Apocynaceae Family (dogbane).

In the summer, the hot sun (in the hotter climates) will burn the Oleander blossoms, as it does the blossom of certain other plantings. The blossoms shrivel, die, and eventually fall off. This will happen if an Oleander gets full sun all day, but if it gets enough shade—for example, it is under or right next to a tree—the blossoms won't shrivel and die so soon (but of course, eventually, they will). Their blossoms are seasonal. Plant and tree blossoms shrivel and die from too much sun exposure, especially in the hotter climates. They may do fine in less hot areas. Still, Oleander blossoms last for a fair amount of time (depending on the outside temperature).

When you buy an Oleander, the label on the pot will indicate what color the blossoms will be and how high the Oleander can get. If you are going to have Oleanders, you should be willing to pick up dropped leaves and perhaps even enjoy doing that. Many people enjoy <u>all</u> aspects of gardening. It is a state of mind, tying in with outlook and attitude. The fact that gardening keeps you fit should keep you going, as well. There are way more plusses for landscaping and gardening than there are negatives. I can't think of any negatives. You have to put some money into the overall endeavor and money spent is not a negative. In the meantime, you'll enjoy the outdoors, get some sun, and get some exercise.

CHOICES, CHOICES, AND MORE CHOICES

When planning out any part of a lot, think about trees and where you want to place them. A very important concern for some is how tall a specific type of tree will end out being, once it is fully grown. Because tall trees can topple, some people are not interested in trees that will get taller, or much taller than the height of their home. If a tree is to be around a building, some people will only want trees to be only so tall. They don't want trees that will produce allergens that a number of people cannot be around. They don't want trees that drop blossoms, pods, seeds, etc., and some people don't like leaves, either, because leaves drop and fall off in the fall. Of course, needles will drop off of conifer-type of trees and certain Evergreens so that is something to think about, too.

You have to rake needles once or twice a year just like you have to do the leaves. Technically, raking needles and leaves once a year can be done but quite often there are still more needles or leaves to come (or drop) and so you end out raking the needles and leaves at least twice a year. Besides the raking chores, every now and again trees will need some trimming, pruning, and shaping. Most people don't mind doing any of these things or paying to have someone else do them. Relative to businesses, most companies will hire out for landscape and lot maintenance.

Don't totally overlook trees that blossom. Yes the blossoms will fall, perhaps blow helter-skelter, and then crinkle up and die, but they can be raked up, too. Blossoms on trees can be pretty, and that is why people will buy trees that blossom and why some trees with blossoms get planted. Still, if you believe you will live in the home you are in for years to come, do you want to be raking up blossoms in your old age? Trees that have blossoms tend to be shorter, or less tall (like Cherry, Peach, Orange, and Lila trees). Some blossom trees can be fruit-bearing trees and this fact will add to the popularity of specific trees that can be selected. Fruit trees can take years before they first bear fruit, though—mainly certain types, like the Avocado, which is grown around California in abundance.

The overall subject of fruit trees will require extra study and so will the overall subject of nut-producing trees. There are many types to choose from and certain ones are more commonly purchased. Some are lesser-known. Crabapple trees are hardy ones. You can make jam out of the crabapples but they are a little sour to eat, right off the tree. As for blossom-related trees, I'll never forget the blossoms on the Lilac trees I observed in more northern areas. The fragrance of blossoms can be quite nice, with certain blossoms, especially, and so some people seek out such trees for their lot. Everyone likes nice fragrances but only some plantings have fragrances that completely take over an area. (As an aside, one of my neighbors planted Jasmine vines at one side area of his lot and you could smell those jasmine blossoms even from some distance. Jasmine vines are not trees, of course, but if it is fragrance you are after, certain vines or climber plantings should be considered, along with certain trees.

Heavy storms have been coming in to specific areas because of Global Warming. Because sea and ocean waters are a little warmer than usual, storms get built up and winds blow into land areas and the rains that come with the winds can be torrential. Too much rain, combined with wind action, can cause trees to blow down (and this has surely been happening, because of tropical storms and hurricanes). Water and flooding softens and loosens the dirt around the tree roots so when winds blow, the tree goes down.

It helps if the tree roots are buried in the best possible way, to begin with. Trees can go in the ground and be buried wrong. None of the roots should be too close up to the top area of the ground. The roots have to be well distributed all around the tree and they have to go down far enough; some of the roots should be pointed downwards, while others won't be, so much. Find out from an expert, though, exactly how the tree you are about to plant should be planted and pay attention to what they say about root distribution. Not all trees have to be planted exactly the same way. You should make up a special natural ground-up mulch, too, and set it all down into the planting hole, mixed in with dirt.

If a tall tree falls, it can damage what it falls down on. A tree can fall down on a roof, garage, shed, car, awning, fence, covered patio, and they've even fallen on pets and people. Rain is, so often, what causes this, but there usually has to be wind. On occasion, tree falling is caused solely by wind action. A neighbor's tall tree can do damage, if their tree falls. So can your own tree. A rule of green thumb for some people is—only plant trees that will not grow too much taller than your home or your neighbor's home. If a home is two stories, the tree could obviously be taller. If buildings are taller, trees can be taller, too. If you have lower trees, your neighbors will probably breathe a sigh of relief. Some trees don't even have branches, per se, like the Italian Cypress tree doesn't, for example. Certain kinds of trees are more vulnerable to falling but there haven't been many studies on this; it will depend on what the soil type and composition is that the tree is planted in, too.

There are so many trees to choose from, including some of the foreign-country trees (but be careful, because of invasive species). Quite often, trees you don't think will do well in your area will do well so a tree you decide to plant can come from anywhere in the world. You can get trees by way of the Internet, too, but most people go to a local mart or plant and tree nursery.

Evergreens are popular around the world. They come in different sizes and shapes. There are various types of Evergreens. People are surprised to learn that they do pretty well in warm to even hot-weather climates. I was quite surprised to find this out. I was surprised about both the Evergreen trees and the Evergreen bushes. In that Evergreen means 'always green', all Evergreens live year round. Many Evergreens simply don't lose leaves or needles, compared with the deciduous plantings. Deciduous plantings lose leaves or foliage in autumn, but there is re-growth in the spring.

A number of Evergreens only lose a few of their needles, but the amount lost will also relate to the size of the tree. Warm weather causes dropping to happen and so does rain. It loosens the needles that are already dry, and so they will fall. Only a few Evergreen trees seem to drop an excessive amount of needles and this almost always has to do with dry and hot weather. Some people don't like such trees because of the needles. There are pros and cons to keeping such a tree. They tend to live a long time, which is a plus. The real tall ones provide considerable shade. My Evergreen tree is really tall. It was there when I moved in. If it ever fell, it could destroy a part of my home. I keep living with it, but should I?

One nice thing about Evergreen Pine trees is the pinecones. They are conifers, i.e., they have pinecones (conifer=cones). I collect these pinecones. They can be sold year-round for craft projects, especially around Christmas. I wash them, let them dry on a towel, and after they dry and plump out again, I organize them as to size. Then, they go in a box. Evergreen trees, if they are tall enough, will provide a great deal of shade and can very nicely shade a considerable part of a home. It would be great if, somehow, all of the home got shade, but that rarely happens. Shade is usually only around one or, at most, two areas and it usually doesn't cover the whole side of a home, just a partial side. Most landscaped lots end out having at least two shade trees. They aren't always so tall, though. They provide ground-area shade, which can be nice.

One Evergreen type that is very popular (and practical) is the Juniper bush, which grows to the same size and dimensions of the average bush. Junipers are from the Cypress family and there are fifty to sixty species of Juniper. There are both Juniper bushes and Juniper trees. Junipers can grow in cold or hot climates. Juniper bushes look good flanking the side of a home, and they're very hardy. They do not drop needles because they don't have what can be referred to as needles. On occasion, you may need to trim some parts off so the shape is more conforming, and you may also need to clip out dead wood, though doing so is rare and will cause gaps. In time, however, the gap areas should get filled in by new growth.

Many people plant a line of Juniper bushes along the edge of their home, or, they may plant one Juniper in a corner somewhere. Juniper bushes are full in shape, and they are a very nice green. They tend to grow to a height of about four feet. Whenever you plant anything next to a home, be sure you know how wide the planting will get to be. For example, Juniper bushes should be planted approximately seventeen to twenty inches away from the edge of a home or building—at least. They tend to end out with a diameter or width of around thirty-five to forty inches so you plant them around seventeen to twenty inches out from the home. Juniper bushes are a nice space occupier and they look good under windows. Yews are also needle-laden Evergreens and they make good hedges.

Other Evergreen bushes (often called shrubs) are the Boxwood, Euonymus, Firethorn (Pyracantha), Holly, and Photinia. These are all broad-leaf ones, however. The Boxwood can be shaped and sculpted quite easily. You can shape or sculpt it to look like a box. Some bushes and shrubs you don't want to shape/sculpt, however.

Holly bushes are quite often used as a hedge. They've been used as trees, too. Their leaves are spiny and they never lose any leaves. Holly berries come out in autumn and sometimes close in to Christmas. Blossoms come out from April to early summer. By June, a lot of different blossoms are showing. Most of them start up in the spring. Some won't last through the summer, though.

Blossoms are different from blooms. Blossoms are a spread of small flower-like blooms but blooms are thought of as being on flowers, not so much on trees and bushes. Whenever there are any blooms at all in a yard, some people don't take time out to observe them, and enjoy them. Sadly, they take the beauty for granted with an 'it's there, so what, it will be there next year', type of attitude. Some people need to take a flower appreciation course because there is beauty… and there is real beauty. Some people will deeply appreciate the beauty of flowers and have a 10 on the Appreciation Gauge; others will have a one on the Appreciation Gauge and flowers will mean little to them and they'll take them for granted and barely even notice them (if they notice them at all).

Many fine artists select flowers as a subject for their art. Artists very carefully look at flowers, and their leaves. Some draw or paint flowers in very detailed ways. Some do the same with trees. Some artists are nature artists. Some of this art is excellent. Some of it is fair. And then there's the art that is in the middle of the two extremes. One television series that follows the life of a nature artist and illustrator (who did many trees, plants, and wildflowers) is titled *The Country Diary of an Edwardian Lady* (1996). It is also a book. The lady, Edith Holden, who lived from 1871 to 1920, did artistry of nature and wildlife found around the English countryside and found during all four seasons.

It's true, people are sometimes too busy to take time out to enjoy and appreciate nature. (Gardening will definitely help this along.) Still, even if one's life is busy and an individual is pre-occupied with survival and personal matters, appreciation for many subject areas can be cultivated in a number of ways. Mere observation of natural beauty can be a start but observers have to go beyond that and one way to do that is to well focus in on details of all that constitutes natural beauty.

If you want an Evergreen bush that has blossoms (as opposed to an Oleander), go with the Camellia, the Gardenia, or the Azalea/Rhododendron bush (or shrub). Evergreens come in different sizes and shapes, whether bushes or shrubs or trees. You might look into growing some Blueberry bushes, too, or Vaccinium. They can grow up to eight feet tall, but check climate-growth conditions first. Some Evergreen trees are quite stately looking. Some people plant nothing but Evergreens. Evergreens can last for decades, too, if they're given adequate care (and if they're generally not all that temperamental). Shrubs are generally thought to be shorter than bushes, but they aren't always. They are considered bushes by many (as well as being shrubs). Because they are not so tall, they are more decorative than functional. Anything tall and full is functional—a windbreaker, property divider, privacy and security enhancer, a noise barrier, and sometimes it can serve as a shield against dust.

There are many Evergreen types around desert and other southern areas, and they seem to live on and on. Some are generic; some have come in from other areas. Originally, they may have all come in from other areas because they tend to be found more up north. Many plantings in all USA desert areas are not generic but they seem to work. Having a variety of plantings makes landscaping fun, quite frankly. You can have Evergreens, leafy vegetation, cacti, succulents, and palm trees all on the same lot. You can also grow flowers. I like to wait until everything else gets planted before I plant any flowers. They're the last to acquire, even if they're to go in pots. I personally don't grow flowers around my home. I tried it, but the ones I selected took a lot of time, especially with the watering, and they tossed seeds all over the place. Ants got to some of them. Some got heat wilt. I perhaps selected the wrong flowers. I tend to prefer plantings—like bushes—that have a number of small blossoms on them (and again, I'm not prone to growing actual flowers). Larger blooms are lovely around a yard, though, and flowers can add a great deal of color to an area. Flowers are really aesthetic. Only certain flowers can grow around desert areas, and they'll all need ample watering. Flowers are natural art.

If you like flowers on your lot, try seeds, bulbs, and tiny plantings, to see what works best for you and what grows the best. Some people like to have flowers around their patio area, their carport, or their stairs because they are able to look at and enjoy them more frequently, compared with if the flowers are over in a remote corner somewhere. In any American states, some people like to grow their state flower, somewhere on their lot. Because flowers tend to need more watering, you have to oversee that and watch over their condition. Sometimes you must water every day. They are generally delicate, and vulnerable to excess sun.

Certain flowers in particular aren't all that easy to grow. Some will die fairly quickly if there's too much water, or too little water. Most always, flowers need much more regular watering than other plantings do. Sometimes, the watering must be frequent and even daily. Some flowers seem to need coddling or Tender Love and Care (or TLC) (especially in areas that get really hot). To keep my lot low maintenance, I will very rarely grow flowers. (They're all-right in pots setting in the carport shade.) I prefer perennials to annuals if I ever do grow them. To each his or her own, though. Certain flowers throw so many seeds in the desert areas. You have to be very careful about flowers because they're vulnerable around intense sun, and sometimes, the petals wilt and dry up really easily. The heat can eventually get them. Even just a very short time with too much sun, and the flower part of a planting can be destroyed. Flowers may thrive in the spring, but not at all in the summer, in a number of hot areas. Ants only eat certain flowers, and who wants to go to war with the ants.

The two flower types I did all-right with in the desert were yellow Sun Ray Mums (Chrysanthemums) and any type of Vinca. I like the Pacifica Red Vinca. Pink Sundrops did well, too. I also liked Candytuft. Marigolds did all-right, too. Still and all, they all needed partial shade. When weather gets to be 110° to 115° F, flowers may need full shade (and lots of water and the more hours a planting is in the shade, the less the watering that will be needed). These noted flowers do well almost anywhere, but you have to tend to them, wherever they are.

Some people lavish their lots with flowers. A number of people go for roses, but roses don't do that well in full sun, not in hot, dry climates. They do great around Florida and all the Gulf states, really. In the dry parts of Texas, Arizona, and California, they don't grow fast, they dry up and can die, and if the roses do bud and bloom, the sun can cause the petals to crinkle and fade. Partial sun is the only way to go with roses wherever they are. Late afternoon sun can get to be too much for them, though, because that is when it is the hottest. Roses should, ideally, be in an area where they only get sun before noon. After noon, the area should be completely shaded. Roses also require skilled trimming or pruning and there are ways to go about doing both. You have to know what you're doing when you grow roses…and especially when you trim and prune them. There's a way of cutting anything growing on a rose bush.

In spring and especially summer, roses should be watered fairly often in warm and hot areas—every other day is reasonable, and assuming the roses are getting enough shade. Some people will water them every day, however, and do the same with other flowers. The more shade any planting gets, the less watering they will need, but they will still need watering. I tend to see rose bushes more in the front of people's homes, than in the back. In desert areas, they sometimes get too much if they are in a front yard or area, depending on how the home is laid out. Roses may do well on one side of the street but not on the other side, if they are in front.

At least consider adding color, here and there, by adding flowers, and even wildflowers. Wildflowers can sometimes be formally grown. Learn which types thrive in your locale. Flower and wildflower roots generally don't go down that far and so you have to be more concerned about soil condition, particularly from the top to sometimes even twelve inches down. Learn about their first blooming time, and their blooming range (of time) because you may want the flowers and wildflowers to be in bloom for as long as possible. In desert areas, only some flowers and wildflowers will thrive and you will always have to be concerned about and focus in on their watering. Very few flowers will stay in bloom for a really long time, in the warmer temperatures.

Realize that flowers and wildflowers can throw quite a few seeds around your lot so be prepared to pull up the ones you do not want in certain spots; you may be able to re-plant the plantings elsewhere on the lot, or put them in pots. Any selected wildflowers for your landscape should be native to your area. They are difficult to re-plant or pot (they're quite frail and will often die when being transplanted). Wildflowers are more difficult to grow than flowers are, as a general rule. They tend to be more temperamental to even get started. Once they get established, they can do quite well, but again, try to learn about their blooming times and lengths, since some stay in bloom longer than others do. Wildflowers come back each year and they are perennials.

Certain floral groundcover does well, but only a very few types do, in the hot-weather areas and desert-climate areas. A groundcover is multiple short plantings growing in close together and growing close down to the ground; it usually has lots of small blooms or flowers so you don't see so much green from the foliage and what you see is mostly color. Around a landscaping or garden area, usually only one type of groundcover is used in one part, but there can be mixed-in groundcover, too. This can be risky because the groundcovers may not have the same bloom times.

Only a very rare type of groundcover will stay in bloom all year round. These ones are hard to come across in the first place. Not very many people even know about them and in desert areas, you don't see the groundcover very often. You have to hunt these few types down, but they will still require regular watering, rest assured, even though they are year-round groundcover plantings. You see all kinds of ground cover wherever the weather is cooler. It can cover a really large area or any sized area, really, even a very small area. You sometimes see groundcover in front yards. It can be there by itself, or can flank flower, plant, or tree areas.

The Bougainvillea plant (that is actually a vine) grows in a warm-weather climate, depending on the area, of course. It grows in desert areas. Whenever I refer to 'desert' in this book, I'm referring to most of the desert areas in America. They tend to be in East Texas, on over to California. Most American desert areas are not like some desert areas found in other countries, since some of those are composed of mostly sand dunes, where nothing can grow. American deserts tend to have decent soil. However, doing a soil sample before choosing plantings is always advisable. Soil varies from area to area no matter where you are living. North areas have different soils from southern areas, but soil compositions vary all over the planet.

The Bougainvillea appears to have a number of blossoms, and the bright red ones will particularly catch your attention. The actual blossoms are fairly small. It's the bracts that surround the blossoms that are large (and bright and colorful). Bougainvilleas are more temperamental than Oleanders, for sure, but they will brighten up any landscape. Their blossoms look large (because of the bracts) and they look like some flowers look even though they're really a vine. Red-flowering Bougainvillea can sometimes even take full sun all day, though some shade would likely be best. But, the white and yellow-flowering Bougainvilleas will always need partial shade because they are a little more sun sensitive. Sometimes that kind of thing happens, with near-identical types of plantings.

Some people have a watering system for their flowers (sometimes called an irrigation system), but they're still using quite a lot of water— even more water than if the watering was done by hand. I do all my watering by hand when the weather is warm and hot. I do little watering when the weather is cool and none when the weather is cold. During warm and hot days, I prefer watering very late in the afternoon or early evening when it is still light out. During cooler days, I prefer watering early a.m. If plantings are in shady or semi-shade areas, watering is more effective during a spring or summer day, but when there is direct sun, the water will evaporate fairly fast. As noted earlier, when I water, I usually douse the area more than once.

All flowers should be in at least somewhat recessed beds or there should be some type of irrigation set-up. Sometimes flowers are put in rows and a recessed irrigating lay-out will work better than if the ground is flat. When there is recessed irrigating lay-out, there won't need to be as much watering. Plantings will get more of the water. do not grow flowers because they make my watering have to be put to too much of a schedule, even when they have been properly planted. With my hardy plantings, that don't require much watering, as a general rule I'm not bound to a watering schedule. Of course, I must still pay attention to numbers of waterings, and times of rainfalls. Some people could make good use of their home computers here, and keep track of watering matters.

Soil is generally good all over America, even in the south and in many of the desert areas. For example, in Tucson, Arizona, the soil is good around most of the city and plantings can be seen all over Tucson. However, a few areas around Tucson have a sand and grit layer along the top and so a soil sample should always be done before too many plantings are planned and purchased, no matter where a person lives, even up in the northern areas. In other words, soil samples can vary, even in one town or city. They can even vary in very small areas. Your soil could even be a little different from your neighbor's. You don't know what was done to your lot's soil by other residents before you moved in, either. For example, the area could have been fertilized, or, it could have been stripped of minerals or nutrients. Having a soil sample done can cost money. If you have time, plant a couple of plantings first, to see how they do. Do not do the lot, though, before knowing what condition the soil is in.

You cannot, necessarily, tell by looking at soil if it is good or isn't, unless something is clearly off-kilter. Special scientific testing might be what needs to be done...or, it might not be needed but such information would be nice to have. Most desert areas in America are livable, and people don't have to go somewhere else. Besides, we now have irrigation. The soil is pretty good or at least decent around American deserts. There are a few dunes in America, here and there, but they are few and far between. They're in fairly small areas—little pocket areas, as it were.

On the subject of soil samples, and also, grading, always consider using native plantings because you may have more success with them. Outside of native plantings can work, and work very well in many cases, but native plants tend to thrive better in the area where they come from (for the most part). They also tend to look like they belong to the area, because they do. Generally, when native plantings are put in native areas, the native plantings aren't so fussy about the native soil they're put in, and they tend to be hardier when it comes to any native insects. In warmer areas, native plantings will usually take its usual amount of water (but not in every setting so be careful) and they may not need any fertilizer or vitamins, unless the soil has somehow changed.

Soil samples will almost always vary from place to place in one area. South-Western areas can have good dark-brown dirt, and not have an abundance of sand in it so do not, necessarily, think that plant growth all over the South-West will be difficult. (And so, too, with southern areas, in general.) Make sure you are familiar with as many native plants as you can before you do your planning so you will have plenty of options. Also, learn what you can about non-native plantings that grow and do well in your area so you'll have even more options. With desert-area plantings, try to ascertain if any of the plantings 'throw thorns'. You might not want those around.

Some people make up their own compost, and they mix it in with actual soil. They might also mix in a planting soil compound that they have purchased with some soil, before they plant something. They dig a large hole, before planting, and put in this soil compound and mix the dug-out dirt in with it. Compost is not the same as potting soil, but people will sometimes confuse the two. Compost is heavier and thicker. Keep in mind that commercially-bought mixed potting soil is very light in weight and particles rise to the top when there is watering. This can become quite a nuisance. This is why it shouldn't be mixed in with the dirt. Compost can be mixed in, though. The natural soil can be mixed in with an actual home-made compost, too. A compost mix can be fresh peels of vegetables and fruit, as carrots, cucumbers, potatoes and apples and anything of the like that's organic. (I, personally, never used orange peelings.) I've even seen coffee grounds and broken-up eggshells go in to make up a compost. Use compost sparingly, though. It's supposed to add nutrients to the soil. Too much can decay and not be good for the planting. It has to be mixed in well with enough of the dirt.

Commercial compost is not as densely packed in as real soil is. You can put in compost but you should never put any potting soil in dug-out holes in the ground. The compost has to at least be well mixed in with actual dirt. Some commercial compost is not dense enough to use as a mix for some plantings, if they end out being tall and heavy from the get go or they become tall and heavy, after a time. Actual dirt holds the plantings in more securely so for some plantings, don't even mix in any compost at all, or, mix in very little. You may only want a little compost to be mixed in at the top area, and it shouldn't go down too far when you plant anything that is or is going to become large. You can use the natural-made compost but not too much of it if the planting will be tall and heavy, like a tree. You want to save any extra dug-out soil or dirt to put back where it came from anytime you dig it out. Real soil and dirt is more compact than what is found in commercial bags or compost and anyone planting anything has to try to save as much real soil/dirt as they can, to put back into the dug-out spot. Sometimes you may want only a little compost or you may not want any compost.

Some will put a layer of compost on top of the dirt, too, and leave it so nutrients will get down into the dirt, like what happens with fertilizer, to replenish soil nutrients. With some gardening projects, some people may even lay down a layer of fertilizer. It is loaded with nutrients. Fertilizer has Nitrogen, Phosphorous, and Potassium in it, predominantly, but there is also Calcium, Magnesium, and Sulfur, secondarily. There are also a number of other nutrients mixed in. Nitrogen is the most important, but all vitamins and minerals are needed.

Fertilizer (from the bags) can be a bit strong for some plants if they directly touch the fertilizer, but not after the nutrients go down into the ground. Before planting anything, after the fertilizer has done its job, you will want to remove the layer of fertilizer that was put down. Then, you do the planting. Fertilizer can be spread on the ground, as from a bag, or sprinkled on the ground, as from a container. Compost or mulch is what gets mixed in with the dirt, not fertilizer. If fertilizer is sprinkled on by a container, you obviously won't be removing it. It seeps into the dirt. You can also buy plant food, but that tends to be nutrients you can use for individual plants; it is not usually used for a large area. Go to a garden shop and check out everything that is available relative to whatever is in bags and whatever you think will be useful for your particular yard and/or garden. Read all the labels and the instructions on all the bags and buy what is most applicable. Again, you can make your own compost (or mulch) and mix it down lower, in with some dirt.

Today, there are organic fertilizers that have no chemicals in them. Other gardening products are also organic; it will note this on the bag, box, or container. If what you are considering buying has the word 'natural' printed on it, be wary because what is purported to be natural may not be of all that much merit and it will not be organic (unless it actually notes 'Organic'). If you want to go Organic, the word 'Organic' should be printed on the product somewhere but be careful of the wording because the wording can mislead you.

Right after putting in the planting (and then putting in the original soil or dirt), the planting has to be watered down and the soil/dirt soaked so the soil/dirt will pack in tightly around or against the planting's roots. Obviously, the planting itself should come up straight from the ground and be straight, after any soaking. If the plant tips, it will have to be braced in better. With trees, some people will put a tall stake in next to the tree, and connect a rope from the tree to the pole so the tree will stay in straight, and also not blow down.

Some people will still put potting soil into a dug-out spot even though the granules in potting soil are light in weight and every time they water the spot, the granules will go all over the place. It's not as bad as the straight compost when you mix it in with the dirt. With potting soil, you'll have granules all over the place when you water the area, even if you do mix it in with the dirt. Compost won't end out being so bad. Potting soil is really only for potted plants, as its name suggests. On the same subject, no one should ever want to use real soil or dirt in pots (as noted earlier). It compacts in so tightly that water never gets down to the roots. There is no aeration so water cannot get through. Most of the dirt stays dry. Water accumulates and stays on top of the soil/dirt in the pot and evaporates before it is able to soak in. Plants can die from lack of water even if you've watered them. Always use potting soil.

Some people end out with a number of potted plants, more than they ever expected to have, in fact; then, they have to figure out what to do with them. They may not want to put any of their potted plantings in the ground and they may want to keep them in pots. If you can find any of those raised-up, wooden-planked platforms (that are used in warehouses to put boxes on and are a few inches up from the ground), you can use one to put a number of pots on. Because they're flat and low to the ground, but are raised up, when you water the potted plants (that are on top of the wood planks), the water goes through the planks down onto the ground. You can paint or redwood stain the planks, to add some color to the landscaping. The pots can be lined up in rows. The wooden platform can be set under an awning or shade tree if you don't want the potted plants to get maximum or full sun. Many people put their potted plants on shelves that are on their deck or patio, or alongside of their carport and against the home. You can put potted plants anywhere around the lot, though—either in groups or as solos. You can put some of the plants in long and thin plant boxes, too. These are rectangular-shaped; some are wood and some are plastic. These can go in certain, selected areas.

There are some beautiful pots and planters available for purchase in large marts or home-building centers. Sometimes, you can go to pottery shops, as well. Design and color can be eye-catching. Ceramic planters can have colorful prints and pictures on them. They can also be plain, with nature colors. Usually, the more elaborate the design, the more expensive the pot. There are also pots that look ceramic but they are made of plastic. They're called Dura-planters®

or something similar. They are much lighter in weight than ceramic planters are. They tend to come in natural colors and earth tones. All planters add to a landscaping. One thing about potted plants—you can always take them with you if you have to move. They also make nice gifts.

In some southern states, access to Mexico is not far. Mexico has many potters. Numerous pots and yard deco items are made and sold in Mexico and people go there and pick up beautiful and wonderful items for their yards. Somehow, they get them home. Some will even go back and get more pots, go briefly through customs, put the pots in their car, and then go back and get even more pots, that very same day. You can even use a baby stroller or a grocery carrier (not a grocery cart) to wheel pots through customs/immigration, and then on over to your car. Pots are never a problem getting past the customs gate, but border officials will likely look inside the pots.

Items that are made in Mexico are also found around the border, on the USA side. They are even found in cities that are up some ways from the border. (If they're found anywhere else—that is further away from border areas—they're probably going to be expensive.) Lawn ornaments, ceramics, and pots that are made in Mexico are generally very colorful, and they're usually affordable but prices have gone up a bit down there and so you really have to work a bargain for yourself, and haggle (which is something they've always done anyway). Many items are handmade and hand-painted. Some of these pots do not do real well in direct sun, over a period of time, because of peeling. The clay part may weather badly, too. Some items are painted really well, and the paint is sometimes baked on. Look the pot over real well before you buy it, Check for cracks and imperfections. Some imperfections may be fine, while others may not be. A small crack can quickly lead to a bigger crack, for example.

As you go west to east and get closer in to where Florida is, there will be other Hispanic art, including pottery and landscape items that have been made by Cubans and Puerto Ricans. Some might be made with shells. Distribution of this Hispanic Art (other than the Mexican Art) goes into or starts in Florida and goes up to Georgia and over to the eastern States of Alabama, Mississippi, and Louisiana. Texas gets a lot of the Mexican Art. So does Arizona and California. Louisiana gets some Mexican Art, too, but they also relish their own Cajun Art. There are also various Indian tribes around the nation that put out Indian art. Some of them do pottery. Not as many do actual yard items.

For the most part, plastic-made items do not do well in direct sun, either, because the color fades and you have to replace the item with something else, after a time. Also, some plastics dry out and crack. Some colored-glass items, if you can find them, don't fade, and they stay a bright color. Coloring up a yard or lot is not hard to do, but certain colorful items don't last very long in direct heat and intense sun.

One must look around and shop around, whether in Mexico or anywhere else, until the right items come along. The thrill is in the hunt. If you can, put ornament items in full shade or partial-shade areas so they will last longer and look better as they're being seen. The one advantage of getting pots from Mexico is that many of them are individually painted by individual artists, and in this way, they aren't mass produced.

You can buy yard and landscape ornaments at any time, but it's best to wait until the lot or yard has taken shape and you've put in most of the pavers, rock gardens, and plantings. Eye-catching yard ornaments and art fill in space and add charm and beauty to a landscape. There's a variety to choose from—colorful pots, ceramic figures of various sizes and colors, wooden items, wind-gauging poles or stick art, metal art, plastic figures or flowers, artistic pots, and the list goes on. If you wait to buy ornaments, you'll also be able to ascertain what size any ornaments you buy should be. It's a good idea to brush on or spray a clear polyurethane paint or just clear paint over anything ceramic that you know will be in the sun and rain. Certain other items might need this spraying, too. It will help prevent peeling and add to longevity.

If I was able to, I'd have a collection of ceramic gnomes and leprechauns, or more likely, some ceramic forest animals. Oh well… maybe one day. In Southern areas, especially the South-Western areas, people try to stay with the South-Western themes but they surely don't have to. You see a lot of the Mexican and/or the Native American motif all around the South-West. Occasionally you see a ranching motif. Forest animals tends to be a more northern theme, but there are three South-West animal motifs you will see in the yards and gardens and these would be the Gambel Quail, the Roadrunner, and the coyote.

Pots, and yard and landscape deco items, can easily be stolen when you're not watching. I don't put any out front. (I don't have a fence.) Some could be put more to the back, in front, but it is at your own risk. Anything loose that can be taken and then resold, or used by the drive-by thief, is vulnerable. Theft can occur more than once, too, and, unfortunately, some things are hard to secure (by anchoring, cementing in, or using a lock and chain, etc.), and so, you may want to put such things in spots that can't even be seen by drivers-by. You will be able to see these items from time to time, but the thieves won't be able to notice them. If you have a fence with a gate in front, the risk of theft will be much less if you put yard items out. I tend to put deco items in corners and under or around certain plantings, but none of these items go in the front of the home. I put some potted plants along or around the carport itself, but they are not in very valuable pots. Real heavy items are less apt to be stolen, but still, it's always a risk if such items are put in front, and sometimes even if they're to the side.

If you go on vacation, you might consider putting your front or side items in back, to minimize the risk of theft. Sometimes at night, thieves drive through neighborhoods not their own (in trucks, vans, or cars) and they steal whatever can be easily grabbed. They come along on big holidays, too—Christmas, Thanksgiving, and the like—and check for cars not present. They assume someone is gone if cars are not there, and then they strike. Sometimes these thieves work in pairs. In other words, the two can pick up heavy items. They've been known to hit mobile home parks, even secured ones that have a security gate and/or guard. Separate homes and businesses are always vulnerable. They will even dig plantings out of the ground, and steal them. Some people's security cameras are on all the time, though, and the cameras can serve to deter some of the trespassing and theft.

On the subject of theft, it's a good idea to have two metal locks on your shed door, too. Thieves might break one lock, but they will be much more deterred if there are two metal locks. If you have plastic hinges on your shed door, replace them with metal ones, even if they aren't broken and are working. Thieves know that the plastic hinges easily break (and so what's the point of attaching an actual padlock). You can put a board behind the shed door in the area where the lock parts go, but behind the door so when you drill in any screws, they will be better affixed because of the board. If you have valuable tools in your shed, especially power tools, and if those tools are in a non-fortified shed, there is a risk there, that they'll be stolen, along with other items.

It's not a good idea to leave anything valuable on a patio, even if the patio is not to the side but to the back. Some thieves will actually enter back yards, too, and they will even jump a fence. Very rarely is a patio in front of a home. Apartments often have front patios but since apartment people don't have yards, they usually don't have anything of much value on their patio. Many potted plants go on such patios, however. So do chairs, wind chimes, and sometimes, bicycles—all of which can be stolen. Bicycles should always be chained and locked to something but it's hard to do that with potted plants.

To emphasize, if you put lawn ornaments or items out in the front area, it is at your own risk (of loss) because they cannot only be stolen, but they can be damaged, as well. Whether you live in a mobile home or a house, you have to always be concerned about vandalism or malicious mischief. Even though it's safer to put yard and landscape ornaments or items along the sides of, or in the rear areas of the lot, it's still at your own risk because of possible theft and malicious mischief. If you have a deck, you're still at risk because you can't be home all the time and thieves will even go up on a deck and carry off what they want to steal. Some neighborhoods are more vulnerable to this happening than others are, but floater thieves can be and will go anywhere.

Some decks (and decks are almost always along the outside wall that walls around the vicinity of the living room) will have valuable items on them, and these can be stolen at night, too, or at any time during the day, especially if the resident isn't home much. Some people put the stairs up to a deck to the back area of the deck so it isn't at the front, or close to the front (i.e., the street). You can also close off the deck/patio area so you can only get to it by way of the house door. Doing this has pros and cons. Open decks/patios are vulnerable to thieves but closed ones aren't, so much. Hanging plants look nice around a deck, and also patios. They're not usually stolen but wind chimes can be. Wind chimes can actually be fairly expensive purchases. Some mobile homes have porches that are lower down and ground level, but there's not much room on porches and anything decorative is not usually put on them because the porches tend to be small.

Thieves tend to steal what they can see. Sometimes, they come around when they think residents are asleep. Again, if a yard is fenced in, items are safer, even if they are in the front area. A gate lock is certainly advisable. You hope that no one will steal anything off your lot, but it's always possible that someone will. Some of these thieves wear dark clothes and dark sneakers so you cannot see or hear them at night. (And, yes, some will wear hoodies.) A few people have security cameras up, so anyone entering the area gets filmed. There's always Neighborhood Watch co-operation, but, of course, if everyone is sleeping and it is dark…. Also, neighbors can't always be relied upon to 'watch', and to even report.

You will want to have decent-looking yard or lawn furniture around if you plan to use the outdoors for rest and recreation and for eating. Before investing too much in lawn furniture, determine if it will mostly be in the sun, or the shade. Some outdoor furniture does not do well in the sun. Also, some outdoor furniture is more adaptive to poolside lounging than other outdoor furniture is. Generally, poolside furniture should be able to take more of a beating. Loungers should, perhaps, not have cushions, but some residents insist on having cushions. The cushions can be placed on top of loungers very easily. Water should not be able to get inside these cushions. Some people will want to have a table that has a shade umbrella that fits in the middle of the table. As for collapsible chairs, they're hard to find. There are plenty of plastic chairs around that don't collapse; they're often white. Plastic Adirondack chairs came in somewhat en masse, in the 2010s. They come in different colors. They tend to force you to sit lower down and nearer to the ground. People who live around the seaside sometimes put them down on the beach.

With many, lounge furniture that is a whole set (be it poolside or just general) is quite popular because the color and print are uniform. Some outdoor furniture is fairly costly. Some outdoor furniture should really stay in the shade all the time but so often, it doesn't.

When it is really hot, it should at least be put in the shade when it isn't being used. Some people go on the Internet or mail order route, to find good outdoor furniture. Shipping costs can add up, especially if each piece is heavy.

Sturdy redwood furniture has always been popular, but it is hard to find, these days. Still, you will want to re-stain it or touch it up every two or three years (if it needs it) and you'll have to occasionally tighten the screws. It's best to keep it in the shade. Usually, redwood furniture has cushions. If your outdoor furniture is hard plastic, you'll have to periodically clean it, and perhaps put a coat of wax on it. Some people use car wax, after washing it well. Some people use car wax on their plastic pots, too, because plastic pots get scratched up and they fade and dry out from sun exposure. I've been known to use ArmorAll® on used plastic pots, but I prefer just putting car wax on them. You can clean and wax your outdoor furniture at the same time that you treat any plastic pots with a wax coat or ArmorAll®.

To add color, you can find colorful concrete stain (it doesn't peel), and you can stain rocks, bricks, blocks, pavers, and walkways with it. You can use different colors around the lot. Concrete stain isn't easy to find because not many companies make it, but it sure can brighten up a place and it holds up well. Walkways, and shed and garage or carport flooring can also be stained with concrete stain. More than one color can be used, even on one project. You can even do artsy things with some concrete stains but a gallon of concrete stain is somewhat costly so you may be limited as to what you can do with the concrete stain. Some people prefer earth-tone colors, but many colors and shades are available with the concrete stain. You can use concrete stain on wood, too, but not very many do. That's not what it's for.

On the subject of concrete staining, if you have any rocks or concrete around that you wish to color or stain, use the concrete stain. The stain is specially formulated for concrete and it comes in a gallon-sized can. You can get it in both the bright colors, and the pastels. You can always buy a gallon of concrete stain and share the price, and the can, with a relative or a neighbor, if you don't need all that much concrete stain for a particular project. A gallon can isn't cheap. You just have to agree on a color, together. You can put the other half in some kind of can with a very good lid. Cans will work all right for storing concrete stain.

Sometimes, concrete stairs can occasionally be re-strained, after some use. If you put the right amount into a small coffee can and do not use the larger can of stain when you do the job, you will only get some debris in the smaller coffee can that you're using, as you are staining. (You should use a coffee can when redwood staining wood, too, so what's still in the larger gallon-sized can stays pure.) If you use a jar, do so at your own risk. You do not want to ever drop concrete or redwood <u>stain</u> anywhere. Whatever you use should really have a secured lid. If there are any spills, it will be a huge mess and the area will stain unless you wipe it up really quickly and even then, some of the stain could absorb and take or become permanent. Always be super careful with an open concrete stain container. Be more careful than careful. (So, too, with redwood stain, which you usually only use on wood, not concrete.)

Again, concrete stain can really add color to a landscape area, and it can be used for different kinds of projects. Again, even concrete stairs can be stained. Usually, it is walk areas and floors that are stained. It is possible to use concrete stain on wood but doing so would be at your own risk so do a sample area first. It's worked for me, but it can depend on wood type and the actual project you're doing.

In addition to planting and using hedges and shrubs as dividers, concrete blocks can be used to section areas, and to serve as boundary dividers around a lot. I have concrete blocks in several areas—in front, to the sides and the back of the home—and they are essentially boundary dividers. Some are behind my carport, to serve as a short barricade or wall. Several concrete blocks are piled up in some spots—one on one and next to other ones. They make up a wall division. Along one side of the home, several of these concrete blocks are piled up, one on one. It saves on fencing. It gets the message across to neighbors, just in case you want the message to get across. It will establish lot divisions and boundaries. These blocks are gray and they can be concrete stained any color. Pavers can be bought in a number of different colors but you can still concrete stain them, if you want to.

You can stack two, three, and maybe even four of these concrete blocks and they're pretty secure. On top of the highest concrete block, (and as a memo, sometimes there doesn't have to be more than one concrete block on the ground to serve as a divider), I put a flat, colored paver (on top of that top block). It has the same surface-area dimensions as the concrete block has but it is not as thick. The paver covers up the concrete block top area because it fits perfectly on top. The paver covers up the two holes that most large concretes block tend to have. If these two holes aren't covered up, the block itself looks unfinished and tacky when it is on its side and being used as a divider. The paver is much thinner than the concrete block is and it may be as thin as only an inch. The paver adds color and a bit of height. Plus it's a cover. The surface of the paver is, of course, flat, and I set one or two good-sized decorator stones/rocks on top of the paver toppers for that extra touch and the natural look. Doing projects like this costs little. The concrete blocks are a little heavy, though. However, once they're set up, that's it. You won't have to lift them again.

I try to find nicer rocks to put on top of the concrete blocks with the paver toppers and I use the natural rocks that you can buy at landscape-material businesses or I find them out in nature somewhere. Usually, landscape-material businesses usually sell by the pound and they charge for delivery. With loose items, they sell by the item. It's great if you can order everything at one time and it saves money if you can go get the materials yourself or can ask a friend or relative to help you do this. If you go there, the employees at these businesses will load your car or truck, but you have to unload it all when you get home. You will then have to spread it, if it is the gravel or landscape or pebble rocks.

Shaped concrete blocks are also found and can be purchased at these businesses. These are the rectangular ones that are used underneath mobile homes, to hold them up. These rectangular blocks are the same ones used to edge an area and make boundary areas on my own lot. (I have just been noting them.) You can also get similar concrete items that are tapered but are blunt on top. The base is quite a bit bigger than the top, obviously. You can also find square concrete blocks. You can use concrete stain on any of these, as well, or you can just leave them gray. Any of them can be used as dividers. Rectangular ones can be set on top of the rectangular-shaped ones, to add height.

You should stain all concrete blocks at the same time—all around each other in one place—before you put them where they are to go, but it would be all right to stain them when they're in the spot where they're to stay. You will need to put a piece of newspaper under each block that you stain. This is why it's better to stain the concrete blocks before you put them in place. You do not want to stack these first. If blocks are stacked first, it's difficult to put newspaper under the bottom ones unless you unstack all of the blocks. All projects require forethought. Each block should really be separate from the other blocks so you can stain all sides of the blocks. You may want to stain all sides in the event you want to turn them or use them in a different way, later on.

Lattice-like pen wood dividers (that are thin and have a criss-crossing pattern) can be used here and there for decoration and function. They can be propped up between two concrete blocks (stained or unstained), and so they can suffice for fencing or dividers. They come in one size, usually, which is 4' by 8'. They can always be cut to size, too. These are usually around a quarter of an inch thick, and some are even thicker, at around a half an inch. These are the ones you want to use—the half an inch size. If you use them as dividers, they must be thicker. Some people like to stain them with redwood stain, but you can also buy the real redwood panels. These dividers come in natural wood, or painted-white wood. You can get plastic ones, too. There's not too much color selection, either way. The plastic ones are white but I've seen beige ones, too. They can have a more tightly-enclosed criss-crossing pattern that allows in less sun, or a more open criss-crossing pattern that allows in more sun. The pattern that is more tightly enclosed gives more privacy because you can't see much through them. These lattice panels are also used as awning panels (the quarter of an inch thick panels are).

On awning posts, they are useful as a sun shield plus they will provide more privacy. They have to be screwed into the awning posts. These are great for carport areas because they provide a lot of protection from the sun (and possibly a little from the dust). Your vehicles are more protected, that way. They provide much-needed shade when it is hot outside. You can put them up on awning posts as single ones or you can do them in a double way so that one is up on top of the other, on the awning posts. The panels will fit double like that if your awning posts exceed eight feet in height, which they usually do. (The two panels are four feet high so that is eight feet right there). The awning posts have to be a certain distance apart but a panel can be set over another panel as long as the screws are right for the job. Large washers are advised, which you can paint over if you wish. I weave somewhat thin rope over the middle area where the two panels meet so they are connected and so the wind does not stress where the screws and washers are. The panels are white so I use thin white rope.

If you do the doubling job and panels are in two rows, once all the panels are up, you really should get strong twine or thin rope and weave it in and out of the middle area where the two panels meet all along where they join and from end to end so that wind action will not stress the panels because they are being held together in the middle area, by the connecting twine or rope. This will keep the panels from splitting in places, over the years. The large washers will help with that, too.

Once the panels are up, think about what you want to plant next to where the panels are. You may not want to plant anything. Lower plants or bushes would be best if you do plant anything. You could put plantings all in a row along there (on the other side of where the panels are, obviously). You don't want any of those plantings to crowd against the wood or plastic panels and put pressure anywhere on them. The pressure could cause the plastic to crack or the wood to split, depending on what material you had used for the lattice job. Again, you can cut these criss-crossing patterned panels (wood or plastic) to use as dividers for fencing (or use them in the size that they come in, depending on how the fencing or dividing project has been planned). It will be more for design, though, because such fencing cannot be used for security purposes since there will be no posts secured down into the ground.

I've seen fencing made of concrete blocks and long wood logs, and the concrete blocks were stained with concrete stain. Two of those 7 ½" x 7 ½" x 15 ½" concrete blocks with the two holes in them (one on top of the other) were linearly placed every so many feet from the ones next in line. The one block was put on top of the other, short side up. A long wood log was put inside of the highest hole in the concrete blocks. More than one block could be piled up on top of the other and then two long logs could go in—one in the very top hole, for sure, and then another log in a hole down from the top hole. You could arrange a higher, or a lower concrete block and long log fence, depending on what you want. This fencing will be somewhat permanent, but you can also move it (unless you put in mortar between the blocks in that mortar will bind the blocks together). You can use this set-up for separating areas on your lot, too, if it is a big enough lot.

You can save money by setting up this type of fence or division. It works well in a front yard area, too. It will not be a security fence, though, and it could be toppled unless some kind of cement/mortar is used to keep the concrete blocks together. This is not really necessary to do but some will want to do this. You can redwood stain the logs; possibly specific-sized long boards could be used, but they wouldn't look as good as the rounded logs. (And by the way, these somewhat thin logs can be used for bed edging, too, just like rocks or stones can) True, people can step over them because they won't be too, very high when made to be fencing, but they can be used to indicate property division and lines and this is the point. If they end out being high enough, people will not want to step over them.

Those 7 ½" x 7 ½" x 15 ½" concrete blocks work well as dividers even without the logs. You can arrange them however you like. They are gray when you buy them, and they tend to be heavy. You can concrete stain them any color or just leave them gray. Any concrete staining lasts a long time, even in the sun. Once concrete blocks are stained, you may not need to stain them again for years. Some of the colors you can select can be quite bright, and quickly noticeable once the blocks are put in place on the lot. Color can be eye-catching—this we all know. What is colorful grabs your attention.

Some people put a concrete path down, somewhere on their lot. A concrete path going along the front of a shed is always nice, and it's great if the floor of a shed is concrete, as opposed to being wood. You can then concrete stain the shed floor, and do the same with the path in front of the shed. You can use the same color, or not. The path may need to be re-stained after several years, though, because of intense sun exposure and foot tread. Usually, people who care about plantings and gardening and landscaping care about these kinds of things, too—these extra projects. <u>They want everything to be nice</u>.

On your average-sized lot, you'll need a seventy-five foot hose. You may need to add a twenty-five footer, to total a hundred feet. If you have a fifty-foot hose, it is easier to manipulate or handle than a longer one is so you might consider buying a fifty-foot one and a twenty-five foot one, or even another fifty-foot one, to get you to a hundred feet. Simply screw on the shorter one to the longer one when you need to, and use whatever length you need when you need it. If you find yourself a little short and you don't have enough hose length, you can always shoot out water (spray it), over to an area from a distance. But, it's best to do some measuring, from the outdoor water spout, and figure out, early on, what total length of hosing you will need. Then, figure out the length or lengths of hose or hoses to buy.

It's hard to find a hose that doesn't crimp. I like beige or brown hoses for lots that have landscape rocks, but they are near impossible to find, at least right now they are. I saw a gray one once. Those match the rocks. I've seen black hoses, too. They don't show up as conspicuously as the green ones do when they are on top of the landscape rocks. I once saw a red hose but it was an indoor one used to put out a fire, should one start up in a warehouse. You can put any hose inside any structure, though, including your own home. A hose is a necessity, and there are hose attachments for watering that you can look into, as well, including an oscillator. An oscillator is a plastic unit that sets on the ground and has tiny holes in it for water to go through. It shoots or sprays out water and the spray amount can be adjusted. The water moves back and forth (oscillates) so water can cover more area. You can leave the area, once it is oscillating (unlike with the hand watering).

A hose, obviously, can be left outside. Generally, hoses don't get stolen. I try to at least keep mine in a shady area (when it is not in use).

Hoses today still tend to be green, but quite a few that are made are now black. A rare one is beige, so it will match the ground (without any grass). And, if you can find a beige one that doesn't crimp too badly (like many hoses today do, leaving an awful crease where it bent), again, it will not contrast with the landscape rocks (like the green one will). It will blend in. To emphasize and as previously noted, more mobile home owners and homeowners in general, even if they live more northerly, are going to the landscape rocks to cover their lot; some people will even remove the grass that's there, especially if it is patchy, because they don't want to have to water the grass in the summer, due to the cost of water and a desire to conserve water. For this reason, perhaps more beige hoses will be manufactured. I'd like to see beige and gray rubber hoses on the market. The rubber hoses are superior to the vinyl ones. The vinyl ones crimp. They are more easily punctured.

Besides the flat pillow, I also find garden gloves to be indispensable. I have thick rubber gloves and the thinner, cloth-made gloves. I use the cloth ones to scoot aside rocks and pebbles, which I occasionally have to do to clean out beds and scoop up leaves and debris. I use the rubberized ones to get down into the soil to remove roots (when the ground area is wet). Both can protect me from thorns, quills, nettles, sharp rocks, and insect bites. For me, insect bites haven't been much of a problem, though, except for occasional ants and very few mosquitoes. You can wear socks to prevent ant bites, and mosquitoes do not like to be out in direct sun. They can be in shady areas, though, and if you expect they could be around, wear sweatpants (with a band at the bottom) and something long-sleeved. You may need to be wearing socks. Some will use mosquito repellent. They come out at dusk and at night, after the sun goes down.

Most spiders can be spotted, as you are gardening. They are classified as arachnids but most people lump them in with insects. Bigger spiders can always be seen. Spiders are not so harmful to plants, bushes, and trees, like insects can be. Spiders tend to eat some of the harmful insects. That is why they hang around gardens. Poisonous spiders are very few, in the USA. The desert areas may have scorpions and tarantulas, but they aren't very common, even there, and they are only in a few areas. They don't like being around noise and people. (Some insects, in general, will only be active when it is dark and this includes some spider types, too.) There are a few areas that have Black Widows but they like quiet, secluded areas where there is some moisture. Avoid any black spider that has a distinctive red area on their abdomen. That would be a stinging Black Widow. The Brown Recluse spider can also sting. Some people can have a very bad reaction to spider bites or stings—even just one bite. Wear gardening gloves if you think you have any of these insects around. Do not wear open-area sandals. Be a little careful about spider web areas. Be watchful. Many areas have very few spiders so you have to do research. When cleaning out beds, just in case any local animals have used the area for a bathroom, the rubber gloves protect a wearer from having to touch whatever might be unsanitary. Of course, I immediately wash my hands when I come inside from gardening. Relative to gloves, some people will use welder's gloves to handle or remove some types of cactus. Welder's gloves are extremely thick. You just have to buy what you need.

I personally never get upset about local animals using any spot around my lot for a bathroom because I love, love, love all animals. I don't even mind if cats spray an area with urine because I just hose the area off. Usually, a cat's spray isn't very much urine at all. I understand their needs and their behaviors and, in fact, I put food out day and night for stray cats. Hose water gets rid of any urine spray. You can also wash the area down with soapy water or pine cleaner but you don't need to if you hose the area off. One-piece tongs and a baggie can be used to get rid of clumps if I ever find fecal clumps anywhere.

I feel sorry for stray cats, and I've taken in many of them and found homes for them. There are many things in life we can overlook and work around, if we care to. For me, cats around gardens and yards are one of those things. Pregnant women have to be careful about Toxoplasmosis, though, and not do gardening projects if cats use their garden areas for a bathroom. Always use tongs when removing fecal clumps.

Lattice can be useful as sun protection, as well as for fencing division. Some attach this lattice to awning posts, sideways, so they keep sun out and provide at least some privacy. You can buy silkscreen material to cover lattice panels. Silkscreen can be thin or not so thin. It will always serve as a sunscreen, but some material screens cut out sun better than other material does. Some call sunscreen, shade-screen. The lattice (again, generally 4' x 8') and the screen material (sold in rolls) can be put inside a wood frame and the finished item can then be mounted on to the awning posts. More than one lattice panel can be purchased, for a longer area. Framework (the framing) for such a construction can be wood or metal but some people don't even bother framing the lattice. They just put it up whole and as it is.

Cut-to-size tubular metal is often used to make a sunscreen area, but it is usually combined with a thick canvas-like fabric that can be used, instead of the open crisscross-pattern wood or plastic dividers (the lattice), that is covered over by some kind of material (or left uncovered). Whatever materials end out being used, latticework or silkscreen/sunscreen can provide shade, privacy, and freedom from at least some rain, wind, and dust. These kinds of projects can be done in different ways using different materials so they have to be well planned out after the options have been considered and looked into.

One or more lattice panels can also be used for shading of particular garden areas. In the summer, when the sun gets so hot that it can burn the leaves of some plants and even burn some cacti, putting up a temporary shade area will save those plantings. You can put in four stakes (wood or metal) and prop the crisscross-patterned open wood or plastic panel in between them so the sun won't shine so harshly on the plantings. The rays will be broken up. You can cut these panels to different sizes. You can also prop a panel in between concrete blocks if you have some extra blocks. I've even set a panel up against a fence (of stacked-up concrete blocks) so the angle of the lattice panel was about sixty degrees. I put one or two 'two by fours' under the lattice panel to better hold it in place because the panel tended to sway or bend, maybe not at first, but it swayed or bent later on. I do a lattice panel covering every year on some plantings, right before the summer heat takes over.

The lattice panel (and anything else that is sun-shielding) stays in place until mid-September when it is no longer too hot. I then set any sun-shields behind some bushes against my shed or anywhere else where I can get them out of sight. I do the same thing with a lattice panel piece in another area, but the panel piece sets more upright. You have to do whatever you can or whatever it takes to protect certain plantings from excess summer heat, especially around desert areas.

Lattice panels could be used as a cover over plantings during snowy and frost and freeze times, too, if you are able to use them as a covering. Some kind of fabric could be securely set on top or stapled on to the panel. And, any positioning of the panel would have to be thought through. The panel would have to be able to keep snow off the plantings. The panel couldn't be blown about by the wind so it would have to be secured, somehow. The same panels you use in the summer to protect your plantings from excessive heat can also be used in the winter. You always want to keep snow off certain plantings, if you get any snow (but not every planting because some aren't bothered by snow). A board (braced on side bricks) would work, too, but it would have to be removed when there is no frost and snow so the planting could get some winter sun. Again, you do all these projects a little at a time. Many times, though, when it comes to doing landscape projects, you must be timely in your efforts because some things you have to do will be seasonal.

When an important project comes around, all needed materials have to be on hand. You will have to buy items and supplies along the way. Some people keep a separate fund aside for these kinds of projects. You don't really have to invest in power tools because hand tools work just fine, but some people like power tools. They're the first items a thief looks for when they break into a shed, though. You can keep power tools in the home. Some power tools can be quite expensive. I've even heard of thieves stealing lawnmowers—power and otherwise. They've even put those lawn-mowing vehicles (that you drive around to mow a lawn) inside the bed of their truck. Then, off they went. Of course, if there is a serial number on it, they'll be, more readily, caught. Thieves get more money if something is powered or electrical. Always think—security. In this day and age, thieves will steal anything, even things that are affixed.

You never know when or where a thief will strike. <u>How</u> they strike is getting more and more ingenious. If there are two thieves, they might use cellphones or smartphones. One will be in a neighborhood, at a property. The other will be a drive-around look-out who will contact the on-site thief if there is a need to do so. When the thief is ready to abscond with the items, the one in the truck, van, or even car is notified to come around. Then there's the grocery sack trick. The stolen items are put in one or more grocery bags and carried from one home to another. It looks like all they have are groceries. This can be an inside-the-neighborhood theft. If a cellphone is being used, one thief carrying the assumed groceries can be picked up by an accomplice in a vehicle and then the two can go virtually anywhere, including to a different neighborhood. Thieves can come up with any excuse for being in a neighborhood they are casing or even burglarizing.

A hoodie of any color is sometimes worn if thieves don't want to be recognized (or seen on camera), but you can't assume that someone wearing a hoodie is a thief—be they local or otherwise. It's not hard to hide a stolen item under a hoodie, though. It's not hard to hide a weapon under a hoodie, either. Hoodies keep cold air and wind off the head so people of all ages wear them. They tend to raise suspicion, though—almost instinctively. Thieves don't always strike in the dead of night—this is the point. Anything loose on the lot is vulnerable to theft, and even to malicious mischief, as, breakage, unwanted spray painting, or damage done in other ways. I've heard of inflated balloon-like items, as a Santa or a snowman, being punctured or slashed. I've heard of nativity scenes (during the Christmas season) being stolen or compromised in some way. Some have called those crimes hate crimes. Some of these crimes, in other words, are anti-religious.

On the subject of crime, the following point or points have to be made, and they have to do with working out in the yard. It used to be that whenever I would work out in my yard or on my lot, I'd leave a door unlocked—the one I went in and out of. I'd go all around the home, doing this and that, so the door area was not always seen and I would feel perfectly safe. Then I heard of a crime case where a man snuck in an unlocked door of a home while the woman was working in the yard. He went downstairs and killed her husband, waited for her to come inside, abducted her, put her in a car trunk, took her to his home, kept her captive for some time, and abused her, physically. By way of a miracle, she was able to escape his clutches.

Since I heard that crime case, I have been locking the exit/entry door that I use when I garden, and I keep the keys with me, on my person. I feel safer when I work, needless to note. It's really not all that inconvenient to have to do this and for me, better safe than sorry (and I would be very sorry, indeed, if anything like that were ever to happen to me).

It is unfortunate that we have to take more precautions, in this day and age. Even if there is a security camera, it is still best to keep all doors locked at all times (and check that your windows are locked, too). You can still work out in the yard. You can't give in to fears. You can still enjoy working in the yard. I'd also note, to women, 'don't wear shorts when you garden' but it is not really my place to do that. But, for a number of practical and safety reasons, I think that slacks, jeans, or sweats are best when working out in the yard. If you wear short, you can brush up against what might be sharp or abrasive. You should get in the habit of wearing a cap or hat, too, whenever you garden, because of both direct and indirect sunlight. The area where your hair tends to part will get sunburned the worst if you don't, but your whole head can get sunburned in spots if there is no hat, especially if there is some wind and breezes.

Something new that gardeners can use are what is known as UV sleeves. These are polyester stretch sleeves that fit over arms and, while the pair fits over hands as well as arms, they have no fingers so that fingers are free to do work but hands and arms are protected— from sun, thorns, bristles, mosquitoes, et. al. The UV notation implies they are sun shields. These weigh little and are washable. They usually come in three sizes. You might want to wear them when you do certain landscaping or gardening projects. They call them sleeves but they are long gloves that cover only some of each finger. They're spandex so they should stay on. They may not give you protection against long thorns, though. When you head out to garden or work in the yard, you have to be prepared, relative to clothing. Don't forget a good pair of sunglasses, too, with UV protection. Get a good pair, if you don't have protective sunglasses.

You have to be wearing clothes that are adaptive to what you are doing. An older or less costly pair of shoes are better than a very expensive pair because they are going to get dirty and maybe even muddy. They're going to get beat up. Don't go outside without your hat. I've done that several times and inevitably have to go back inside to get it. I now wear long sweatpants banded at the bottom at the ankles and a partially long-sleeve blouse, especially when it is mosquito season. I wear less-costly canvas athletic shoes because of the ants and general wear and tear on the shoes. Any canvas-type shoes would work. They should not be too heavy, depending on what is being done. If you are shoveling dirt, though, you might want them to be heavier. Most of the time. I prefer a lighter-weight pair of athletic shoes. Never garden in an expensive pair of shoes. Also, you want washable shoes or shoes that can be easily cleaned.

Because of ants, I have learned to not garden in sandals. They are just too open for stinging ants. You never know where ants are going to be on a lot, or how many you will run into when and as you are gardening. One thing about ants—they seem to increase around a generally undisturbed lot, every year, unless you find effective ways to control them. Again, I wear the athletic/sports shoes (aka sneakers) and a pair of socks so I don't get ant bites. When there is a band (at the ankles), on a pair of sweatpants, there is even more protection from ants.

There's been times when I've worn a longer cotton dress and a pair of jellies when I've done work out in the yard but that was before the increasing of ant numbers. I can wear such clothes now if I only have one or two things to do that take little time. What sometimes happens, though, is that I keep finding more things to do than what I had planned. I end out doing more than I'd planned and doing yardwork longer than I'd planned and so I ended out getting stung. Ideally, you initially plan out how long you will be doing yard work and you wear appropriate clothing. You want to be wearing long pants and non-open shoes when you are spraying pesticides and weed killer, too. The less such chemicals get on your skin, the better. You have to be very careful about any spray, especially when there are winds. You do not want to breathe in any fumes and you should probably wear a protective mask.

Wearing T-shirts or similar kinds of tops will be less problematic for certain kinds of yard and landscape tasks. Really loose clothing can catch on something that juts or sticks out and can cause an accident so bewear . . . of what you wear.

When landscaping any lot anywhere and when gardening, you have to wear practical clothes. I used to garden in a casual somewhat faded older dress, and still do, on occasion. The dress is longer and it is blousy and airy. Personally, I don't know how anyone can garden in tight clothes. It is too hard to bend and to move around. I've seen people doing it, but count me out. Some people wear shorts when they garden, but again, count me out for that, too, and for a number of reasons. I am concerned about brushing up against bushes and branches. Sometimes branches stick out and they can scrape your skin. Principally, though, I just don't like my skin to be so exposed when I work in the yard because I don't always know what I'm going to end out doing. Often, I end out doing much more than I was expecting to do and that can include some heavier work. I don't like wearing shorts when I'm doing heavier work (like moving heavier items around). Also, I like my clothes to cover me so I'll be protected from the sun. Loose clothes that 'breathe', like cotton-made ones, work best for me, except for the sweatpants, but they 'breathe' well enough. Being better covered protects you from mosquito and chigger bites, too.

Most people are pretty smart when it comes to what clothes to wear when they are working out in the yard. You have to wear work-appropriate clothes because gardening and yardwork is work. It can be hard work, at times, but there are times when the work is light, too. It is rewarding work, either way. It can also be enjoyable work as long as you pace yourself. I prefer sweatpants, a loose blouse, socks, and canvas shoes when I know I will be doing a lot of work or heavier, more energetic work. Anyone can bend easily when they wear sweatpants. Often, I'll go out to do one project but I end out doing several projects and work longer than I had expected. I also wear a brimmed hat so my head can't get sunburned.

You can end out doing a lot of physical work—twisting, reaching, bending—and so personally, I feel like I have no choice but to work in sweatpants when I know I have a lot to do. They are loose fitting and they have an elastic band at the waist so you can turn and twist and bend and move around. As noted earlier, I prefer that the sweatpants have bands at the lower leg areas, around the ankles, but they don't have to. Because sweatpants are thick, they are very protective. I have sweatpants that I only use when gardening. I usually wear a somewhat loose, airy blouse on top so air can get inside and keep me cooler. The sleeves are longer but they are somewhat loose, too. Mosquitoes and ants can't bite through sweats (and not through blouses and sleeves), and again, legs can't get scraped or scratched.

When it concerns clothes, to each his or her own. As a footnote, I have no idea what the woman who was abducted when she was gardening had been wearing and it wouldn't have mattered, anyway. The man would have committed the crime regardless of what she'd been wearing. Thank God he got caught. When you are gardening, be concerned about any children inside your home, too. Keeping home doors locked while gardening, or doing anything outside, is an important effort to prevent crime. Try not to forget to lock the door as you work outside. If you round a corner of your home, you cannot see someone entering that door so if it is locked, you will feel better about rounding that corner.

Yes, we live in a real world and there is evil out there. We have to take precautions. Still and all, nice yards can be spiritually refreshing to have and to see. They are a positive, and can lift everybody up. Anything nice, can. There is a lot of good in this world. It's good to put our focus on what is more pleasant, but we always have to be thinking ahead, and be careful.

MAINTAIN YOUR INVESTMENT

Most of the items you need for garden and landscape do not cost that much. All in all, they add up, but you don't need to buy everything at the same time. The various projects you will do over a period of time will add up in cost but certain items, you will need at the beginning. You can start off with most all items in hand, and some will do that from the beginning, but you don't have to do everything at one time. You can do projects in sequence, gradually. Most people can afford to do a little at a time, but not everything, at once. Whether you own the lot or don't, any home will go up in value after it is landscaped and the resident(s) can enjoy the area in the meantime.

If the home is a mobile home and it is being sold, the buyer might want to move the mobile home off the lot, in which event, you can simply decline to sell the home to them because their bid will be too low if they're going to do that, since they will probably be discounting the value of the yard (the work put into the lot) in their offer or bid to buy. You can always add the words 'recommend mobile home not be moved' to your selling ad. The right buyer will eventually come along, and he or she will appreciate moving into a mobile home that has an exceptional, easy-to-maintain landscape and yard and they will be willing to pay a decent price for it.

Keep in mind that you can take some of your plantings with you to your next home if you wish. You can take some of your lawn and garden materials with you, too, even special pavers or concrete blocks. You can remove certain items, and then reorganize the lot so it still looks nice. You won't be the first to have done that, if you do. Anything too heavy, though, and you might want to leave it (which would include any concrete blocks). Usually, a seller takes yard decorator items with them.

Mobile homes vary in price and some parks and communities are picky about what mobile homes come in to the complex. They may bar some if they are past a particular year or if they are in bad condition. In some cases, a mobile home community may require some landscaping after it comes in to the park, and they'll set forth specific guidelines. Usually, there's some latitude, though, for individual choices. Usually, watering systems aren't needed on mobile home lots because the lots aren't all that large. Still, some people have them. A few mobile home parks and communities have larger lots than others have, but even those aren't all that large. Some people who retire (not all) don't want large yards to take care of (unless they can pay for a gardener), but they will likely want a yard with plantings on it that they like and enjoy looking at and tending to.

Different regions and areas where vegetation is found tend to have different vegetation but one thing is for sure—there are always many plantings to choose from in every area. The areas or area types (and there are seven main ones) are Desert, Plains and Prairie, Hill, Rain Forest, Forest, Near Coast, Coast, and perhaps a few other more minor ones that are similar but slightly different when compared with at least one of the principle seven areas that were noted. These areas can be in different places in a country and are not always in just one area. Some of the areas or area types overlap with other areas or area types. There is also Swamp, but it can fit in with Rain Forest because there are usually trees in swampy areas. Like Rain Forests, swamps are humid. Various plantings are found around swamp areas too, but landscaping in swamp areas can be problematic.

Plantings will vary in price wherever they are found. Some can be quite costly. Some might be rare or hard to obtain. All plantings will add up and it is a good idea to keep a general accounting of how much money is being put into the plantings that go into the ground so when you go to sell, you will have it on record. Keep a tab on everything, in fact. The tendency is to let too much slide, relative to accounting and when you go to sell.

Each of the seven regions has their own different kinds of vegetation, which is there to sustain the local wildlife, really. Other vegetation types have been brought into a region and will likely also do well. Thus, you will see many kinds of potential plantings that are available at the local home marts and plant nurseries. If you stick with regional vegetation for plantings, generally the plantings survive quite well. Naturally, they will look like they belong to the area and won't look out of place. If you venture out and try outside plantings, realize that the plantings may be more temperamental than the local plantings are. If you decide to have both kinds of plantings, you will have the generic and the non-generic on your lot, which is a common thing to do.

Plantings are like indoor treasures that people select and buy. It's enjoyable to look at indoor treasures and it's enjoyable to look at outdoor treasures (i.e. the plantings). You design and you plant, and you try to accent the plantings. Some people want their landscaping to resemble natural scenery. Some choose that which is unique and different—even that which is unusual. Landscaping can look immaculate and precise, random and spontaneous, or anywhere in-between. Mine is something in between but it's a little more in the immaculate and precise realm, too.

Some people like to set Standards in pots on their lot. A Standard is a shrub with a single trunk and the shrub grows in the form of a small tree. They only get to be two to three feet tall. They are clipped and shaped. These shrubs can stay in their pot or planter for years. They should be fertilized every summer, and only fertilized half that amount during the winter. They're kept outside, generally near and even next to the home, and sometimes they are near the front entrance. They can be kept on a patio, too. Many times, they are brought inside for the winter, after any pests have been sprayed/ killed or somehow removed. Of course, trees are sometimes put in big pots or planters, too. Some trees never get very large so they may be all right for some time, in the large pot or planter. Other trees will need to be transplanted when their roots get to be too big.

A Bonsai Tree is not really a Standard because most people keep their expensive Bonsai Trees inside. Some consider them to be a type of Standard. On occasion, they're put outside, though—it all depends on the home. Bonsai Trees tend to be miniature-sized trees that are shaped, and purposely stunted, to be art pieces. They originated in Japan and more Japanese people tend to have them than anyone else does, but they're now sold in the mass market and are currently enjoyed by many people. Essentially, the trees are purposely dwarfed. Actually, quite a few Bonsais are not all that miniature; all are 'relative' in their size. When you see a Bonsai, you know them. They have a distinct look about them, even if they are the larger ones. Essentially, Bonsais are thwarted in their growth so they take on a much smaller proportion. There is skill involved in the making of these trees and both Art and Science are involved. Only certain types of trees are forced to conform to certain growth patterning. Do Bonsai Trees ever blossom, and can any of the types they use ever bear nuts or fruit? You might want to look into that before you purchase a Bonsai.

I have quite a few potted plants around the lot, but I don't yet have Standards. They're kind of heavy. Some of the pots I use are pretty. Some are plain. They're all different sizes. None are all that big. Sometimes I re-use planters that the plantings first came in at a mart or home center. I find tiny plantlets around the yard that are growing from seeds thrown from already-established plants or that started growing next to a parent plant. I put these tiny plantings in planters and I nurture them until they are larger. Then, I find a place around the yard where I can plant them or I put them in a bigger pot. Sometimes, I sell them. I like to line potted plants along my carport, but I have a section in back for potted plants, too. A few of them are to the other side of the home, under an awning. One good thing about potted plants is that you can always move them around. And I do.

When you re-pot and plant, it may end out taking more time than you first think. It is not an easy job because of all the lifting and bending. You may need to put some plants into larger pots, for example, and keep in mind that handling potting soil can be cumbersome and messy. Depending on how many pots and plants you have to do will determine the amount of time you must put into the project. You have to be very careful to not spill potting soil on landscape rocks, too. Potting soil gets set in between and amongst all the rocks and you cannot get it out and have to remove all the rocks and then remove the spillage. Then you need to replace the rocks.

If you are prone to having potted plants, you'll need to buy good potting soil. Some brands are certainly better than others are. Top brands can be somewhat expensive, some are cheap and maybe too cheap, and then there are those in the middle of the two polarities. You really don't need real expensive potting soil, but some people will prefer it. To each his or her own. Bag sizes vary as to weight so you have to do a per ounce cost analysis, in addition to reading what all is printed on the different bags.

It takes time to initially pot plants, and then to re-pot them. Any plant going into a pot should obviously be smaller in proportion to the pot size. Some plants, once potted, grow fast. As noted earlier, ground dirt should never be used in pots because it isn't porous enough and when the plant is watered, the water won't soak in. If the ground dirt ever does get too saturated, as from a long-enough rain, it takes a long time to dry and the plant will get so waterlogged that it will wilt and die.

Store-bought potting soil has vitamins and minerals in it and they enrich the plant. After a while, the plant uses the vitamins and minerals up, so the potting soil needs to be replaced with new potting soil. The best time to do this is when you re-pot, i.e. when the plant and the roots get too big for the pot. Until a plant gets to be its maximum size, it is a good idea to use inexpensive pots. When the plant is its maximum size, then a nicer and more expensive pot would be in order. Potting soil should be changed every year, but some people change it less often than that. Whenever you re-pot, you should use new potting soil, unless there is little time between the re-potting times because then, the potting soil may still be useable.

Regarding ground dirt, when you dig some out of the ground before placing a plant or tree into the ground, save any leftover dirt and put it in one particular container (for example, a cheap plastic pot that you don't care about all that much). Put it away, from sight, somewhere, if you can, and use it later on to fill up a space in the ground when you have to dig a planting out of the ground to put elsewhere. There may be too much of a hole left there from where the plant had been so that other ground dirt will be needed to fill the hole in better. (You always want to save ground dirt in case you need to use it for something later on.)

Once you remove something from a pot, you may not be able to use the pot and the potting soil that is left in that pot. Some people will throw away previously-used potting soil because they think that the previous plant soaked up the vitamins or minerals in the potting soil. But new plantings will still grow in previously-used potting soil so you can reuse it for a new plant, up to a certain time. You don't want to use previously-used potting soil more than twice, though. Buy a new bag of it and use that. Keep watch over the condition of potting soil in your pots. Potting soil can acquire certain types of micro-organisms, after a time, which are not good for the plant.

Regarding potted plants, and re-potting or transferring potted plants into the ground, keep in mind that potted plants can become root-bound if they're in a pot too long. The roots wind around the other roots and the roots eventually all grow in too tight. You have to take care of root-bound plants right away. Sometimes, you cannot untangle a root-bound plant and sometimes you can. Eventually, a plant, bush, tree, etc. can become too large for a pot. On occasion, a pot will crack or break because of it. Pots have to be deep enough and wide enough for a plant at all times. When you buy a planting anywhere, the planting might already be root-bound. Either they put it in that way or it was in the pot too long and grew that way. Unfortunately, some commercial potted plants will always be root-bound, inside of their pots, but you can't know that they are when you buy them because you can't see the roots. Keep in mind that anything you pot can also become root-bound, so you have to keep general tabs on this. Some plants grow more roots than others do. Some grow roots faster.

Root-bound plants, after they're been planted, may not get good root-hold, under the ground. They may be fine, but the root-hold won't be the best. Some plantings you may not want to plant if they are tightly root-bound, especially if you can't disentangle them. You might want to return them, or exchange them at wherever you bought them.

If you put a significantly root-bound plant into the ground, it may have trouble flourishing, from the start. It could even die because the roots are so wound around and entangled. They could rot, for one thing. Roots shouldn't go under the ground if they are all jammed together. You should try to disentangle some or all of the roots, but be very careful as you do. Sometimes, you can do nothing about entangled roots and you'll hurt the plant if you even try to disentangle them because too many roots will break off. All you can do is either try to plant such a planting and then hope for the best, or return it to the place where you bought it. Look all roots over before you put any planting into the ground. Some, you will need to disentangle or separate, if you are able to. You want them to end out being splayed outwardly, down in the ground.

Sometimes, root-bound plants will survive if you plant them, but, of course, it would have been better to plant a planting that had loose and free roots so the roots could have grown normally over time and so the planting would have ended out being more secure and stable down in the ground. Planting a root-bound tree, for example, can be dangerous because if the roots are unable to go deep down (as the taproot tends to do), and if they are unable to spread out and go down deep enough, as they are supposed to do, then, when a high wind comes about, the planting could be blown over and if it is a heavy tree, that will not be good.

Mainly, you want to dig a hole deep and one that is wide enough when you plant something so you can see that the roots are spread out evenly and symmetrically. You cannot do that when roots are all tangled in together. You always hold a planting up so roots dangle in the hole; then, you fill in some dirt all around the dangling roots, as you are holding up the planting. But, you spread some of the outer roots out a little as you do this. In some ways, it's better to put plantings into the ground when they are smaller (as long as they aren't root-bound in the pot to begin with since plants of any size can get root-bound). The roots of a somewhat smaller planting are likely to have a better chance of going down deeper and being more evenly distributed around the planting. In other words, the planting is apt to end out being well secured. Strange as it may seem, roots seem to be inclined to grow a certain way, barring any obstacles. There seems to be a pattern to root growth.

I was able to utilize much more space than I first thought possible, with my landscaping. In large part, it's because I used so many of my outer edges. I ended out with close to a hundred plantings (not to mention my potted plants—those are separate). I enjoy looking at each area on my lot now—very much. I enjoy my life more, because I'm continually able to enjoy my yard. Some things are worth more than money, quite frankly.

It took me a long time to finally finish my lot to my satisfaction and to where the areas around the lot that I wanted filled in got filled in. It took years, in fact. Keeping to a balanced life, I was nonetheless able to go out and work in the yard, periodically. When I could, I went outside and worked (if you want to call it work because I enjoyed it). I do, of course, always want to have a balanced life so landscaping and gardening will never dominate my life (except maybe at times, if some of the work projects were to add up or accumulate). Still, it's been more of a sideline, or hobby for me. Again, I spaced the work out over the years and that, really, was the best way for me to do it. I especially enjoyed going outside after it rained. I'd pull weeds up and get rid of those ugly and obtrusive eyesores rather quickly. And I'd clean out beds, too, because there would be no dust or insects around after a rain. I'd do whatever needed doing, because I loved being out in the fresh, clean, moist, and crisp air, after a rain. Again, you always want to take time out to inspect your lot. My lot has four check-points—the front, the east side front area, the east side back area, and the west side back area. The west side front area is really more a part of the front. As you inspect your lot, think of each check-point area. You can even number them, in your mind. If, say, number four needs attention, using a number can be easy to remember. My check-point areas are not exactly quadrants because they do not have equal dimensions or the same lay-out.

Frankly, now I can rest on my laurels, except for the routine maintenance that is required every once in a while and throughout every year. I enjoy getting out and doing these physical tasks, and if I added up the number of hours I put in to routine maintenance of my yard and landscaping, they would be few in comparison with the number of hours counted up for other kinds of totally different work I have done or projects I have completed. As previously noted, the yard and lot was a sideline or a hobby, but, over the years, I had done a lot. (There's that pun again.) It's all been worth it—the planning, the money spent, the time, and the physical work. I'd do it all over again if I had to. I would want to do it all over again, but I don't have to because I've already done it. Of course, any new place I would move to would get the royal treatment regarding this kind of work. It seems to be in my blood. I'll go about it a little slower, though, and hire out more, since I am now much older. (You really don't want to hire out, though, unless you absolutely must. I still do lots, and will until I can't.)

There are only a few things I'd do differently, were I to start a new yard in a warm or hot area. I'd put in more Mexican Bird of Paradise plants, fewer Oleanders (but I'd still have some), add some Jasmine vines, add a few other types of bushes that blossomed (like Gardenia bushes do), and I would stay with the varied cacti and succulents and with the Evergreen bushes and trees, especially the Italian Cypress ones and especially the Arborvitae ones. I'd try to find one or two shade trees that would end out being tall enough to actually shade areas around and/or over the home, but no shade tree would be too tall (like some shade trees can come to be). I'd also probably do more overall research, relative to my overall purchase options.

If you are moving into a new home, and the landscaping is incomplete or unacceptable, then I say, meet the challenge, see the vision, and get started, no matter what age you are. Plan it all out. Do one project at a time and keep on doing them. The day will come when you will know you are done and then you will be able to rest on your laurels and coast along.

Again, a lot is a lot is a lot so the principles and ideas found in this book can apply to a house lot, a mobile home lot, or a business lot. If you go into a house, if you go into a mobile home, if you go from a house to a mobile home or from a mobile home to a house, this book will be useful. If you purchase business property, you can also use the book as a reference. Not only can it be a guide to use for your business property, but it can also be a guide to use for a friend or relative's business property. It can be a guide for whenever anyone starts landscaping any lot anywhere. There are times when little can or should be done because you might not be living at a certain place for very long, but sometimes you end out staying at one place longer than you had been expecting so you may as well get started and do what you can towards the landscaping. Maybe just do a little, if you think you'll be somewhere temporarily. Doing something is certainly better that doing nothing. At least try to get a start. But, if a home you are living in is owned by someone else, you probably shouldn't do too much. On occasion, an owner will reduce rent for landscape and garden work that is done by a renter so be sure to save all your receipts. Always check that all out with any landlord first, before you spend money on miscellaneous. Of course, a few small plants don't cost much at all.

Landscaping tasks and yard work projects have to be done in a timely way. When it's time to trim, get rid of pests, water, remove leaves and debris, de-weed, control insects, plant, etc., when it's time to do those things. You don't want to defer these tasks for very long, although some people do and then the lot or yard suffers. You can, and should, get into a routine or schedule, in that certain tasks need to be done at certain times of the year. Tasks and timings, of course, will vary from place to place, and usually there are time-range latitudes.

On your average-sized lot, with a number of fairly easy-to-care-for plantings, you should be outside for a couple of hours or more doing something at least once a month, as a general rule. You should be out there for a half a day or a full day doing something, at least every two or three months. That is, if your yard or lot is one that is more, shall we say, bountiful. Personally, I prefer putting in half and sometimes whole days when I do my yard work, unless it's really hot outside. I often put in more cumulative time than what I have just noted, though, especially at certain times of the year. I'm one of those people who likes to do several things at around the same time just so I can get it all done. If the work is strenuous, though, then go with the work/rest, work/rest scenario. Working a full day, then resting a full day, then working a full day, then resting a full day is a good way to go. Or, just work a half a day, especially if it is real warm outside. Many people will work on their yard and landscaping during the week-ends.

Resting is so important when you are doing strenuous work. You shouldn't overdo it in the first place but when you do physical work past a certain point, you have to, then, rest. Keep in mind that sun exposure can tire out a person when they do physical work. Trimming, sawing off branches, picking up branches, shoveling, raking, lifting or dragging heavy bags or boxes filled with clippings and debris, and walking all over the lot can become physically draining. There are low-maintenance lots that will require even less time and work but they will still require work. No yard or garden is work-free. As an older person now, a low-maintenance yard is the best way for me to go, but that doesn't mean there aren't a lot of plantings all over the lot. Au contraire. All my plantings were put in before I became an older person. Maintenance and occasional replacing of what might die requires effort and I'm able to keep up with it all.

When you plan out a low-maintenance yard, simply stay clear of the more temperamental plantings. As I am in the South-West (but this would work in the South and most parts of the South-East, too), I stay with bushes like Oleanders, Boxwoods, and Gardenia bushes and I like Jasmine vines because of the fragrance but they need some day shade. I plant a variety of cactus and they are in a number of rock enclosures. I have some Evergreen bushes, and two giant Evergreen trees, one being the Arborvitae, the other being a very tall South-Western White Pine tree (that sheds too many needles so next time, I would seek out a needleless tree and probably a podless tree, too, since pods can get thrown all over the place, as well). The Mesquite tree tosses off many pods, for example. These Pines get up to forty to fifty feet tall and twenty to thirty feet wide. I have many Oleanders because they are wonderful windbreakers. Italian Cypress trees are, too, if they are planted side by side. They are a haven for bird's nests if you like birds. I have other plantings, too, but they all thrive in very warm to hot, dry weather. This all includes for my low-maintenance lot.

As part of maintenance, you must do occasional walkabouts to see if too many leaves have been falling and if the more leafy plantings need some watering, or any planting does, for that matter. It is good for the soul to go outside and walk all around the lot to check to see if all is fine. When you go about the lot, you get to see your landscaping handiwork. Again, I personally tend to stay away from flowers or floral groundcover. Flowers take more time for upkeep. The larger bushes bloom and blossom so there is enough of a floral addition to the yard, unless they've been cut down to be a certain height or are considerably trimmed back. You can reduce blossom amount by cutting bushes back and some people want to do that so they don't have to pick the blossoms up when they fall, later on. On Oleanders, there can be so many blossoms that older people will especially tend to trim their bushes back (or have them trimmed back). Not only do the blossoms fall from certain bushes, but the leaves fall, as well, so if there has been ample trimming, there will be less to pick up or remove later on.

If someone is a Senior Citizen, after a point it might be a good idea to hire a gardener to come in on occasion, to do certain jobs. Some seniors are able to hire a year-round gardener. Sometimes only four or five times a year will work. Those who are older can have their projects listed for the gardener to do, so they'll all get done. Some homes require less assistance; some will require more.

With my low-maintenance lot, I can go out quarterly and do general garden maintenance. I can even just go out two times a year but I would really have to spend more time maintaining certain areas of the yard. Still, occasional walkabouts will need to be done during the whole calendar year. I pull weeds year-round, as needed. The more landscaping rocks you have on the lot, the fewer weeds you will get. Some put down landscaping rocks (River Rock, etc.) quite thick so there is not just one layer of them. In the long run, time and money is saved (since time is money) when plenty of landscape rocks are put down. I wait until after a rain every time, to pull any weeds. On occasion, I spray weeds, but I usually get my trusty pillow, plop it down, and pull them out by their roots (after a rain, preferably). It's probably all right for most people to pull up a few weeds while standing up and bending, and I'll do this if there are only a few weeds to pull up, but if there's quite a few weeds, I get down on my knees on my protective pillow and I use the pillow because of the hard edges on the landscape rocks.

When it comes to my 'intermittent' maintenance, I will first do all the trimming, all around the lot. I wait to do the bed cleaning until all the trimming is done, which includes removing dead branches and twigs. If any leaves, dead branches, or twigs fall into the beds, I clean out the beds. If I have evergreen needles in my beds. I am able to roll them up when I remove them. You can also pick up a whole clump of pine needles because they pile up on top of one another. If you have landscape rocks, you may need to pick up leaves, pods, and debris by hand, rather than rake them up. The raking doesn't always go so well because of the small rocks. The hand-picking goes fast if you use a low box, set on the ground, and then dump those collected contents into a bigger box, or a large bag. If you rake up pods and especially leaves, they can break up into bits, plus you will lose a lot of landscape racks when you go to pick it all up. It really does go fast if you pick up everything by hand (and use your knee pillow). You do not want to bend your knee more than at a 90° angle, ever.

As a gardener, the less you have to bend your knees, the better, especially if you are a Senior Citizen. Past a certain age, and you have to be careful about bending and twisting. It's the leaves and the debris that need to be picked up by hand. Leaves break up into pieces and the bits nestle in between all the rocks. Debris is really clutter, and sometimes it is actual trash, like candy wrappers, Styrofoam pieces, paper, plastic, etc. You must also get on your knees when pulling weeds. Again, I get down on my knees rather often, and use a pillow.

Spraying for insects will be up to you. Frankly, I sprayed very little for insects. But you have to spray, if you live in certain areas. Either you must look for them, or call in the insect inspector. They will show you the insects and evidence that insects are there. If they don't, then ask that they do. If you've trimmed around your lot and you see insects, spray after trimming when there are more open areas for the spray to get into. I have a number of ants and I don't even spray for ants, anymore. I just wear canvas shoes and socks so they can't bite me. There are non-toxic products you can use to get rids of insects. Some spraying can cause leaves to end out with spots that are sometimes white. Early detection of insect types is important, so insects can be kept under control.

Anytime there is an infestation of the wrong type of insect, bring out the right kind of spray. Some insects really don't harm certain plantings, and some do not harm them all that much. You will probably want to leave those ones be. Some insects even eat the more culprit insects that do damage, so they should be left alone, if possible. You have to be careful of termites, though; you don't see them because they live under the ground. They'll find wood wherever it is and really go to town with it and ruin any wood they've been chomping on. If you have termites, it's more than a good idea to call in professional people to spray for them and keep the numbers down as much as you can. Routine spraying may even be needed, so it is done according to a schedule.

Termites can harm parts of some plants, but most people spray for termites because they want to protect any wood that was used to construct their home or office building with. I've seen where termites will chew on dried parts of cactus. Sometimes some of the base of a Saguaro, for example, will dry and become brown and termites will go after that part because it has essentially become wood. They come in from under the ground to get to it and they can be difficult to detect. Hardly anybody stops to look for them.

It's a good idea to keep an actual landscape notebook with a calendar as part of it so you become aware of all the tasks you need to do at different times of the year. If you do this, you'll soon realize what some landscape jobs need to be done by certain dates. There will be routine jobs and also random jobs that will need to be done. On occasion, there will be unexpected jobs, and there will also be occasional emergencies to tend to.

There are what can be called patterns of yard or lot care. Depending on where you live will determine these patterns. What plantings you have in your yard or your lot will determine the patterns, too. You might consider recording these patterns, and then plan a year-round maintenance program based on these patterns. Write down what you do and when you do it so that you will have a guide to follow for the next year. You can't always go by what your neighbors or local people are doing because every lot is different. Yours will not be like theirs.

Sometimes you hit a glitch. For example, you may get ground termites, in which event the ground areas (the top of the soil) has to be specially treated. You may get a rash of ants somewhere, too. (I usually just leave the ants alone but some people try to get rid of them.) Another glitch is that you may hit a dry spell, or, an overly rainy time. Though there are patterns of yard and lot care, there are also occasional interruptions, changes, differences, and improvisations, especially in this day and age, and with Global Warming.

Planting can take place in the spring or even the summer. Occasionally it can even be done in autumn. Spring, however, seems to be the more usual time for this. There are generally some rains in July and August, and even September. Leaves can fall any time (amounts will vary), and you'll have to remove leaves whenever you see enough of them collected. If rain has been little, more leaves will drop. With some vegetation, when it gets cold, leaves change color and then drop, but we all know that they will come back in the spring. This trend generally applies to certain trees, but it applies to some kinds of bushes and shrubs, as well. Watering is done much more so during warmer months—sometimes regularly and sometimes not, depending on the plantings. Overall, trimming should be done at least once a year but sometimes more than that; trimming should be done sometime in the spring and sometime in early autumn, but it should especially be done in the spring.

You can create, for yourself and your family a low-maintenance yard or a high-maintenance one, or, you can create one that is somewhere in between. This all hinges on what kind of yard or lot you want to have. Some people want, and plan out, a high-maintenance garden. They may grow fruits and vegetables, or they may grow several kinds of flowers. Some gardens can be low-maintenance ones, but most are not. If you have little available time, then you will want a low-maintenance yard or lot and/or garden.

A low-maintenance yard or lot can still have many plantings. It will need at least some upkeep. Frequency of watering (or infrequency) has great bearing on maintenance. Trimming, pruning, etc. does, as well. Leaf and debris removal, raking, watering, transplanting, etc. ties in, also. So does weed removal, and pest extermination or removal. Some people don't have much trouble with pests, however. A high-maintenance lot doesn't necessarily mean it is better than the one that isn't. It doesn't necessarily mean it is more costly to establish, either.

Yard work should be enjoyed even though it isn't always easy. When endorphins get charged up, this contributes to that good feeling or euphoria. Creativity and accomplishment contribute to a good feeling, too. You are in sole charge of your outlook and attitude about all things, all the time, and this would include yard work and landscaping. Yard work comes easy to most people. Usually, it's not real hard work. At times it can be but overall, it isn't. The key word is pace. Always pace yourself. Never be rushed.

Yard work forces you to exercise, which is good, but never overexert yourself, and if you suspect it is too strenuous for you, hire a gardener, or see a physician to ascertain how much you can actually handle. If heat is a problem, only work in the earlier a.m. hours, or when it is overcast. Heat will tire anyone out but especially older people, or people who are overweight. I know that doing yard work has helped to keep my weight down. It has burned up calories. If you do a lot of yard work, you may not have to go to a gym or go jobbing. When endorphins are activated, this is good for both body and mind.

Once a yard is established and near complete or completed, an ecosystem exists, which makes it interesting. The yard birds eat the insects. Some insects eat other insects—for example, ladybugs eat aphids. The birds need water, and for that reason, people make sure there is water out for the birds. And the birds also need trees and shrubs, for shade and nesting. People put birdseed out for birds and will even put a birdbath out for them so the birds can drink the water and enjoy splashing about. Sometimes these are termed, water stands. They have to periodically be cleaned out, without fail, because they can get dirty very fast. Some will put up hummingbird feeders, with special sweetened water. Some bird lovers will organize their lot just for birds, quite frankly. Everything they do is to help their feathered friends. Some people want a yard for this reason, alone; they may also feed other wildlife. Also, quite a few people want to go with a completely natural-looking landscape. This sometimes relates to their wanting to feed wildlife, but not always. In any event, a natural landscape is sometimes planned by a Landscape Architect.

Children should be involved in yard care, too. They can pick up leaves and debris in beds. They can water plants, and they can rake and bag leaves. They can pull out weeds, too. When I was young, my mother paid us for pulling weeds. If the ground was dry, we'd use an old table knife, push it down to cut the root of the weed down a few inches, and then pull the weed up. Too many parents don't think to involve their children in yard-care and chore-related tasks. This work can be a part of their allowance, if they're given an allowance. Furthermore, children don't generally ask to take on such tasks. With encouragement, they might but quite often, they have to be told what to do—with or without receiving an allowance. Every experience a child has stays with them. Also, some teenagers could be paid to do some yard-care tasks. Teenagers usually like that idea. All teenagers should earn money when they are younger. It's a part of growing up. They may need some guidance, though. For example, they should not just trim a tree unless they are first trained and know what they are doing.

When it comes to your yard or lot, you are the overseer. No one else is. You will have to be the watchman or watchwoman. To a degree, you can train your children to be inclined to be work and chore oriented (but they are not yet mature adults, responsible for a home).

Therefore, like with pet care, final and ultimate responsibility falls on the adult. The adult will have to watch over the yard and lot, and perhaps a garden (if there is one), just like a lifeguard watches over a group of swimmers at a pool or a beach. The adult will have to have the perspective that the yard or lot needs year-round, intermittent care, to look its best and to survive. Prevention is worth an ounce of cure so the adult will have to focus in on that and have forethought. In other words, keeping a yard or lot well landscaped and maintained will be a personal challenge.

Some people have a green thumb, and take to yard and lot tasks like a duck takes to water. <u>Many people grow to like and enjoy landscaping and the yard and lot tasks that go with it</u>. At times, you will have to push yourself, as you establish and maintain the yard and landscape. Sometimes, you will have to <u>make</u> time for these tasks, and anyone can, if they want to bad enough and see the overall value of it all. Nothing gets done by itself. Nothing ever has and nothing ever will. Nothing will come of nothing. It gives a person a good feeling to look around and see tasks around their lot that have been completed.

Establishing a landscaping can contribute to the establishing of a balanced life, so that life can be better enjoyed. Life shouldn't be viewed as drudgery or as something to avoid. Some people already realize this, but some people don't. Some people realize this only in part. Like a plant grows, so do people.

Remember that anything you do for any lot, as long as it is an improvement, it will be an investment. You are either investing, hoping for a financial return, or investing, expecting a return on the improvement of your quality of life. Even the simplest of landscapes can have beauty. Being around beauty, which you yourself have created, can enhance your life. However, it is important to get outside and enjoy the beauty (and the sunshine). Just going outside to drink a favorite beverage can be enjoyable. This is why people barbecue and even eat outside, from time to time. Many people will buy nice outdoor furniture, principally so they can enjoy the outdoors. People usually have a table of some sort, which they put in with the other outdoor furniture.

Sadly, there are uninspired people out there who do the very minimum, if even that. There are people out there who don't care to learn much, and who may also have little drive. There are some who don't make good use of their time. They may not be well organized. They may procrastinate, or prioritize wrong. Some people just get off balance and some live outside the realm of moderation and they live in the realm of excess. The world is what it is. Therefore, there are some who are unable or unwilling to handle doing yard and lot tasks, and, in most cases, they won't even start them up. Of course, you have to be willing to spend a little money. You have to have some motivation. Sadly, too, some people don't have the confidence they need to be gardeners. Such people need a little nudging. There really are people who don't have much extra time and are always really busy, though; also, things come up. There may well be good, and even compassionate reasons why some people lack this or that or do what they do, or don't do what you might want them to do. Where there is a will, there isn't always a way. People just need to examine themselves. Also, if someone doesn't want to garden, for whatever the reason, it really is their business. You can plant seeds to help motivate them, but that's all you can do.

With the coronavirus around (COVID-19), more people wanted to get out and work on their yard and garden, or start up some garden and landscape projects. Because of the quarantine, they wanted to get out of the house but they didn't want to be around people and the yard and garden was isolated from people. People everywhere put more hours into garden and landscape projects and work.

A yard and lot can be thought of as a thing in progress. It can take years to establish an exceptional yard and lot. Most people go the in-progress route, but some will get their landscaping done in one haul and then rarely do another thing to it, except for general maintenance. Some will do quite a lot at first and then do some additional projects along the way. To each his and her own. To each their own regarding many aspects of gardening and landscaping, really, because gardening and landscaping is and always will be individualistically done, and it will always involve a number of choice—initially and along the way. Individuals make their own choices and this is why there are so many different landscapes all over the world. All lots are different. All are unique. A landscaped lot can reveal much about a person, a couple, and, sometimes a whole family. It may not, necessarily, reveal anything about a business, however. Topiary might, though,

When shrubs and bushes are clipped in the shape of something specific, there has been what is known as topiary art. In the main, Topiary started during Roman times. Most plantings selected for Topiary are Evergreens, and they tend to have small leaves or needles. The planting does not have to be a recognized object or Topiary character; it can be any kind of design. The planting can be rounded, as a ball, layered-looking, flattened at the top, and just generally shaped—in a traditional or a modern-looking manner. Art d'objects have been top-hats, cones, boxes, which aren't so hard to do, but there have been dragons and Disney characters and airplanes, et al., which are not so easy to do. Pretty much any animal imaginable can be done. Birds are cool. The clipped and trimmed form has to look like what it is representing and some objects really can't be topiaried. Forms of people have even been done. Usually, Topiary artists are specially hired. The art is rarely seen and is not very common. It has to be maintained because everything will grow out unevenly after a time.

Landscaping a lot can be a hobby and it can be shared with loved ones. It has many benefits. And you get to see some of those benefits every time you're outside or look out the window. If you buy the smaller plantings, or end out getting plantings that are no-cost, landscaping can be very affordable. Some people go rock hunting and bring back rocks for their lot. (You can get some nice rocks at a gem and mineral show, too, but you usually have to pay for them. Some of them may be reasonably priced, for what they are. If they are too costly, you might not want them on the lot, especially in front.) There are places around most towns and cities where you can find the larger edger rocks, but you may have to hunt them down. It's easier to find the smaller landscape layer rocks. There's many ways to cut corners when it comes to spending money for landscaping. Landscaping doesn't have to be expensive. People sell landscape materials by way of shopper ads and the Internet, too. Furthermore, some items can be picked up at garage sales or at second-hand stores. Many landscape materials show little wear and tear and yet they are still 'used' and you can get them for low prices.

As you are going along, consider working on a scrapbook or photo album that features your landscaping labor and projects. Photograph areas before, and then after you complete a project or area. Then, photograph areas after plantings have grown. It will be great to have these remembrances, and it might be helpful to show them to people who are thinking of buying your home, when and if that day rolls around.

Be careful to not jam plantings in so that there are too many and the lot or areas around the lot look or are cluttered. You want to have room to walk around your lot. The day may come when you acquire too many plantings to put into the ground. You'll dig up baby plantings, because they have a way of showing up in random places on your lot, and you won't have any more room to re-plant them and your pots will already have plantings in them. At this point, it's time to start selling your extra plantings, or to start giving them away to friends, relatives, or neighbors.

You can, of course, be giving plantings away all along the way, but only give plantings away to people who strongly indicate they will plant the planting somewhere on their own lot. In other words, they must want the planting. Otherwise, they may just let the planting sit somewhere, get too big for the pot, and die. Of course, eventually, all plantings must die, but plantings shouldn't have to die prematurely. Think in a utilitarianism way. Nothing that grows from the ground is eternal; still, you want your plantings to live as long as possible so you watch over them with at least some tenacity and interest. You tend to the plantings with some consistency, too. The goal is to not lose plantings prematurely and to keep the plantings as healthy as possible all along the way. The goal is to keep the yard and lot looking nice.

When you see well-planned landscaping, yards, and gardens—and some are quite grand—you realize that a great deal of time and money has been put into the endeavors. Botanical gardens, estates, grounds, parks, and the like—some of these are well known for their landscaping and plantings. You can pick up ideas from such places and apply them to what you want to do with your own lot and garden. You can borrow books about gardening from the library or buy such books at bookstores. You can get them online, very easily. There are also gardening shows on television you can watch. This particular book canvasses the overall subject of landscaping, and gives you some essential and specific basics, but you never stop learning if you are an active, practicing gardener. It is not difficult to landscape a lot. From every effort made and project completed, you learn something new, and this, of course, makes your life more interesting.

My book ended out being a <u>lot</u> more work than I first thought it would be. (I kept on adding to it.) Of course, you likely recognized that play on words. Well, a lot can be a lot of work but, again, you usually do it bit by bit and over the course of time. Don't let the idea of landscaping any-sized lot overwhelm you. It's the easiest thing in the world to do as long as you pace yourself and know what you are doing. You will have to spend some money along the way, but everyone has to spend money, and so, you won't be alone there. Do what you can as you can, and don't ever let a landscape and garden go to ruin. Some people do. You get overgrowth, large, full weeds that are helter skelter on the lot, dead plants, leaves all over the place, a fading out of any colors, a fading out and chipping of whatever can fade and chip, insect infestation, and an overall unkempt look. You can be a fast worker, a steady plodder, or both, but you can't be inattentive—not for too, very long.

As noted earlier, there are many reasons why people want their yard areas or lot to look nice. It's similar to wanting your external appearance to look nice. People see it, and they get an impression. The biggest reason, though, is that people want to enjoy their home, which includes their landscape and garden, which is a part of their home and adds to their enjoyment. My thinking is that people should do 'just enough and a little bit more', when it comes to yard work. No one should become a slave to it. Remember, you can always hire some of the work out. I never did, but when a person gets to be in the Senior Citizen range, probably some work should be given over to the more agile and adept. Joints and bones start to change when people get older. Bending and lifting can become problematic. Movement becomes slower. It would be great if no one ever aged past fifty, but if that had been the case, people continued to live and would have crowded one another out years and years ago because they would have all kept on living. We're already bursting at the seams in some areas, as it is. That is one reason why people like to have a landscape and garden. It makes people feel closer to country living with its open spaces and natural landscape, even if their home is in the city. That's one reason why people zealously work on their yard. You go outside, see nature, look at the sky, feel the sun, and breathe in the fresh air. Air is much nicer outside than it is inside.

Having a nice garden helps a person to be closer to nature and to an outdoor kind of life; at least for a time and on one level, urban life gets blocked out. Being in a landscape and garden area, at their home, can bring about a temporary reprieve from work and business. It can bring about 'family time', when there is just the family. It's great to go out in the yard and barbecue, entertain guests, watch the kids play, sit and enjoy a beverage, lay down and sunbathe, or just sit and visit with family members or friends. When outside, the eyes go from spot to spot and the brain takes in whatever is in sight. The outdoors can be an escape from the indoors. It can be 'that other place'.

This is the gist of what rock or stone-edged gardens can look like, but you have to find the rocks somewhere. I use small, medium, and large rocks. This one uses the large rocks. You have to maneuver each rock in place. As separators, note the concrete blocks to the side, topped with pavers. You can see concrete paver blocks packed in, in front, which gives a resident a little more space for whatever they might need it for. You can use these for shed flooring, too. Notice the different colors of the landscape rocks. On one side, they are white, which reflects heat. On the other side, they are gray or gray/brown.

These edged rock gardens can go all over a lot. They give any planting their own place and break up the monotony. They work for any and all plantings, which would include flowers and vegetables.

INDEX

A

abusing the law 16
accuracy iv
acid rain 9
adaptive plants 18, 161
Adirondack chairs 218
aeration 212
aesthetic 51, 203
Africa 58, 86, 94, 133, 161
African 40, 71, 144
African countries 71
Africanized killer bees 130
Africanized Killer Bees 130, 141, 143,
        144, 145
African Violets 40
afternoon sun 50, 55, 204
agave 72, 95, 98, 100, 101, 102, 107
agave Americana 98
Agave americana 98
agaves 70, 72, 93, 95, 100, 101, 102, 106,
        107, 117
agave tequilana 100
agave Tequilana 100
Agave tequilana 100
aggressive 61, 140, 141, 142, 143, 144, 145
agreement 29
Agriculture Department 139
ailments 15
Alabama 148, 214
alligators 147
allotment gardening 5
allotments 3, 5
allowance 255
aloe 17, 72, 95, 101
aluminum ladders 89
ambiance 52, 55, 62, 80, 88, 91, 181
amenities 46, 47

America 5, 58, 71, 92, 94, 101, 130, 139, 144,
        159, 206, 207, 208
American deserts 206, 208
anacondas 148
angle xiii, 24, 31, 36, 69, 87, 172, 192, 230,
        244, 251
animal 67, 130, 141, 143, 215, 258
animal motifs 215
animals 3, 7, 44, 59, 61, 71, 72, 73, 102, 106,
        135, 141, 143, 146, 148, 215, 228
anise 17
ankles 146, 153, 234, 236
annuals 203
anomalies 62
Antarctica 85, 185, 193
ant bites 146, 227, 234
antioxidant 7
anti-venom 147
ants 23, 129, 130, 149, 204, 227, 234, 236,
        251, 253
aphids 166, 254
Apocynaceae Family (dogbane) 194
approaching a hive 59
April 67, 123, 125, 126, 201
aquifers 162
Arab countries 86
Arborvitae 51, 92, 102, 120, 179, 180,
        246, 249
Arctic 193
areoles 65, 66, 93, 97, 99
Argentina 58
Argentine Cardon 57, 58
arid 116
Arizona 9, 55, 58, 60, 80, 108, 145, 167, 181,
        204, 207, 214
ArmorAll® 219
arms 54, 56, 57, 62, 63, 106, 107, 108, 146,
        147, 233

aromatherapy 16
art 15, 26, 27, 40, 92, 128, 201, 203, 213, 214, 240, 258
artificial grass 163
artists 201, 214, 258
Ash trees 131
Asia 61, 71, 94, 185
assemble 78, 143
athletic shoes 234
attack 61, 134, 137, 139, 141, 143, 145, 146
attackers 61, 144
autumn 54, 68, 73, 96, 97, 104, 117, 121, 122, 127, 130, 149, 150, 180, 199, 201, 253
avenues 84
Avocado 197
awning 90, 106, 179, 198, 212, 223, 229, 241
awning posts 223, 229
awnings 1, 89
Azalea 202
azureus 108

B

baby palm 82, 85
baby plantings 73, 95, 107, 113, 259
baby plants 112, 118
back yards 159
bacteria 178
bag xii, 158, 181, 186, 191, 210, 211, 242, 251, 255
bags xii, 182, 183, 188, 210, 231, 241, 248
baking soda 136
balance 150, 257
balanced life 245, 256
ball 32, 106, 108, 109, 162, 258
Ball cacti 108
balls 97
barbecue xi, 153, 189, 256, 262
barbecue area 153
barbecue skewer xi, 189
barbecuing 34, 181
bark 131, 132, 166
Bark Beetles 131
bark strips 166
barley 9
Barrel 108
Barrel cacti 108
Barrels 108, 120
barricade or wall 221

base 51, 52, 57, 72, 80, 81, 82, 84, 86, 87, 88, 106, 122, 172, 173, 174, 175, 189, 222, 252
bases 84, 174
basil 16
battery-driven mowers 158
battery-powered mowers 158
beard 79, 80, 81
beards 80, 88, 91
beauty 11, 13, 201, 202, 214, 256
bed 25, 44, 66, 69, 109, 112, 144, 150, 151, 152, 164, 169, 190, 225, 231, 250
bed areas 150, 164, 169, 190
bed cleaning 250
beds 38, 105, 109, 110, 112, 119, 149, 151, 152, 156, 165, 169, 171, 178, 179, 186, 207, 227, 228, 245, 250, 255
bee 59, 60, 61, 137, 138, 139, 140, 141, 142, 143, 144, 145, 146
beehive 142, 143, 145
beehives 23, 61, 142, 144
beekeeper 142
bees 58, 59, 60, 61, 130, 137, 138, 139, 140, 141, 142, 143, 144, 145, 146, 149
bee tissues 139
beetles 131, 132, 182
bell peppers 8
below-zero 193
below-zero temperatures 193
bending 236, 241, 250, 251
berries 8, 10, 99, 201
beta-carotene 7
beverages 17
biochemical 7
bird 52, 55, 187, 249, 255
birdbath 255
Bird of Paradise 98, 246
birds 50, 52, 55, 56, 59, 62, 146, 188, 249, 254
birdseed 254
Bird's Nest 109
blackberries 8
black-eyed peas 9
black tea 10
Black Widow 228
blade 70, 72, 76, 87, 100, 102, 111, 116, 117, 172
blade joint 87
blades 70, 72, 87, 93, 95, 96, 98, 100, 101, 102, 106, 115, 117, 128, 157

blocks 2, 30, 36, 46, 154, 219, 220, 221, 222, 224, 225, 230, 238
bloom 126, 188, 190, 204, 205, 206, 249
blooming 108, 126, 205
blooms 11, 14, 58, 62, 67, 109, 126, 137, 188, 201, 203, 205
blossom 122, 126, 194, 195, 197, 240, 249
blossoms 16, 18, 58, 67, 99, 100, 106, 125, 126, 127, 129, 132, 144, 169, 181, 182, 185, 189, 190, 194, 195, 196, 197, 201, 202, 203, 206, 249
blower 186, 191
blowers 191
blue 12, 52, 100
Blue Agave 98, 100
Blueberry bushes 202
board 1, 26, 90, 97, 154, 216, 230
bombycina 110
Bonsai Tree 63, 240
book iv
books 20, 91, 96, 132, 135, 260
border 50, 54, 100, 160, 194, 213
Botanical gardens 260
Bougainvillea 206
boundary dividers 220
boxes xii, 182, 183, 212, 248, 258
Boxwood 185, 200
Boxwoods 248
bracts 206
brain cells 7
branch 50, 70, 72, 99, 100, 101, 102, 108, 122, 128, 138, 188, 189, 192
branch cactus 108
branches 50, 51, 54, 57, 70, 72, 87, 89, 93, 95, 99, 100, 101, 102, 104, 106, 108, 122, 124, 125, 126, 128, 132, 144, 181, 182, 187, 188, 191, 192, 193, 198, 235, 248, 250
Brazil 58
breakage 77, 124, 186, 232
breezes 40, 80, 94, 111, 233
breezy 20
bricks 2, 25, 69, 109, 150, 151, 219, 230
brimmed hat 236
Bristle Brush 110
British Columbia 61
broccoli 7
broom 90, 125, 129, 184, 187
brown 21, 38, 79, 81, 121, 122, 123, 128, 153, 154, 166, 176, 184, 209, 226, 252

browning 53, 127, 166
Brown Recluse 228
bug 82, 132, 133, 135, 136, 166, 251, 261
bug control 132
bug poison 136
bugs 6, 46, 82, 83, 85, 129, 130, 132, 133, 135, 136, 166, 177, 245, 251
bug spray 133, 135, 166
bug types 251
building owners 41
building structures 59
bulbous roots 115
bulbs 20, 203
bump 59, 72, 141
bumped 141, 142
bump the intruder 59
buried 32, 33, 75, 198
burrowed holes 148
bush 99, 112, 121, 122, 125, 161, 185, 188, 189, 190, 200, 202, 204, 243, 246
bushes 4, 8, 11, 19, 25, 28, 38, 92, 105, 118, 120, 121, 123, 125, 126, 166, 181, 184, 185, 188, 189, 191, 192, 194, 199, 200, 201, 202, 203, 204, 224, 230, 235, 246, 248, 249, 253, 258
business 1, 35, 59, 91, 132, 139, 163, 181, 247, 257, 258, 262
businesses 82, 83, 86, 139, 167, 196, 216, 221, 222
business property 1, 247
butterflies 137
buzz 137, 138

C

cable xiii, 33
cables xiii, 32, 36
cable tv lines 33
cable TV lines 33
cacti 28, 40, 57, 58, 62, 63, 64, 65, 66, 67, 69, 70, 73, 82, 92, 93, 94, 95, 96, 97, 98, 99, 100, 101, 103, 105, 106, 107, 108, 109, 110, 111, 112, 119, 120, 152, 184, 202, 229, 246
cacti dividing 97
cactus xi, xii, 11, 54, 57, 58, 62, 63, 64, 66, 67, 69, 70, 76, 77, 79, 92, 94, 99, 101, 103, 107, 108, 109, 110, 111, 115, 118, 119, 152, 182, 183, 192, 228, 249, 252
cactus flowers 109

cactus fruit 58, 67
Cactus Wren 55
Cajun Art 214
Calcium 210
calendar 39, 250, 252
California 9, 40, 52, 54, 80, 86, 145, 160, 197, 204, 206, 214
California fan palm 80
Camellia 202
cameras 216, 218
camping 44
camptotricha 109
Canada 47, 61
cancer 7, 67
candida 109
candy 58, 182, 251
Candytuft 204
candy wrappers 182, 251
cannabis 17
canopies 6, 9
canvas-like fabric 229
cap xii, 115, 233
cap or hat xii, 233
caraway 17
cardboard boxes xii, 182, 183
Cardon 57, 58
Caribbean 71
Carnegiea gigantea 54
carnivorous 136
Carolinas 148
carotene 7
carotenoids 7
Carpenter Bees 137, 138, 143
carport 30, 156, 203, 212, 215, 219, 220, 223, 241
Carson 135
Carson, Rachel 135
car wax 219
Case Study ii
cassava 9
castor bean 17
Cathedral Plant 98, 100
cats 52, 71, 88, 102, 105, 146, 228, 229
CBD 15, 16
Cedar 131
Cedar trees 131
cellphones 231
cells 7, 8, 63, 103
Celsius 95, 97, 193
Central America 58, 71, 94, 101

Central and South America 71, 94
Century Plant 98, 100
Century Plants 98, 100
ceramic 26, 212, 214, 215
ceramic figures 214
ceramic planters 213
ceramics 213
ceremonies 34
Cereus 101, 108
Cereus peruvianus 101
chairs 97, 217, 218
chambers 61, 137, 144
chamomile 17
check-points 245
chemical insecticides 139, 140
chemicals 139, 177, 211, 234
Cherry 197
chervil 17
chia 9
chickpeas 9
chigger 235
Chikungunya 71
children 2, 47, 59, 60, 102, 148, 236, 255
China 61, 71
Chinese fan palm 83
chipped rocks 156
Chlordane 133
Chlorosis 121
choices 158, 196, 238, 258
cholesterol 7
Cholla cactus 64, 79
Christmas 28, 35, 199, 201, 216, 232
Christmas lights 28
Christmas lights and displays 28
Chrysanthemums 13, 204
cider vinegar 134
cinchona 17
cinnamon 16
city workers 31, 33
clean out beds 149, 186, 227, 245
climate 47, 71, 83, 120, 122, 132, 156, 159, 160, 202, 206
climates 12, 48, 51, 58, 102, 116, 120, 122, 136, 165, 185, 195, 199, 200, 204
climber plantings 197
clip 64, 72, 115, 193, 200
clipper xi
clippers xi, 21, 78, 192
clipping 72, 108, 158, 176
clippings 158, 182, 183, 248

clothes 35, 146, 218, 233, 234, 235, 236
clothing 102, 140, 143, 233, 234, 235
clove 17
clump 97, 250
clumps 110, 168, 178, 186, 228, 229
clutter 27, 251
cluttered 259
coast 61, 86, 157, 246
Coast 238
coastal areas 8, 40, 82, 158
cobblestones 153
cockroach 133
coconut palms 83
Coconut Palms 83
codeine 17
cold 23, 37, 54, 61, 67, 68, 69, 73, 82, 90,
    96, 102, 103, 104, 105, 117, 122, 137,
    144, 149, 171, 180, 184, 193, 200, 207,
    232, 253
colder months 68, 105, 146
collagen production 8
color 10, 25, 26, 31, 37, 54, 95, 98, 99, 100,
    103, 121, 128, 132, 137, 144, 153, 154,
    157, 169, 195, 203, 205, 212, 214, 218,
    219, 220, 221, 223, 225, 231, 253
colored 31, 98, 139, 153, 156, 167, 169, 186,
    194, 214, 221
colored-glass items 214
colored rock 169
colorful 83, 99, 101, 206, 212, 213, 214,
    219, 225
colors 14, 153, 156, 157, 212, 214, 218, 219,
    220, 221, 225, 261
columnar 57, 66, 93, 108, 109
columnar cactus 108
commercial 4, 6, 134, 135, 136, 168,
    209, 243
commercial compost 209
commercial insecticide 135
commercial pesticides 6
commercial remedy 136
commercial spray 168
common names 110
communal 3, 5
communal gardening 3, 5
communities 40, 45, 47, 238
community gardening 5
compare notes 3
compost xii, 113, 209, 210, 211
compressa 109

computers 207
concrete xiii, 2, 34, 36, 153, 154, 156, 219,
    220, 221, 222, 224, 225, 230, 238
concrete block 2, 36, 154, 220, 221, 222,
    224, 225, 230, 238
concrete blocks 2, 36, 154, 220, 221, 222,
    224, 225, 230, 238, 263
concrete floor xiii, 36
concrete path 154, 225
concrete stain 219, 220, 221, 222, 224, 225
coneflower 17
cones 199, 258
confidence 257
conifer 196, 199
conserve water 158, 227
constrictor 147
content vii
continents 85, 185
control 59, 83, 132, 158, 173, 234, 247, 251
cooking 15, 17, 45
cord 31, 32, 33
cord or wire 32
cords 31, 32, 33
cords or pipes 31
core 100, 101
coriander 16
coronavirus 71, 162, 257
cosmetic 51
cotton 234, 235
country 4, 67, 89, 133, 137, 141, 147, 159, 184,
    198, 238, 261
Country Diary of an Edwardian Lady 201
cover rocks 155
COVID-19 71, 257
cowpea 9
coyote 215
crabapples 197
Crabapple trees 197
create 3, 30, 41, 42, 46, 55, 69, 105, 119, 151,
    154, 162, 168, 185, 253
crest 62, 63
Crested Saguaro 62, 63
Crested Saguaro Society 62
crickets 133
crime 5, 232, 236
Crime and Rehabilitation ii
crime case 232
criss-crossing pattern 222, 224
crops 8, 9, 62, 133, 139
crowns 84

Cubans 214
cucaracha 133
cucumbers 7, 209
culprit bugs 252
cultivating 5
cumin 16
curbside pickup 183
cushions 218, 219
customs 40, 213
cutting 73, 79, 86, 88, 125, 126, 158, 167, 172, 204, 249
cyads 91
Cypress 52, 53, 102, 120, 152, 166, 179, 198, 200, 246, 249
Cypress tree 52, 53, 102, 120, 152, 166, 198, 249
Cypress trees 52, 53, 102, 152, 249

D

dahlia 17
damage 7, 8, 35, 36, 50, 63, 96, 132, 136, 167, 180, 198, 232, 252
damaged cells 63
damaged plantings 104
dandelion 17
dangling roots 244
database for Global Warming 162
Date Palm 83
Date Palms 83
DDT 135
dead 38, 79, 80, 81, 86, 116, 122, 127, 128, 129, 133, 136, 139, 163, 168, 173, 176, 182, 183, 184, 185, 186, 187, 188, 189, 190, 191, 192, 193, 200, 232, 250, 261
dead bees 139
dead leaves 122, 127, 129, 184, 187, 189, 190, 193
dead plants 261
dead wood 191, 192, 200
deadwood 191, 192, 193, 200
death 59, 96, 113, 127, 135, 141, 149, 177, 178
debris xi, xii, 77, 110, 129, 181, 182, 183, 186, 187, 188, 191, 220, 227, 247, 248, 250, 251, 254, 255
deciduous 94, 102, 121, 127, 180, 199
deck xiv, 1, 35, 89, 116, 180, 190, 212, 217
deco item 213, 215
deco items 213, 215
decoration 88, 222

decorations 2, 28, 35
decorative 190, 202, 217
definition 25
de-fronded 81, 91
de-fronding 91
delicate 101, 203
delivery 221
Dendrologists 54
Dengue fever 71
de-root 88
desalination 159, 160, 163
descaling 82
desert 12, 47, 51, 57, 77, 79, 82, 89, 91, 93, 94, 97, 98, 103, 104, 116, 120, 122, 123, 136, 159, 160, 167, 178, 184, 193, 202, 203, 204, 205, 206, 207, 208, 209, 228, 230
desert areas 47, 51, 91, 93, 94, 104, 116, 120, 122, 123, 159, 178, 184, 202, 203, 204, 205, 206, 207, 208, 228, 230
desert palm tree 57
Desert Palm Tree 57
desert plants 77, 184
desert vegetation 94
design 24, 112, 150, 212, 224, 239, 258
details iv
diameter 80, 200
die 18, 52, 71, 74, 76, 81, 94, 95, 97, 100, 103, 113, 117, 122, 127, 128, 129, 130, 131, 134, 145, 149, 157, 163, 165, 168, 172, 175, 176, 177, 188, 191, 193, 195, 197, 203, 204, 205, 212, 242, 243, 248, 260
dig 31, 32, 33, 69, 70, 74, 75, 76, 85, 112, 115, 129, 153, 154, 155, 159, 165, 167, 168, 175, 192, 209, 210, 216, 242, 244, 259
digging 7, 31, 33, 70, 74, 146, 167
dill 16
dimension 25, 43, 200
dimensions xiii, 6, 43, 200, 221, 245
dirt xi, xii, 31, 32, 33, 37, 68, 70, 74, 75, 76, 77, 87, 88, 89, 107, 111, 112, 113, 146, 151, 153, 155, 165, 168, 170, 171, 172, 187, 198, 209, 210, 211, 234, 241, 242, 244
dirt clumps 168
diseases 67, 71
disentangle 243
dish detergent 136, 177
dish soap 134
disorders 15
divider 194, 202, 221
dividers 194, 220, 222, 224, 225, 229

diving board 26
dog 31, 102, 105
dogs 71, 88, 106
Dongbei 61
doors 15, 60, 233, 236
doors locked 233, 236
double lock 35
doublewide 3, 6, 44
doublewides 43
douse 119, 207
drainage 7, 30, 113, 128
dried leaves 38, 182, 184, 191
drip 4, 53, 54, 104, 116, 122, 123, 128, 160,
    163, 165
drip-method systems 160
drip systems 163
driveway 156
drooping 53, 116, 123, 127
dropped leaves 124, 127, 188, 191, 195
drought 8, 9, 121, 160
drought-resistant 8, 9
dry 9, 15, 25, 51, 53, 54, 58, 80, 93, 94,
    100, 104, 105, 111, 117, 121, 122, 123,
    124, 128, 138, 142, 154, 157, 159, 161,
    163, 172, 176, 180, 182, 187, 190, 199,
    203, 204, 212, 214, 219, 242, 249, 252,
    253, 255
dry leaves 187
dry-out 123, 124
dryout 123
dunes 206, 208
Dura-planters® 212
dust 129, 131, 157, 187, 194, 202, 223,
    229, 245
dustpan 125, 129, 187
dwarfed 240
dwarfism 62
Dwarf Palm 83
dying 53, 121, 127, 139, 143, 165, 177

E

Earth 68
earth tones 213
Easter Lily cactus 108
Easy Flowering 109
eaves 60, 85, 122, 123, 124, 137, 138, 182,
    185, 186, 253, 255
Echeveria 101
Echinocactus 108

Echinocereus 66
Echinocereus engelmannii 66
Echinocereus stramineus 66
Echinopsis 108
Echinopsis subdenudata 108
eclectic garden 94
ecosystem 254
edge 38, 51, 70, 109, 150, 151, 152, 156, 169,
    179, 190, 200, 222
edger xi, 66, 151, 187, 259
edger rocks 66, 151, 187, 259
edges 52, 96, 100, 105, 106, 119, 156, 157,
    179, 190, 245, 250
edging 102, 150, 151, 152, 167, 225
Edith Holden 201
eggs 61, 71, 133, 134
elastic 236
electric 158
electric mowers 158
elevation 103
ellagic acid 8
emergencies 252
emergency 60, 147
emergency care 60
emissions 161, 163
empty boxes 183
encephalitis 71
encroach 154
endorphins 34, 254
Engelman prickly pear 64
England 3, 5
English vii
enhancement 27
enigmas 62
enjoy 1, 11, 30, 34, 36, 41, 46, 58, 107, 117,
    190, 195, 201, 203, 233, 237, 238, 245,
    246, 255, 256, 261, 262
enjoyment 261
entangled roots 243
Entomological Science 136
EPA 6
errors iv
Espostoa lanata 108
established 6, 37, 48, 52, 53, 65, 68, 69, 74,
    115, 118, 151, 152, 159, 169, 193, 205,
    240, 254
estates 260
Eulychnia saint-piena 108
Euonymus 200
Europe 6, 143

European 5, 144
evaporation 160, 162
evaporative cooler 90
evergreen 51, 102, 127, 129, 185, 200, 202
Evergreen 51, 99, 102, 120, 123, 127, 129,
        178, 180, 185, 199, 200, 202, 246, 249
Evergreen nettles 129
evergreens 94, 199, 202
Evergreens 52, 94, 131, 178, 180, 184, 196,
        199, 200, 202, 258
exaggerated interruptions 27
exercise 171, 189, 195, 254
exotic 83, 86, 93
exotic palms 86
experience 17, 30, 255
expert 198
experts 33, 34, 138, 140
exterminate 60, 132
extermination 60, 254
exterminator 141, 146
eyes vii, 32, 34, 60, 71, 120, 148, 156, 262
eyesore 27, 176

F

fade 94, 128, 204, 214, 219, 261
fading 123, 261
Fahrenheit 95, 97, 193
fall 51, 73, 75, 86, 87, 122, 195, 253
family 5, 12, 17, 23, 29, 110, 133, 200, 253,
        258, 262
Family 110, 194
family time 262
fan palms 80
fan parts 80
fans 84
farm animals 143, 146
feathered friends 255
fecal clumps 228, 229
Federal Government 60, 142
feet 55, 57, 80, 83, 84, 106, 107, 108, 112,
        125, 126, 146, 156, 180, 189, 194, 200,
        202, 223, 224, 226, 239, 249
fence 7, 32, 45, 106, 146, 148, 171, 198, 215,
        216, 225, 230
fencing 7, 151, 194, 221, 223, 224, 225, 229
fern 80, 84, 99
fern-like 80, 84, 99
fern-like leaves 84
ferns 99

Ferocactus 108
fertilize 57
fertilized 208, 240
fertilizer 57, 208, 210
fibrous roots 77
Fig Beetle 132
Figi 83
figs 132
Fiji 83, 88
fines 17, 57
fire 81, 129, 131, 191, 226
Fire ants 130
fire fodder 131
fire hazard 81, 129, 191
Firethorn 99, 200
fish 34, 148
flat box 38, 129, 183
flat grade 30
flat rocks 25
flavors 17
flax 9
flooding 49, 59, 198
floor xiii, xiv, 36, 41, 153, 225
flooring 36, 153, 154, 219
floors 35, 220
floral 137, 138, 142, 205, 249
florals 97
Florida 40, 80, 82, 86, 142, 147, 148, 149, 160,
        167, 204, 213
flower 10, 13, 14, 93, 101, 108, 109, 120, 123,
        201, 203, 204, 206
flower appreciation 201
flowerettes 203
flowers 2, 4, 9, 10, 11, 12, 13, 14, 15, 18, 19,
        21, 28, 40, 62, 67, 68, 92, 97, 101, 105,
        109, 123, 134, 138, 141, 164, 166, 181,
        201, 202, 203, 204, 205, 206, 207, 214,
        249, 253, 263
Flowers 10, 11, 12, 13, 15, 19, 21, 36, 203, 249
folds 94
foliage 40, 52, 166, 199, 205
Folk Medicine 17
foods 7, 16, 17, 67
footpath 153, 154
foreign plantings 4
Forest 101, 131, 215, 238
forest animals 215
forethought 28, 130, 222, 256
fossil fuels 161, 163
foundation 1, 36

four seasons 68, 201
foxglove 17
fragrance of blossoms 197
fragrances 13, 16, 197
fragrant 194
frame 25, 229
framing 26, 154, 229
free plantings 112, 118, 151
freeze 63, 96, 103, 122, 230
freezes 102, 103
freezing 184
fresh air 19, 34, 261
fresh air and sunshine 19, 34
fronds 79, 80, 81, 82, 83, 84, 85, 86, 87
frond trimmer 81
front entrance 240
frost xii, 58, 67, 103, 116, 136, 230
froze 184
fruit 2, 4, 5, 7, 8, 10, 11, 20, 22, 26, 28, 37, 57,
    58, 67, 83, 117, 132, 134, 197, 209, 240
fruit-bearing trees 197
fruit flies 134
fruit or nut trees 4
fruits 5, 9, 253
full shade 95, 204, 214
full sun 69, 97, 98, 101, 195, 204, 207, 212
functional 202
fungus 121, 136
furniture 26, 57, 218, 219, 257

G

gallons of water 9
Gambel Quail 215
Gap Theory ii
garage 30, 35, 156, 158, 198, 219, 259
garage sales 259
garbage xii, 47, 70, 173, 182, 183
garbage can lid xii, 70
garbage pick-up 47, 183
garden xi, 2, 3, 4, 5, 6, 8, 9, 10, 11, 14, 16, 17,
    19, 20, 22, 23, 24, 25, 29, 35, 63, 85, 94,
    112, 113, 117, 119, 130, 132, 133, 136,
    140, 142, 143, 147, 149, 150, 151, 152,
    161, 170, 173, 182, 183, 205, 211, 227,
    229, 232, 233, 234, 235, 237, 238, 247,
    248, 250, 253, 256, 257, 260, 261, 262
garden areas 2, 6, 151, 229
garden center 140, 161
garden centers 161

garden clippings 182, 183
gardener 74, 76, 78, 88, 146, 186, 238, 250,
    251, 254, 260
gardeners 3, 73, 102, 130, 141, 146, 188,
    233, 257
garden gloves 227
Gardenia 202, 246, 248
Gardenia bush 246, 248
gardening ix, xi, xii, xiii, 2, 3, 5, 9, 10, 11, 18,
    19, 24, 29, 32, 35, 38, 39, 41, 42, 49, 58,
    63, 70, 73, 74, 77, 78, 102, 105, 111, 126,
    129, 130, 143, 147, 149, 150, 160, 182,
    187, 195, 210, 211, 226, 228, 229, 233,
    234, 235, 236, 245, 258, 260
gardening bag xii
gardening club 73
gardening gloves 78, 228
gardening items xiii
gardening shows 3, 260
gardening supplies 35, 182
gardening tools xiv, 32, 35, 78, 111
garden raiders 10
garden specimens 85
garden tools 35
garlic 16, 135
gas lines 31
gasoline 158
gate lock 218
gatherings 13, 34
gators 147, 148, 149
gem and mineral show 259
gem/mineral show 259
generic 4, 102, 160, 202, 239
Genus 110
Georgia 148, 214
germinating 177
Giant Hornets 60, 61, 130, 137, 142, 144
Global Warming vii, 8, 12, 53, 58, 100, 120,
    124, 130, 131, 159, 162, 197, 253
Global Warming Causes 163
Global Warming Causes and Solutions 163
gloves xii, 78, 227, 228, 233
gnats 130, 134
gnomes 215
Golden Barrel 108, 120
Golden Barrels 108, 120
gophers 67
grade 30, 154
grading 31, 49, 208
grafted 62

grafting 92
granules 113, 132, 211
grapes 5, 133
grass xi, 25, 38, 156, 157, 158, 159, 163, 165, 167, 168, 177, 181, 182, 227
grass clippings 158
grasshoppers 133
grass killer 159
grass lawns 167
grass squares 25
gravel 25, 156, 222
green 7, 9, 10, 29, 52, 53, 64, 81, 91, 96, 98, 100, 101, 104, 105, 108, 115, 121, 122, 123, 128, 129, 130, 154, 166, 167, 184, 185, 198, 199, 200, 205, 226, 227, 256
greenery 29, 123, 124, 126
Green Giant 180
green gram 9
greenhouse xiii, xiv, 26, 161, 163
greenhouse gases 161, 163
green tea 10
green thumb 29, 105, 128, 130, 198, 256
green vegetables 7
ground xiii, 4, 5, 6, 7, 8, 12, 15, 18, 19, 25, 26, 28, 30, 31, 33, 36, 37, 38, 51, 53, 57, 60, 61, 67, 68, 69, 70, 72, 75, 76, 77, 81, 85, 87, 88, 89, 92, 104, 105, 107, 112, 113, 115, 116, 117, 118, 121, 122, 123, 124, 125, 129, 132, 138, 142, 146, 150, 151, 153, 154, 156, 158, 159, 164, 165, 166, 168, 171, 172, 173, 174, 175, 176, 177, 181, 187, 189, 198, 200, 205, 206, 207, 209, 210, 211, 212, 216, 217, 218, 221, 224, 226, 227, 239, 242, 243, 244, 251, 252, 253, 255, 259, 260
groundcover 4, 205, 206, 249
ground dirt 68, 113, 241, 242
ground hollows 138
groundnut 9
ground plant 115
growing season 5, 37, 39, 58, 139
grubs 131
Gulf of Mexico 160

H

hahniana 109
hail 102
handling cactus xii
hand painted 213

hand saw 72, 79, 90
hand spade 33, 112
hand tools xii, 21, 35, 231
hanging baskets 93
hanging plant 115
Hardiness Zone Map 82
hard work 25, 29, 112, 235, 254
harm 67, 68, 76, 97, 133, 150, 251, 252
harmful 18, 135, 184
harmony 150
harvest 58, 100
harvesting 5
hat ix, xii, xiii, xiv, 3, 6, 7, 8, 10, 15, 16, 17, 22, 28, 29, 34, 36, 38, 41, 47, 51, 52, 53, 54, 55, 57, 58, 61, 62, 64, 65, 66, 67, 70, 75, 77, 79, 80, 81, 82, 83, 84, 86, 88, 93, 94, 95, 98, 99, 100, 102, 103, 105, 106, 108, 109, 110, 111, 115, 117, 118, 119, 125, 126, 131, 132, 133, 134, 135, 136, 137, 138, 140, 143, 145, 151, 154, 158, 159, 160, 161, 167, 168, 170, 171, 172, 176, 177, 178, 179, 181, 184, 187, 188, 189, 190, 197, 198, 200, 202, 204, 206, 209, 211, 212, 213, 218, 220, 221, 226, 229, 231, 233, 236, 239, 240, 242, 244, 245, 246, 247, 249, 251, 252, 261
hate crimes 232
Hawaii ix, 82, 83
health 7, 16, 37, 53, 65, 95
health value 16
heartworms 71
heat 12, 69, 91, 94, 96, 123, 162, 202, 203, 214, 230, 254
heat wilt 202
heavy equipment 30
heavy items 215, 216
hedge 66, 180, 185, 194, 201
Hedgehog cactus 66
hedges 40, 92, 194, 200, 220
height 25, 63, 76, 81, 83, 84, 86, 92, 94, 108, 125, 126, 188, 193, 194, 196, 200, 221, 222, 223, 249
hendriksonianus donsilanatus 108
herbalist 17, 18
herbs 16
Hesperaloe parviflora 98
high-maintenance 253, 254
high winds 36, 51, 180
Hill 238
hillside 166

hire 2, 24, 29, 30, 78, 83, 132, 134, 158, 196, 246, 250, 254, 261
hired gardeners 188
hire out 29, 30, 83, 132, 158, 196, 246
Hispanic 213
Hispanic Art 214
hissing 147
hitches 45
hive 59, 60, 61, 62, 137, 138, 139, 141, 142, 143, 144, 145
hives 59, 137, 138, 139, 142, 143, 144, 146
hobby 38, 245, 246, 258
Holden 201
hole 51, 55, 56, 59, 60, 61, 70, 71, 75, 76, 100, 112, 113, 133, 142, 198, 209, 224, 242, 244
holes 55, 56, 59, 62, 113, 131, 148, 209, 221, 224, 226
holidays 216
Holly 200
Holly berries 201
Holly bushes 201
home xiii, 1, 2, 6, 10, 18, 24, 26, 28, 29, 30, 31, 34, 35, 36, 39, 40, 41, 42, 44, 45, 46, 47, 48, 50, 51, 55, 56, 64, 81, 89, 92, 123, 127, 133, 134, 137, 138, 145, 150, 155, 164, 167, 169, 177, 178, 181, 183, 187, 189, 190, 196, 197, 198, 199, 200, 202, 205, 207, 209, 212, 213, 215, 216, 217, 220, 222, 226, 227, 231, 232, 236, 237, 238, 239, 240, 246, 247, 252, 255, 259, 261, 262
home center 240
homeowners 143, 227
homes xiv, 2, 26, 31, 33, 35, 36, 40, 41, 43, 44, 45, 46, 47, 48, 55, 133, 138, 144, 146, 157, 158, 163, 164, 167, 204, 216, 217, 222, 229, 238, 250
honey 58, 137, 140, 141, 144, 145
Honey Bee 60, 61, 137, 138, 139, 140, 141, 142, 143, 144, 145
Honey Bees 60, 61, 137, 138, 139, 140, 141, 142, 143, 144, 145
hooks 92, 100, 102
hook-ups 45
hope vii
hoppers 6, 85
hornets 90, 137, 149
horses 59

hose xii, 4, 9, 25, 37, 54, 72, 75, 77, 96, 105, 112, 122, 124, 164, 167, 175, 176, 226, 228
hose off 77
hot tub 26
house 1, 6, 30, 41, 45, 46, 63, 89, 133, 155, 164, 217, 241, 247, 257
house lots 1, 155
houses 3, 26, 35, 41, 47, 48, 137
humid 8, 40, 238
humidity 40, 157, 167, 180
hummingbird feeders 255
hybrids 94, 97, 101
hyssop 17

I

ice 58, 102, 160, 171
illegal 17, 143
improvement 256
improvisation ix, 253
increased temperature 58, 162, 163
indents 165
India 71
Indian art 214
Indian Paint Brush 17
indirect lighting 95
indirect sunlight 233
Indonesia 71
indoor 18, 93, 106, 116, 163, 178, 226, 239
indoor plants 18, 93, 116
indoors 18, 115, 262
infestation 131, 189, 251, 261
inflorescence 87
insect 23, 82, 83, 132, 133, 134, 135, 136, 139, 142, 149, 166, 189, 227, 251, 261
insect bites 227
insecticide 135
insecticides 134, 135, 139, 140, 143
insects 6, 46, 61, 82, 83, 85, 120, 129, 130, 132, 133, 134, 135, 136, 137, 140, 146, 149, 151, 166, 177, 180, 182, 190, 208, 228, 245, 247, 251, 254
insect spray 133, 134, 135, 166
intercropping 9
interim pots 119
Internet 3, 8, 20, 91, 110, 140, 185, 199, 219, 259
interruptions 25, 27, 253
invade 133

invaders 142
invasive species 3, 17, 198
investment 42, 120, 237, 256
Iron 121, 169
irregularity vii
irrigation 4, 53, 159, 160, 207, 208
irrigation system 160, 207
Italian Cypress 52, 102, 120, 152, 166, 179, 198, 246, 249
Italian Cyprus 52, 120, 152

J

Jalisco 100
Jalisco, Mexico 100
jam 75, 108, 197, 259
Japan 240
Japanese 185, 240
Japanese Boxwood 185
Japanese people 240
jar 220
Jasmine 197, 246, 249
Jasmine vines 197, 246, 249
joint project 29
Joshua tree 51
juniper 17, 200
Juniper 17, 200
Juniper bush 200

K

kale 7
keys 232
kill 58, 59, 61, 85, 96, 131, 133, 134, 135, 136, 139, 142, 143, 145, 149, 166, 168, 176, 177
kill bugs 133
Killer Bees 59, 60, 61, 130, 137, 138, 140, 141, 142, 143, 144, 145, 146
Killer Hornets 142
Kingdom 6, 110
kitchen knife 171, 172
knife xi, 87, 88, 111, 147, 171, 172, 255

L

ladder xii, 22, 81, 86, 89, 90
ladybugs 254
landlord 247
landscape ix, xiii, 1, 2, 19, 25, 28, 29, 30, 33, 34, 38, 39, 47, 78, 83, 92, 94, 95, 112, 113, 128, 130, 133, 142, 150, 155, 156, 158, 163, 164, 167, 168, 170, 172, 176, 177, 178, 181, 186, 187, 188, 190, 196, 205, 206, 213, 214, 215, 217, 220, 221, 226, 227, 231, 235, 237, 241, 247, 250, 252, 255, 256, 257, 259, 260, 261, 262
Landscape Architect 2, 255
landscape-material business 221
landscape-material businesses 221
landscape planning 33
landscape rocks 25, 38, 156, 158, 163, 168, 172, 176, 177, 178, 186, 187, 188, 190, 226, 227, 241, 250, 263
landscapes 256, 258
landscaping ix, x, xi, xii, xiii, 1, 2, 10, 11, 12, 18, 25, 28, 29, 30, 33, 34, 35, 41, 42, 45, 46, 47, 48, 49, 52, 58, 60, 78, 79, 89, 105, 114, 117, 118, 119, 124, 126, 130, 136, 146, 150, 152, 160, 161, 164, 171, 182, 183, 187, 195, 202, 205, 212, 213, 226, 233, 235, 238, 239, 245, 246, 247, 248, 249, 250, 254, 256, 258, 259, 260
Las Vegas 167
lattice 69, 179, 223, 224, 229, 230
lattice panel 69, 223, 229, 230
lava rock 169
law 16, 100
lawn 6, 27, 63, 158, 163, 167, 183, 217, 218, 231, 237
lawn and garden 6, 183, 238
lawn furniture 218
lawnmower 158
lawnmower repairs 158
lawnmowers 231
lawn mowing 158
lawnmowing vehicles 231
lawn ornaments 217
lawns 9, 158, 167, 175
layer rock 155, 156, 158, 159, 167, 168, 169, 179, 181, 187, 188, 259
layer rocks 155, 156, 159, 167, 168, 169, 179, 181, 187, 188, 259
leaf 127, 133, 175, 176, 200
leaf chompers 133
leafy 92, 97, 99, 104, 124, 130, 175, 176, 184, 193, 194, 202, 249
leafy vegetation 130, 202
leaks 163, 164
leaves xi, 7, 10, 18, 38, 51, 53, 56, 65, 84, 85, 93, 97, 104, 121, 122, 123, 124, 125, 126,

127, 128, 129, 132, 166, 169, 173, 174,
176, 179, 180, 181, 182, 183, 184, 185,
186, 187, 188, 189, 190, 191, 192, 193,
195, 196, 199, 201, 227, 229, 247, 249,
250, 251, 253, 255, 258, 261
Lebanon 131
legal 16, 17
leprechauns 215
Lethal Yellowing 85
leveling 31, 49, 146
levelling 49, 146
lifting 112, 241, 248, 261
lights 2, 28
Lilac trees 197
line 33, 60, 68, 84, 165, 200, 224, 241
linear footpath 153
linear ladder 89
lines 21, 31, 33, 133, 225
liquor industry 100
littoralis 108
Livistona chinensis 83
loamy 82
lock xiii, xiv, 35, 215, 216, 218, 236
locks xiii, xiv, 216
Locustidae 133
locusts 133
logs 151, 224, 225
long-sleeved 146, 227
loosened dirt 87, 172
lot ix, xi, xiii, 1, 2, 4, 5, 6, 19, 24, 25, 28, 29,
30, 31, 33, 34, 35, 39, 41, 42, 44, 45, 46,
47, 48, 50, 52, 53, 54, 57, 62, 63, 64,
65, 66, 68, 69, 70, 71, 74, 78, 79, 84, 85,
86, 88, 89, 91, 93, 94, 95, 98, 99, 100,
101, 104, 105, 106, 108, 109, 110, 111,
112, 113, 115, 118, 119, 120, 121, 123,
127, 137, 143, 148, 150, 152, 153, 154,
155, 156, 157, 158, 159, 164, 165, 167,
168, 169, 170, 171, 174, 176, 177, 178,
179, 181, 182, 183, 184, 186, 187, 188,
190, 191, 193, 194, 196, 197, 201, 202,
203, 205, 207, 208, 212, 214, 215, 217,
218, 219, 220, 222, 223, 225, 226, 227,
228, 232, 234, 235, 236, 237, 238, 239,
240, 245, 246, 247, 248, 249, 250, 251,
252, 253, 254, 255, 256, 257, 258, 259,
260, 261
lot area 3, 35
lots 1, 29, 34, 41, 44, 83, 86, 118, 130, 155,
168, 194, 204, 238

Louisiana 148, 214
lounge furniture 218
lounging 34, 218
lower-edged box 182
lower ring 72
low maintenance 119, 171, 190, 203
low-maintenance 28, 99, 248, 250, 253, 254
lumber 57, 142
Luteum Plenum 194
LY 85
lycopene 7

M

Magnesium 210
maintaining 5, 34, 121, 250
maintenance 5, 28, 30, 35, 83, 99, 119,
128, 167, 171, 177, 179, 183, 190, 191,
196, 203, 245, 248, 249, 250, 252, 253,
254, 258
maintenance men 191
maintenance workers 191
malaria 71
malicious mischief 217, 232
Mammillaria 93, 109, 110
Mammillaria compressa 109
management 155
managers 48
Manchuria 61
mandrake 17
manufactured housing 45
map 31, 33
March 67, 144
Marginata 98
Marginata variety 98
Marigolds 13, 204
marijuana 15, 16, 17
marijuana plant 15, 16
mash 100
material vii
materials xiii, 30, 109, 222, 229, 231,
238, 259
maximum-growth size 28
May 67, 123
M. bombycina 110
M. camptotricha 109
M. candida 109
medicinal 15, 16
medicinal herbs 16
medicinal marijuana 15

medicine 16
Mediterranean 185
Mediterranean climate 160
Mediterranean fan palm 83
melon 134
Mental Assessment ii
Mescal 100
Mesquite tree 181, 249
metal cables xiii
metal locks 216
metal siding 46, 56
metal stakes xiii, 36
Mexican 57, 58, 80, 98, 214, 215, 246
Mexican Art 214
Mexican Bird of Paradise 98, 246
Mexican Cardon 57, 58
Mexican fan palm 80
Mexico 54, 55, 57, 60, 71, 73, 80, 82, 94, 100,
    101, 145, 160, 213, 214
M. germnispina 109
M. hahniana 109
micro-organisms 243
Middle-East 86, 94
mildew 136
milk 136
millet 9
minerals 208, 210, 242
minimal 25
Minnesota 47
mint 10, 17
Mississippi 148, 214
mites 130, 180
M. nejapensis 109
mobile home 1, 2, 6, 29, 30, 31, 34, 36, 40,
    41, 42, 43, 44, 45, 46, 47, 48, 55, 56,
    64, 89, 137, 146, 150, 155, 164, 167, 181,
    183, 190, 216, 217, 222, 227, 237, 238,
    246, 247
mobile home community 47, 238
mobile home park 3, 29, 40, 41, 44, 45, 46,
    47, 48, 155, 183, 216, 238
mobile home parks 3, 40, 41, 44, 45, 47, 48,
    183, 216, 238
mobile homes 2, 35, 37, 41, 43, 44, 45, 46,
    47, 48, 55, 146, 217, 222, 238
moisture 40, 53, 77, 82, 105, 119, 228
money 2, 11, 23, 25, 28, 29, 47, 48, 65, 73,
    86, 88, 89, 96, 113, 144, 152, 160, 164,
    167, 195, 208, 222, 225, 231, 239, 245,
    246, 247, 250, 255, 257, 259, 260, 261

Montana 47
morning sun 55
morphine 17
mortar 225
mosquito 70, 71, 146, 234, 235
mosquito bites 146
mosquitoes 70, 71, 130, 146, 227, 233
mother plant 107, 112
motivation 257
mound 88
movement 50, 64, 146, 182
mow 231
M. parkinsonni 110
M. pilcayensis 110
M. pringlei 109
M. rhodantha 109
M. spinosissimi 109
mulch xii, 6, 19, 198, 210
multiple watering 116
Mums 204
mutation 62
myrrh 17
M. zeilmanniana 109

N

National Park areas 131
native 67, 93, 94, 101, 161, 205, 208, 209
Native American motif 215
native plantings 208, 209
native plants 93, 161, 208, 209
Natural 155, 211
natural beauty 202
natural ingredients 177
natural products 135
natural remedies 135
natural remedy 136
natural rocks 109, 150, 152, 221
natural scenery 239
natural weed spray 177
natural wood 223
nature 15, 18, 67, 135, 151, 153, 201, 212,
    221, 261, 262
nature artists 201
Near Coast 238
needles 51, 52, 53, 65, 72, 82, 89, 92, 97,
    102, 110, 131, 169, 171, 178, 179, 180,
    181, 182, 183, 188, 196, 199, 200, 249,
    250, 258
neighborhood 27, 231

Neighborhood Watch 218
neighbors 46, 65, 71, 73, 91, 141, 150, 181,
    190, 197, 198, 208, 218, 221, 252, 259
nejapensis 109
Neonics 6
Nerium 185, 194
Nerium Luteum Plenum 194
Nerium Oleander 194
nest 52, 55, 56, 61, 86, 90, 137, 139, 142, 144,
    182, 188, 251
nesting 55, 56, 59, 254
nesting birds 56
nests 23, 55, 56, 61, 90, 137, 138, 143, 144,
    182, 187, 249
nettles 127, 129, 186, 188, 227
Nevada 9, 145, 167
New Mexico 55, 145
night blooming 108
Nitrogen 121, 210
Nitrogen deficiency 121
non-generic 239
northern areas 39, 47, 48, 92, 102, 158, 167,
    197, 208
notebook 252
notes 3, 31, 33, 39, 120, 211
nourishment 118
nuisance 59, 134, 149, 156, 209
nurseries 8, 140, 152, 239
nursery 52
nutmeg 16
nut pick xi, 77, 110
nut-producing trees 197
nutrients 113, 208, 209, 210
nuts 4, 22, 240
nut tree 4
nut tree growers 4

O

offshoot 70, 72, 87, 107, 115
offshoot planting 115
offshoots 107, 115, 124, 126, 192
oils 16
Oklahoma 148
old age 121, 197
Old Lady 109
Oleanders 36, 102, 120, 121, 122, 125,
    126, 127, 181, 182, 184, 185, 187, 189,
    190, 191, 192, 193, 194, 195, 206, 246,
    248, 249

Opuntia engelmannii 64, 66
Orange 40, 197
orange peelings 209
Order 110
oregano 16
Oreocereus 108
organic 4, 5, 6, 7, 23, 28, 209, 211
Organic 5, 211
organic fertilizers 211
organic food 5
organic gardening 5
organization viii
Organ Pipe Cactus 108
origin 101
ornament 214
ornaments ix, 213, 214, 217
oscillator xii, 175, 226
outdoor furniture 26, 218, 219, 257
outer edges 106, 190, 245
outside plantings 239
overgrowth 177, 261
overhead system 4
overhead watering systems 160
owl 55
owls 56
Owl's Eyes 110
owners 3, 31, 33, 41, 47, 48, 227
oxidate 10
oxidation 10
oxidized 10

P

Pachycereus 57
Pachycereus pringlei 57
pachycladus 108
Pacifica Red 204
padlock 216
pads 64, 65, 93
palms 80, 81, 82, 83, 84, 85, 86, 91
palm tree 57, 79, 80, 81, 82, 83, 84, 85, 86,
    87, 88, 89, 90, 91, 92, 202
palm tree beards 88, 91
palm trees 57, 79, 80, 81, 82, 83, 84, 85, 86,
    87, 88, 90, 91, 202
palm tree seedling 87, 88
Palo Verde tree 181
panels xiv, 69, 223, 224, 229, 230
panicles 87
papery material 61

parent plant 107, 112, 115, 241
park 29, 46, 47, 48, 155
parkinsonni 110
park management 155
parks 3, 40, 41, 44, 45, 47, 48, 183, 216, 238, 260
parsley 16
partial-shade 214
particles 209
parties 34
partitions 150, 152
pastels 220
path 36, 105, 153, 154, 190, 225
pathway 36
patio xiv, 1, 2, 35, 84, 153, 198, 203, 212, 216, 217, 240
patios 217
pattern ix, 62, 63, 128, 179, 184, 223, 229, 244
patterns 68, 100, 128, 252, 253
paver 35, 154, 221, 263
pavers 2, 30, 153, 154, 163, 190, 214, 219, 238
paver toppers 221
Peach 194, 197
Peach Oleander 194
pebbles 155, 156, 163, 168, 169, 227
pebble stones 222
peck 55, 56, 62
peckers 55
peeling 213, 215
peelings 209
peels 209
pegs and board framing 154
pellets 132
perennials 203, 205
permanent 26, 45, 104, 151, 220, 225
permit 33, 57
permits 31, 85, 100
Peruvian Old Man 108
pest 59, 134, 135, 254
pesticide 5, 6
pesticides 5, 6, 139, 141, 145, 234
pest removal 135
pest-rid business 59
pests 23, 56, 134, 135, 136, 140, 149, 240, 247, 254
pet 51, 139, 148, 149, 185, 256
petals 70, 93, 97, 101, 203, 204

pets 18, 59, 61, 102, 106, 139, 147, 148, 181, 185, 198
petticoats 80
pharmaceutical companies 17
Philosocereus 108
Philosocereus azureus 108
Philosocereus pachycladus 108
Phoenix 167
Phosphorous 210
Photinia 200
photo 259
photograph 259
Picoides Arizonae 55
picture 31, 109
pictures 52, 96, 109, 110, 212
pigeon pea 9
pilcayensis 110
pillow xii, 38, 173, 176, 181, 182, 183, 186, 187, 227, 250, 251
Pincushion 110
pine 89, 92, 131, 169, 171, 178, 179, 181, 182, 199, 228, 250
pine cleaner 228
pine cones 199
pinecones 199
pine needles 89, 92, 131, 169, 171, 178, 179, 180, 181, 182, 250
Pines 249
pine trees 199
Pine trees 131, 179, 180, 199
Pink Crown 109
Pink Sundrops 204
pipe 31, 32, 33
pipes 31, 32, 33
pitchfork xi, 64
Plains and Prairie 238
planning ix, 2, 8, 19, 25, 30, 33, 48, 79, 154, 161, 171, 189, 196, 209, 246
plant boxes 212
plant covers xii, 103
plant deterioration 127
plant enclosures 34
planter 77, 78, 111, 239
planters xii, 35, 77, 152, 212, 240, 241
plant-exchanging program 73
Plant Hardiness Zone Map 82
planting 5, 6, 10, 20, 22, 23, 25, 28, 37, 50, 51, 53, 54, 58, 62, 65, 66, 67, 68, 69, 71, 72, 73, 74, 75, 76, 77, 78, 79, 95, 99, 102, 103, 106, 107, 108, 111, 112, 113, 115,

116, 119, 121, 123, 127, 128, 136, 152, 154, 156, 160, 164, 165, 179, 182, 184, 185, 186, 189, 190, 192, 193, 194, 198, 200, 203, 204, 209, 210, 211, 220, 230, 242, 243, 244, 249, 258, 260

plantings 2, 28, 29, 36, 48, 52, 53, 54, 64, 65, 67, 70, 71, 73, 74, 77, 78, 82, 85, 88, 92, 94, 97, 99, 103, 104, 106, 109, 110, 111, 112, 115, 116, 117, 118, 119, 120, 122, 128, 129, 150, 151, 154, 165, 169, 184, 192, 193, 194, 195, 202, 203, 206, 207, 214, 215, 229, 230, 237, 238, 239, 241, 242, 244, 245, 247, 252, 253, 254, 259, 260, 263

plantlets 14, 20, 240

plant nurseries 152, 239

plant parts 15

plant resurrection 128

plants 2, 28, 29, 54, 64, 70, 73, 75, 77, 92, 93, 95, 100, 102, 103, 104, 107, 108, 112, 116, 117, 118, 128, 130, 151, 152, 166, 167, 184, 191, 193, 199, 217, 229, 240, 241, 243, 244, 255

plant types 73, 94

plastic xii, xiv, 32, 45, 46, 56, 69, 70, 97, 119, 182, 212, 214, 216, 218, 219, 223, 224, 226, 229, 230, 242, 251

plastic chairs 97, 218

plastic-made items 214

plastic pots xiv, 119, 219

plastic resin/polymer 46

plastics 214

pleating 94

pleats 63, 94

plot 3, 4, 5, 6, 7, 10

plots 3, 5, 6, 8

plumbing 31, 142, 163

pods 97, 169, 179, 181, 188, 196, 249, 250

points viii, ix, 19, 36, 47, 72, 93, 102, 121, 232, 245

poison 136, 166

poisonous 147

poisons 177

pollination 62

polyurethane paint 215

pond 34

pool 2, 26, 84, 163, 256

pools 26, 47, 71, 90, 163

poolside 218

poolside furniture 218

poppy 17

porch 116

porches 217

porous 71, 241

Potassium 210

potatoes 5, 7, 21, 209

potholders xii, 111

pots ix, xii, xiii, xiv, 18, 112, 113, 118, 119, 202, 203, 205, 211, 212, 213, 214, 215, 219, 240, 241, 242, 243, 259

potted plants xiii, 2, 71, 112, 211, 212, 213, 215, 216, 240, 241, 243, 245

pottery shops 212

potting soil xii, 71, 77, 78, 108, 112, 113, 118, 209, 211, 241, 242

powder 131, 132

power saw 72, 79, 90

power tools xii, xiii, 216, 231

practical 19, 51, 80, 161, 167, 170, 190, 200, 233, 235

precautions 232, 236

preserves 58

previously-used potting soil 113, 242

Prickly Pear 64, 65, 66, 79

pringlei 57, 109

prioritize 257

privacy 46, 62, 147, 180, 194, 202, 223, 229

private garden 4, 8

process ix, 10, 29, 65, 70, 92, 154, 159

project 23, 29, 39, 42, 78, 86, 219, 220, 224, 231, 235, 241, 246, 259, 260

projects ix, xiii, 10, 39, 42, 67, 78, 89, 92, 113, 129, 130, 149, 171, 182, 186, 189, 199, 210, 220, 221, 222, 226, 229, 230, 231, 233, 236, 237, 245, 246, 247, 250, 257, 258, 259

propagated 107

property 1, 11, 26, 33, 45, 50, 53, 59, 71, 100, 143, 202, 225, 231, 247

property division 225

prune 14, 124, 204

pruner xi, 64, 192

pruning 68, 180, 192, 196, 204, 254

Puerto Ricans 214

pull weeds 149, 174, 176, 186, 245, 250

purple 12, 96, 103, 104

purple areas 103

push yourself 256

Pyracantha 99, 200

python 148, 149

Q

quarantine 257
queen 144, 145
queen bee 144, 145
quills xi, 64, 65, 66, 67, 77, 82, 92, 93, 97, 99, 110, 111, 227
quinine 17

R

Rachel Carson 135
railroad ties 151
rain 9, 21, 37, 40, 53, 58, 61, 68, 70, 78, 87, 88, 93, 96, 99, 100, 104, 109, 120, 121, 122, 127, 128, 129, 138, 149, 156, 161, 164, 171, 173, 174, 175, 176, 189, 197, 199, 215, 229, 242, 245, 250, 253
rainfall 37, 82, 105, 119, 124, 161, 162, 164, 177, 193, 207
Rain Forest 101, 238
Rain Forests 238
rain patterns 100, 128
rains 9, 36, 55, 58, 65, 68, 87, 94, 99, 104, 111, 120, 122, 123, 128, 129, 132, 149, 164, 165, 167, 174, 193, 197, 253
rainwater 9, 99, 104, 120, 166
raised foundation 36
rake xi, 21, 38, 78, 127, 129, 167, 178, 179, 180, 182, 186, 187, 188, 191, 196, 250, 255
raked 124, 158, 171, 191, 197
raking 38, 179, 187, 196, 197, 248, 250, 254
ranching motif 215
range 58, 59, 82, 94, 108, 131, 132, 205, 247, 261
range of temperature 58
raspberries 8
rating 29, 41
rationing 159
rattlesnakes 147
rattling 147
real property 26, 45
receipts 247
recess 165
recessed 75, 151, 164, 165, 207
recipes 17, 58, 136
recreational marijuana 16
recreational vehicle 44
Red-Headed Irishman 109

red pepper 135
Red Tip Yucca 98
redwood 151, 212, 219, 220, 223, 225
redwood furniture 219
redwood logs 151
redwood stain 212, 220, 223, 225
regional vegetation 239
relish 58, 214
remote-control 158
remove iv
renter 247
renters 41, 48
repetition vii, 118
re-plant 67, 73, 74, 76, 78, 85, 111, 112, 186, 205, 259
replant 67, 76, 78, 85, 112, 259
re-planting 73, 74, 78, 111, 112, 186
re-pot 18, 77, 112, 241, 242, 243
re-potting 18, 112, 242, 243
reproduction 134
reptiles 148
resistant to frost 58
rest 19, 24, 61, 66, 102, 106, 136, 172, 206, 218, 245, 246, 248
retirees 40
retirement 40
retirement communities 40
rewarding 235
re-wet 75
rhodantha 109
Rhododendron 202
rhubarb 17
ribbed 108
ribbing 94, 97
ring 13, 40, 72, 165, 230, 251
River Rock 156, 250
River Rocks 156
road 156
Roadrunner 215
roads 156, 190
rock ix, 88, 105, 110, 112, 118, 124, 150, 151, 152, 156, 158, 159, 167, 168, 169, 187, 190, 214, 249, 259
rock company 158, 167
rock-edged bed 151, 152, 168, 169, 190
rock-edged beds 151, 152, 168, 169
rock garden 150, 151, 214
rock gardens 150, 151, 214
rock hunting 259
rock pile 88

rocks xi, 2, 25, 38, 66, 77, 88, 109, 110, 112, 115, 118, 124, 150, 151, 152, 153, 155, 156, 158, 159, 163, 167, 168, 169, 172, 176, 177, 178, 179, 181, 186, 187, 188, 190, 219, 221, 225, 226, 227, 241, 250, 251, 259, 263

rodents 46

roll layers 178

rolls of grass 25, 157

root 7, 31, 51, 53, 57, 68, 74, 77, 84, 87, 88, 107, 111, 136, 172, 175, 198, 243, 244, 255

root-bound 243, 244

root bumps 51

root distribution 198

root growth 7, 68, 84, 244

roothold 243

roots xi, 9, 21, 28, 32, 37, 46, 51, 52, 53, 54, 57, 67, 68, 74, 75, 76, 77, 78, 84, 85, 87, 88, 94, 99, 104, 107, 111, 112, 113, 115, 118, 119, 121, 123, 132, 149, 160, 165, 168, 169, 171, 172, 173, 174, 175, 176, 177, 198, 205, 211, 212, 227, 240, 242, 243, 244, 250

roots of trees 51

root system 68, 74, 77

rose bushes 192, 204

roses 204

rosettes 97, 101

round indents 165

roundular 65, 93, 144

routine 128, 245, 247, 252

routine maintenance 128, 245

Royal Palms 86

rubber gloves 227, 228

rules vii

runoff 30, 54, 166

rural 31, 137, 141, 143, 147

RV 44, 45

RV parks 45

S

Saguaro 52, 54, 55, 56, 57, 58, 60, 62, 63, 94, 106, 120, 252

Saguaro National Park 58, 60

Sahara Desert 193

salads 58

salt 135, 177

sand 206, 207, 209

sandals 156, 228, 234

sandalwood 17

sand dunes 206

sandy 82

sap 185

Satellite 109

saturate 76, 85

saw xi, 72, 73, 78, 79, 81, 87, 89, 90, 106, 226

saw blade 73

scale 2, 25, 67, 81, 82, 130, 141, 159

scale insects 130

scales 81, 82

scalloped bricks 109

science 34, 49, 71

scientific 30, 208

scissors xi, 72, 73, 97, 102, 175

scorpions 89, 228

scrapbook 259

screen 70, 180, 229

season 5, 17, 37, 39, 86, 97, 111, 129, 139, 160, 232, 234

seasonal 71, 195, 231

seasons 5, 40, 52, 58, 68, 97, 122, 123, 201

security 47, 84, 180, 189, 202, 216, 218, 224, 225, 231, 232

security cameras 216, 218

security gate 216

security purposes 224

seed bank 9

seedling 87, 88

seedlings 87, 88, 111, 118

seeds 7, 8, 14, 20, 83, 87, 111, 118, 152, 155, 157, 173, 174, 177, 181, 188, 196, 202, 203, 205, 240, 257

Senior Citizen 250, 251, 261

senna 17

seven regions 239

seven region types 238

Sevin 131

sewer 32, 133, 163

sewer lines 32, 133

sewer water 163

Sex Trends in Society ii

shade 7, 9, 50, 51, 68, 69, 73, 79, 90, 95, 97, 116, 149, 178, 179, 180, 190, 195, 199, 203, 204, 207, 212, 214, 218, 219, 223, 229, 246, 249, 254

shadescreen 229

shade tree 50, 178, 180, 200, 212, 246

shade trees 50, 178, 180, 200, 246

shade umbrella 218
shading 6, 7, 69, 181, 229
shady 68, 207, 226, 227
shape 6, 12, 41, 44, 50, 72, 73, 92, 99, 108,
    109, 125, 128, 150, 153, 180, 185, 188,
    192, 193, 194, 200, 214, 258
shaping 38, 126, 188, 193, 196
shed xiii, 2, 26, 35, 36, 38, 51, 52, 89, 90, 138,
    148, 153, 178, 179, 190, 198, 216, 219,
    225, 230, 231
shed floor 36, 225
sheds xiii, 35, 90, 249
shock 37, 60, 76, 103
shoot 72, 98, 106, 115, 118, 124, 188, 226
shoots 88, 98, 100, 117, 122, 125, 126, 188,
    189, 192, 193, 226
shortage 159
shortages 159
shorts 19, 233, 235
shovel xi, 21, 32, 33, 70, 76, 78, 168, 186
shovel blade 76
shoveling xii, 234, 248
shrub 99, 184, 185, 202, 239
shrubs ix, 4, 11, 28, 40, 51, 92, 123, 164, 191,
    200, 202, 220, 239, 253, 254, 258
side branches 125, 192
siding 46, 55, 56, 187
Silent Spring 135
Silken Pincushion 110
silkscreen 229
Silver Arrows 109
singlewide 3, 6, 64
singlewides 43
Sister Agnes 194
skin 7, 8, 67, 102, 103, 135, 185, 234, 235
skin cells 8
skin irritation 185
skirting 1, 45, 89
slab 36
sleeves 233, 236
slow drip 53, 54, 104, 122, 123, 165
slow-drip 4, 53, 116
slow-drip method 4
slow dripping 54
small lot xi, xiii, 3, 6, 7, 10, 26, 27, 29, 47, 156
small rocks xi, 110, 118, 155, 156, 169, 170,
    191, 251
smartphones 231
snake bite 147
snakeproof 148

snakes 89, 147, 148
sneakers 218, 234
snow 39, 58, 63, 102, 105, 136, 150, 160, 171,
    184, 230
snow and freeze 63
snow-and-ice winters 105
Snowball 109
snowfall 184
socks 130, 146, 227, 234, 235, 251
soil xii, 5, 6, 7, 9, 19, 20, 21, 25, 30, 37, 49, 71,
    75, 77, 78, 82, 85, 108, 111, 112, 113,
    118, 121, 131, 159, 168, 169, 173, 174,
    177, 188, 198, 205, 206, 207, 208, 209,
    210, 211, 227, 241, 242, 253
soil composition 6, 7, 37, 206
soil condition 30, 205
soil sample 49, 206, 207, 208
soil samples 49, 208
solo plantings 152
Sonoran Desert 54
sorghum 9
South ix, 10, 11, 40, 52, 54, 55, 61, 62, 71, 73,
    86, 92, 94, 95, 100, 101, 130, 132, 144,
    147, 157, 160, 161, 178, 181, 185, 209,
    215, 248
South America 71, 94, 101, 130, 144, 161
South American plants 161
South-East 40, 71, 94, 147, 185, 248
South-East Asia 71, 94, 185
southern ix, 38, 39, 40, 48, 68, 71, 82, 92, 94,
    96, 102, 104, 105, 115, 116, 123, 130,
    133, 139, 145, 147, 148, 159, 161, 171,
    184, 185, 190, 202, 206, 209, 213, 215
southern areas 38, 48, 68, 83, 92, 96, 102,
    104, 116, 123, 130, 133, 148, 161, 190,
    202, 206, 209, 215
South Korea 61
South Seas 86
South-West ix, 10, 11, 52, 54, 55, 62, 73, 92,
    95, 100, 132, 160, 161, 178, 209, 215, 249
South-Western 11, 62, 73, 92, 178, 209,
    215, 249
South-Western White Pine 92, 178, 249
soybeans 9
spade xi, 21, 33, 76, 77, 111, 112, 175
Spartan look 29
specialist 83, 131, 132, 136, 143, 166
Species 110
spice 15, 17
spices 9, 15, 16, 17, 19, 136

spider 180, 187, 228
Spider plant 115, 116, 117
Spider plants 115, 116, 117
spiders 227
spider web areas 228
spill 70, 241
spillage 241
spinach 5, 7
spines 58, 65, 66, 70, 92, 93, 99
spray 4, 14, 23, 31, 90, 131, 133, 134, 135,
     136, 140, 163, 166, 167, 168, 173, 174,
     175, 176, 177, 180, 215, 226, 228, 232,
     234, 250, 251, 252
spray bottle 136, 175
sprayed 6, 85, 115, 133, 134, 135, 139,
     240, 251
spraying 4, 132, 134, 135, 168, 174, 176, 177,
     215, 234, 251, 252
spray paint 232
spray system 4, 163
spray weeds 176, 177, 250
spread 51, 61, 75, 117, 149, 159, 167, 169, 201,
     210, 222, 244
spreading 61, 142, 154
spring 37, 56, 68, 73, 90, 96, 99, 104, 121,
     123, 125, 128, 130, 146, 147, 150, 158,
     188, 199, 201, 203, 204, 207, 253
Spring 104, 123, 135, 253
spring showers 123
sprout 23, 108, 111, 118, 152, 155
sprouts 108, 111, 112, 115, 118, 152
stain 212, 219, 220, 221, 222, 223, 224, 225
staining 154, 219, 220, 225
stairs 26, 35, 190, 203, 217, 220
stake 76, 144, 211
stalks 100, 124, 174, 189, 191, 192
Standards 239, 240
standing water 71
State tree 181
steel cables 36
stem 14, 115, 166, 172, 173, 174, 175, 176
stems 12, 18, 173, 174, 175
Stenocereus pruinosus 108
Stenocereus thurberi 108
stepping stones 154, 155
step-stone 153
sting 60, 134, 137, 142, 144, 228
stinging 61, 129, 130, 137, 140, 144, 228, 234
stinging insects 61, 130, 140
stings 59, 130, 143, 145, 228

stolen items 231
stone 76, 153
stonework 25, 34
storage 45
storm 87, 179
storms 162, 179, 197
stray cats 52, 228, 229
Strickland woodpecker 55
stubby look 125
stung 59, 60, 87, 143, 234
Styrofoam 182, 251
Sub-family 110
succulents 28, 40, 66, 73, 92, 93, 94, 95, 96,
     97, 98, 99, 101, 102, 103, 105, 119, 120,
     164, 184, 192, 202, 246
Sulpher 210
summer 68, 69, 73, 90, 96, 99, 105, 116, 119,
     130, 150, 171, 178, 195, 203, 207, 229,
     230, 240, 253
summer months 69, 124
sun xii, 6, 7, 14, 24, 38, 40, 50, 53, 55, 58, 68,
     69, 73, 78, 95, 96, 98, 99, 101, 116, 123,
     149, 161, 172, 176, 184, 189, 190, 193,
     195, 203, 204, 207, 212, 213, 214, 215,
     218, 219, 223, 225, 226, 227, 229, 230,
     233, 235, 248, 261
sunbathe 262
Sun Belt 8, 40, 48
sun blockage 50
sunburned 95, 97, 233, 236
sun contact 69
sunglasses 233
sun-hardy 95, 190
Sun Ray Mums 204
sunscreen 229
sun sensitive 95, 96, 207
sun shield 223, 233
sun-shield 230
sun shields 233
sunshine 19, 34, 104, 129, 171, 256
supplies xi, xiii, 35, 78, 182, 231
survival 75, 160, 201
survive 67, 127, 161, 193, 239, 244, 256
Swamp 238
swamps 238
swap 73
sweatpants 146, 227, 233, 234, 235, 236
sweats 233, 236
sweet potato 7, 9
sweet potatoes 7

swimming pool 26, 90, 163
swollen area 84
Sylvester Palm 84
symmetry 150, 193
synthetic pesticides 5

T

table knife xi, 87, 88, 111, 172, 255
Tahiti 83
Taiwan 140
tall trees 180, 196
taproot 57, 74, 75, 76, 77, 244
tarantulas 228
tarragon 16
tarwi pea plant 9
task calendar 39
tax dollars 31
taxes 45, 46
tea 9, 10, 15, 17
teenagers 10, 255
teeth 102, 106
temperature 7, 58, 82, 95, 97, 103, 149, 160,
    162, 184, 195
temperature dip 184
tenants 46, 47, 48, 56
Tepari bean 9
tequila 106
termites 46, 106, 130, 149, 151, 252, 253
terrariums 77, 78
tetracycline antibiotics 85
Texas 9, 54, 82, 145, 148, 204, 206, 214
THC 15, 16
THC amount 16
The Case Study ii
theft 215, 216, 217, 231, 232
the South 10, 11, 40, 54, 55, 73, 86, 92, 94,
    95, 100, 132, 157, 161, 181, 209, 215, 248
the South-West 54, 55, 95, 100, 157, 161, 181,
    209, 215
thief 215, 231, 232
thieves 215, 216, 217, 218, 231
thorax 138
thorns 56, 64, 66, 77, 99, 172, 209, 227, 233
throw pillow xii, 173
Thuja 180
thyme 16
tie-downs xiii, 36
time vii
timer 157, 160

tips 3, 95, 98, 102, 211
tomatoes 7, 21, 134
tongs xi, 64, 107, 111, 228, 229
tools xii, xiii, xiv, 21, 32, 35, 78, 111, 216, 231
toothbrush xi, 77, 110
Topiary 258
topsoil 113, 159
toxic 18, 23, 139, 140, 143, 185, 251
Toxophene 133
Toxoplasmosis 229
trailer 44, 45, 46
trailer park 44, 45
transpiration 65
transplant 73, 85, 95, 118
transplanted 77, 103, 205, 240
transplanting 50, 70, 74, 77, 78, 112,
    205, 254
transport 69, 70
travel trailers 44
tree 4, 5, 31, 32, 50, 51, 52, 53, 54, 57, 59, 60,
    79, 80, 81, 82, 83, 84, 85, 86, 87, 88, 89,
    91, 92, 97, 102, 106, 112, 120, 127, 131,
    138, 152, 161, 165, 166, 178, 179, 180,
    181, 184, 186, 194, 195, 196, 197, 198,
    199, 206, 210, 211, 212, 239, 242, 243,
    244, 246, 249, 255
tree falling 198
tree hole 60
tree root 31, 198
trees ix, 4, 6, 8, 11, 19, 22, 28, 32, 38, 40, 50,
    51, 52, 53, 54, 55, 59, 61, 63, 79, 80, 81,
    82, 83, 84, 85, 86, 87, 88, 90, 91, 102,
    105, 106, 117, 118, 120, 121, 123, 126,
    130, 131, 132, 146, 152, 161, 163, 164,
    165, 166, 178, 179, 180, 181, 184, 191,
    192, 196, 197, 198, 199, 200, 201, 202,
    211, 238, 240, 246, 249, 253, 254
tree trimming 50
tree types 50, 79, 80, 82, 83, 84, 88, 131
trial-and-error 96
Tribe 110
Trichocereus pasacana 57
trim 79, 80, 81, 89, 91, 99, 104, 117, 124, 125,
    126, 154, 188, 192, 194, 200, 204, 247,
    249, 255
trim-happy 192
trimmed 80, 81, 91, 102, 126, 171, 184, 249,
    251, 258

trimming 38, 50, 51, 68, 79, 90, 91, 99, 124, 126, 146, 179, 180, 188, 192, 193, 196, 204, 249, 250, 251, 253

triplewide 3, 44

triplewides 43

tropical 80, 198

trunk 53, 80, 84, 166, 181, 232, 239

T-shirts 235

tubercles 66, 93, 97

tubular metal 229

Tucson 58, 60, 167, 207

Tucson, Arizona 58, 60, 167, 207

tumeric 16

turquoise rocks 25

twig 128, 188, 192

twigs 132, 192, 250

type xii, 1, 4, 9, 12, 18, 36, 44, 46, 47, 58, 60, 61, 64, 66, 69, 72, 79, 85, 89, 90, 92, 95, 96, 98, 100, 103, 108, 113, 116, 125, 130, 132, 133, 142, 148, 153, 164, 165, 169, 171, 178, 187, 194, 196, 198, 200, 201, 204, 206, 207, 220, 225, 234, 240, 251

Type Divisions 97

typical height 83

U

underground 31, 32, 53, 59, 129, 132, 159, 166

underground cords or pipes 31

underground pipes 32

underground water 53, 159

underground water table 53, 159

unfinished 221

uniformity 151

United States ix, 6, 8, 11, 38, 39, 40, 54, 71, 94, 101, 130, 144, 167, 185

unlocked door 232

upright xiv, 57, 70, 76, 230

U.S. 94, 101

USA ix, 5, 61, 83, 86, 116, 142, 145, 147, 160, 171, 178, 180, 185, 202, 213, 228

uses of cacti 67

utility 31, 33

utility lines 31, 33

UV protection 8, 233

UV sleeves 233

V

Vaccinium 202

value of the yard 237

Vancouver Island 61

vandalism 5, 217

variegated 98, 115

varieties 10, 92, 95

variety 7, 10, 17, 52, 77, 82, 98, 106, 109, 115, 118, 119, 186, 202, 214, 249

vegetable 2, 6, 7, 10, 26

vegetable and fruit garden 2, 10, 26

vegetables 2, 4, 5, 7, 8, 9, 10, 11, 19, 20, 28, 37, 209, 253, 263

vegetation ix, 9, 40, 59, 85, 94, 102, 109, 130, 132, 136, 139, 160, 166, 202, 238, 239, 253

velocity 54

Vinca 204

vine 8, 206

vinegar 134, 136, 177

vines 11, 61, 144, 197, 246, 249

virus 71

Vitamin A 8

Vitamin C 8

Vitamin D 189

vitamin deficiency 6

vitamins 208, 210, 242

W

walkabout 123, 127

walk area 105, 108, 220

walkway 105, 119, 154

walkways 25, 154, 219

warning 59, 141

Washington 60, 61

Washingtonia filifera 80

Washingtonia robusta 80

wasps 82, 86, 90, 137, 144, 149

wasp spray 90

water 8, 9, 18, 20, 25, 30, 31, 34, 35, 36, 37, 40, 47, 52, 53, 54, 57, 65, 68, 70, 71, 74, 75, 76, 77, 80, 85, 90, 91, 93, 94, 95, 96, 99, 100, 103, 104, 105, 107, 110, 113, 116, 117, 118, 119, 120, 121, 122, 123, 124, 127, 128, 131, 135, 142, 148, 157, 158, 159, 160, 161, 162, 163, 164, 165, 166, 167, 175, 177, 184, 186, 188, 189,

193, 203, 204, 207, 208, 211, 212, 226,
227, 228, 241, 247, 254, 255, 256
water amounts 54
water costs 127
watered 33, 75, 96, 100, 103, 105, 108, 109,
110, 113, 119, 120, 128, 157, 160, 164,
171, 204, 211, 212, 241
watering 4, 6, 8, 9, 20, 22, 34, 36, 37, 53, 57,
68, 91, 96, 99, 103, 104, 116, 117, 119,
120, 121, 122, 123, 124, 127, 128, 157,
160, 163, 164, 167, 202, 203, 204, 205,
206, 207, 209, 226, 238, 249, 254
watering application 116
waterings 53, 96, 99, 116, 124, 160, 203, 205,
206, 207, 254
watering system 4, 157, 160, 163, 164,
207, 238
watering systems 4, 160, 164, 238
water levels 162
waterlogged 113, 242
watermelon 8, 63
water meters 163
water pond 34
water rationing 159
water reduction 164
water runoff 30, 54, 166
water shortage 159
water stands 255
water table 53
water velocity 54
wax 219
weather 5, 37, 39, 40, 50, 53, 54, 68, 69, 90,
96, 103, 104, 105, 116, 117, 120, 133,
146, 162, 180, 193, 199, 204, 205, 206,
207, 213, 249
weather reporting 162
weed 14, 23, 130, 135, 146, 168, 171, 172,
173, 174, 175, 176, 177, 188, 234, 247,
254, 255
weed killer 234
weeds xi, 20, 23, 88, 111, 118, 129, 130,
149, 155, 171, 172, 173, 174, 175, 176,
177, 182, 183, 186, 192, 245, 250, 251,
255, 261
weed seeds 173, 177, 188
weed spray 135, 168, 173, 175, 176, 177
weed-sprayer 177
weedsprayer 177
weed stems 175
weed-whacking 146, 174

weedwhacking 146, 174
weight 78, 85, 89, 113, 152, 156, 169, 209,
211, 213, 233, 234, 241, 254
wells 53
well water 33, 53, 159
West Nile Virus 71
wheelbarrow xii, 70, 167
white 12, 108, 126, 153, 156, 177, 194, 207,
218, 223, 251
whiteflies 130
White Pine 92, 178, 249
White Wool 109
width 25, 34, 84, 200
wildflowers 4, 15, 201, 205
wildlife 135, 201, 239, 255
wilt 12, 76, 113, 117, 202, 203, 242
wind xii, 15, 50, 55, 60, 64, 84, 97, 106, 110,
122, 140, 161, 173, 176, 179, 182, 194,
197, 198, 214, 217, 223, 224, 229, 230,
232, 233, 243, 244
wind action 197, 198, 224
windblown seeds 157
windbreaker 180, 181, 202
winds 36, 51, 55, 84, 111, 180, 197, 234
wind snapping 179
winter 38, 39, 96, 103, 104, 116, 117, 122, 123,
124, 130, 144, 147, 149, 150, 157, 180,
230, 240
Winter 104, 105, 123, 124, 230
winter rain 104
wires 32, 33
wires and pipes 32, 33
wonder foods 7
wood 6, 9, 35, 51, 69, 71, 76, 106, 129, 131,
142, 148, 151, 169, 180, 191, 192, 200,
212, 219, 220, 222, 224, 225, 229,
230, 252
wood chips 169
wood dividers 222
wooden-planked platforms 212
wooden platform 212
wood floors 35
wood logs 224
woodpecker 55, 56
woodpeckers 55, 56
wood rot 131
wood stake 76
Wooly cactus 108
work xiii, 3, 5, 11, 19, 20, 21, 24, 25, 29, 33,
34, 38, 39, 49, 51, 56, 60, 63, 67, 72, 73,

76, 78, 93, 96, 107, 112, 113, 124, 129, 130, 134, 141, 146, 149, 150, 151, 155, 166, 170, 172, 175, 176, 177, 178, 179, 182, 183, 187, 189, 190, 191, 192, 202, 207, 208, 213, 216, 220, 225, 229, 230, 231, 232, 233, 234, 235, 236, 237, 245, 246, 247, 248, 250, 254, 255, 257, 260, 261, 262

work-appropriate clothes 235
worms 6

X

xeriscaping 9

Y

yams 7
yard ix, xii, xiii, 1, 2, 18, 29, 30, 34, 39, 40, 41, 42, 44, 47, 48, 60, 64, 65, 74, 89, 110, 112, 119, 130, 134, 137, 140, 147, 148, 149, 153, 158, 164, 171, 186, 189, 191, 193, 201, 203, 204, 211, 213, 214, 215, 217, 218, 225, 232, 233, 234, 235, 237, 238, 240, 245, 246, 247, 248, 249,

250, 252, 253, 254, 255, 256, 257, 260, 261, 262
yard huggers 64
yard ornaments ix, 214
yards 29, 34, 47, 48, 141, 159, 206, 213, 215, 216, 229, 236, 238, 260
yardwork 34, 63, 149, 189, 234, 235, 247, 254
year-round gardener 250
yellow 7, 12, 53, 71, 85, 98, 100, 108, 117, 121, 122, 123, 127, 128, 137, 181, 184, 191, 194, 204, 207
yellow fever 71
yellow jackets 137
yellow leaves 53, 85, 121, 122, 127, 191
Yews 200
Yucca plants 51

Z

Zika fever 71
zone 83
Zone 83, 109
Zone 12 83
zones 82, 160

Printed in the United States
by Baker & Taylor Publisher Services